The
AMERICAN
DREAM

The

AMERICAN DREAM

Stories from the Heart
of Our Nation

DAN RATHER

WILLIAM MORROW
75 YEARS OF PUBLISHING
An Imprint of HarperCollins*Publishers*

Back jacket photography credits from top row, left to right:

Anthony and Adam Rapp—© Jamey O'Quinn • Sox Kitashima—courtesy of Ms. Kitashima • Trung Dung—courtesy of Mr. Dung • Karen Altland—courtesy of Ms. Altland • Rubylinda Zickafoose—© Milken Family Foundation • Star Detective & Security Agency—by Bruce Powell, courtesy of Star Detective & Security • Chris Gardner—courtesy of Mr. Gardner • The McDonalds—© 2000 by Eskridge Photography • Jacquelyn Mitchard—© 2000 by Patricia Kelly • Enrique Camarena—courtesy of Mr. Camarena • Melissa Nelson—by Sharon W. Gradischnig • Nosrat Scott—courtesy of Ms. Scott • Evelyn Sirrell—by Ralph Morang • Curtis Aikens—courtesy of Food Network • Michael Cruz—courtesy of Mr. Cruz • Sister Sylvia Schmidt—courtesy of Sister Sylvia Schmidt • Wayne Ford—© 1998 University Photo • Adam Ballard—by Dita Photography • Deborah Cline—courtesy of Ms. Cline • Shawn Carlson—by William Sandidge • The Green Family—courtesy of Stacy and Mark Green • Eileen Collins—courtesy of NASA • Joshua Marcus—courtesy of the Marcus family • Ryan Clark & Family—courtesy of the Clark Family • Margaret Gilleo—by Charles J. Guenther, Jr. • Jesus Serrato—courtesy of Mr. Serrato • Trish Milines Dziko—courtesy of Technology Access Foundation • Dr. George Hatsopolous—courtesy of Thermo Electron Corporation • Delores Pass Kesler—by Kelly LaDuke • Oscar Acosta—courtesy of the Acosta family

HarperCollins books may be purchased for educational, business, or sales promotional use. For information please write: Special Markets Department, HarperCollins Publishers Inc., 10 East 53rd Street, New York, NY 10022.

FIRST EDITION

Designed by Bernard Klein

Printed on acid-free paper

Library of Congress Cataloging-in-Publication Data

Rather, Dan.
 The American dream: stories from the heart of our nation / by Dan Rather.—1st ed.
  p. cm.
 ISBN 0-688-17892-8 (alk. paper)
  1. National characteristics, American—Anecdotes. 2. United States—Social life and customs—1971—Anecdotes. 3. United States—Social conditions—1980—Anecdotes. 4. United States—Bibliography—Anecdotes. I. Title.

E169.12.R36 2001
973.92—dc21   2001030031

01 02 03 04 05 RRD 10 9 8 7 6 5 4 3 2 1

For Jeannie
and
all other believers in the dream,
past, present, and future

Because those who lived before us in this nation were able to imagine a new thing, a thing unheard of in the world before, a thing the skeptical and tired men who did not trust in dreams had not been able to imagine, they erected on this continent the first free nation—the first society in which mankind was to be free at last.

—Archibald MacLeish

CONTENTS

ACKNOWLEDGMENTS

Fighting Heart Jean Grace Goebel Rather was the inspiration for this book, as she has been for every good and decent thing I have attempted for most of my adult life. Our children, Robin and Danjack, and their spouses, David Murray and Judith White Rather, also have been, as always, strong in support. Judy earned special mention for having helped to edit and fact-check the final manuscript. So did my sister Patricia Rather Thompson and my ever-reliable old friend Perry Smith.

At HarperCollins, a big thank you to Executive Editor Mauro DiPreta, who took over from Zach Schisgal midstream and patiently and expertly guided this project to the other shore. His assistant, Joelle Yudin, also merits thanks here, as do Dee Dee De Bartlo, Lisa Gallagher, Andrea Molitor, and Derek Gullino.

Bill Adler was my agent for this book, as he has been for a number of others. But this time he did much more. He was a key part of the book's creation, and he guided, directed, and nurtured the germ of an idea all the way through to publication. Gloria Adler helped in innumerable ways. So did my friends and agents for many purposes Richard and Carole Leibner.

Allen Mikaelian worked above and beyond the call to provide editorial guidance and invaluable research. Eric Wybenga works as my in-house editor on all writing projects. He more than once saved this one. This book would not be in your hands without his herculean efforts.

At CBS News, Kim Akhtar and Claire Fletcher worked tirelessly at my side on behalf of this book and deserve special mention for all they have done trying to make it successful. I'd also like to thank Jamie Kraft and Lourdes Aguilar, who produced the "American Dream" segments that ran on the *CBS Evening News.*

I am indebted to Mel Karmazin, Les Moonves, and Andrew Heyward for the daily opportunity to work with the best in journalism while practicing my craft at CBS News and living my own American dream. My thanks are also extended to every member of the team that creates the *CBS Evening News, 60 Minutes, 60 Minutes II, 48 Hours,* the CBS website, and all our broadcasts, especially Jim Murphy, Jeff Fager, Al Ortiz, Susan Zirinsky, Harvey Nagler, Janet Leissner, Wayne Nelson, Mary Mapes, Tom Anderson, Steve Glauber, Paul Fischer, Jerry Cipriano, Hugh Heckman, Toby Wertheim, Debbie Margolis Rubin, Mylene Hollant, Michelle Peltier, Terri Belli, Susan Shackman Adler, A. J. Warren, Eric Shapiro, Susan Martin Cipollaro, and Mike Singletary.

For this and most other endeavors, I continue to rely on the counsel and friendship of Don and Maxine Rather, Bill and Carolyn Johnston, Eunice Martin, Mary Ann Quisenberry, Betsy Smith, Tom and Claire Bettag, Herb and Pat George Rowland, Frank and Luella Bennack, Red and Charline McCombs, Howard Stringer and Jennifer Patterson, Suzanne Meirowitz Nederlander, Toby and Joel Bernstein, Charles and Mary Catherine Ball, Connie and Neal Spelce, Don and Gayle Canada, Donna Dees, Terri and Tim Vanackern, and David and Susan Buksbaum.

As before, I again acknowledge the happy inspiration of M. L., now working on his young life's version of the American dream while continuing to fuel my own.

Finally, I'd like to thank Kenneth Rayborn, Jeff Valdez, Troy and Carol LeBlanc, and Alexander Scherbakov, who all gave generously of their time to be interviewed for this book but whose stories we were unfortunately unable to use. And of course thanks also to all of the American dreamers who appear in these pages.

INTRODUCTION

The Republic is a dream. Nothing happens unless first a dream.

—Carl Sandburg

*W*hen we describe this land of ours, in deep-down essence and everyday spirit, it is the phrase we reach for most often. As an idea, it is older even than the nation and the words that give it name. It has reflected and informed what is best in us as a country and as a people from the beginning and it has been there to remind us that we should be doing better when we have failed to live up to the ideal it describes. It is the American dream, and it has filled me with awe for as long as I can remember.

I do not think it a stretch to call the American dream one of the most powerful ideas in the history of human achievement. As a young boy growing up in Houston, Texas, during the Great Depression, the dream was something taught by my parents. Not explicitly, but by example. By the way they lived their lives I grew to understand—could just *tell*—that it was something in which they were deeply and clearly invested. I could feel its truth in my father's tireless drive to build a better life for himself and his family and in my mother's determination to make the best of what we already had.

The dream kept them going through their dark hours, just as it sustained an entire nation of families—many worse off than mine—through that time. And it also left a bitterness in the mouths of those Americans who had reached for it, brought it to their lips and, like John Steinbeck's Joads, tasted nothing but dust. Such is the nature of dreams, when even dogged pursuit fails to catch them.

It was during this era of national trial, after the stock market crash and between the World Wars, that the historian James Truslow Adams became the first (so far as we can tell) to use the phrase, in an article he wrote in 1931 for the *Catholic Worker*. For him, the American dream was "the dream of a land in which life should be better and richer and fuller for every man, with opportunity for each according to his ability or achievement." The dream was, in short, the promise of freedom and opportunity.

My work has taken me around the world. And no matter where I go, when people find out where I'm from, they want to talk about the American dream. For some, it is an object of ultimate aspiration, often desperately so. For others, it is a hollow ideal to be scorned or spoken of only in the most sardonic of terms. But it is always there, always pulling and pushing those who see in us the embodiment of *something* that can only be expressed in those terms.

I have heard it too, in speaking to our country's soldiers in the deserts of Arabia, in the squalor of Somalia, in the jungles of Vietnam, and along the mine-infested roads of Bosnia. The dream is what keeps them fighting when every rational fiber may be telling them to quit, and it is what they dream of returning to when the fight is done. And again I have seen the Dream's power to sustain those who call America home.

Must this not be the same belief that saw General Washington's troops through the Valley Forge winter? The phrase "American dream" may have been coined in the twentieth century, but the Dream itself long predates it, predates, in a sense, America itself. In the Age of Discovery, the dream was of riches and of the fabled Northwest passage to what was then called the Orient. Years later, the Pilgrims found their dream of a City Upon a Hill fulfilled in a new land where they could worship God according to their beliefs. In their immigrant quest for freedom, the American dream as we know it first took wing.

It has soared ever higher over the years, lifted by the actions of those

Americans we have placed in our historical canon. From George Washington, the founder, who surrendered control of first a victorious army and then the presidency to the workings of democracy, to Abraham Lincoln, the emancipator, who fought to hold this nation together. From Franklin Delano Roosevelt, who rallied America to the fight against fascism and expanded our notions of human rights with his Four Freedoms, to Dr. Martin Luther King Jr., who shared with us a dream "deeply rooted in the American Dream . . . that one day this nation will rise up and live out the true meaning of its creed: 'We hold these truths to be self-evident: that all men are created equal.' "

It seems obvious, but it's worth remembering just how different was our nation's birth from anything known before to humanity. Far from tracing our lineage back through the mists of time to legendary battles and half-forgotten kings, we can fix our birth in a moment. The United States of America was willed into being when the first Founding Father set his inked quill to the Declaration of Independence. The American dream? It brought us into existence.

This last, I believe, cannot be stressed strongly enough. We were the first nation on this earth to be founded on an ideal. As the poet and World War I veteran Archibald MacLeish once wrote, "The courage of the Declaration of Independence is the courage of the act of the imagination." Don't believe it? Quick—name the date of British General Cornwallis's surrender at Yorktown. Can't do it? Well, neither could I. But every schoolchild knows the day we declared ourselves a free people.

The American dream was the idea that guided us through the early days of the republic. And it was the ideal that was compromised in the drafting of a Constitution that, for all its strength and stirring appeals to universal law, left African Americans in chains and women without franchise. It is the vision that has brought millions of immigrants to a land where a better life is possible, and it held the blind spot that allowed the massacre and scattering of the Native American nations that called this continent home long before any European imagined it. It demands noting here that theirs were the first American dreams.

This is how the American river has run, from the highlands of our best thoughts to the valleys of our lowest actions. Like all rivers, it flows to the sea. That sea, it strikes me, is We the People. And just as there is a cleansing power in the vastness of the ocean, so have the American people, driven by history's tides, worked toward an alignment of our American dream with the realities of American life.

So we came into the century just past, a nation feeling its way—in brave strides and awkward lurches alike—toward a more perfect union, toward the establishment of justice. Our progress has been spurred by those poets and citizens of conscience who have invoked the dream—directly and indirectly—as a mirror of our better selves, and encouraged America to make dream reality. Recall that James Truslow Adams's first invocation of the dream came during the depths of a depression that led many to part faith with the dream. So, too, we have F. Scott Fitzgerald's scathing critique of our first boom times in *The Great Gatsby,* and the works and words of Jane Addams, Susan B. Anthony, and Eleanor Roosevelt. We are heir to the postwar probing of playwright Edward Albee's *The American Dream* and Richard Yates's groundbreaking novel *Revolutionary Road.* We have been urged to find the answer to Langston Hughes's question, "What happens to a dream deferred?" But not, unfortunately, before we learned the answer: it explodes.

Looking back, it is apparent that this thing that we call a dream has had a very real impact on how we Americans have lived and have grown. It has, in a concrete sense, made us a nation of idealists, pointing us toward tomorrow and teaching us to struggle toward social justice. It has also touched so many of us on an individual level. It has certainly touched me.

One part of my early introduction to the dream took shape around the family radio set, my young ears spellbound by Edward R. Murrow's World War II dispatches from London during the Blitz: I wanted to be a reporter. I was a poor kid, but not among the poorest by the standards of our tough neighborhood. It was not a place that led me to think that I was anyone special or that I should be reaching for such a faraway star. I had the love and encouragement of my family, but I was also surrounded by examples of capable adults who were thankful to have any job at all, and plenty who had none. College was a distant rumor, a place thought of more in terms of local football heroes than as part of any realistic "career path."

Yet, and this still gives me a thrill today, within twenty years that boy who listened with such rapt attention to Murrow's reports from London was in New York City meeting his childhood hero. The American dream, you see, holds me in its grasp because I have been blessed to live my own personal version of it. Perhaps this could have happened somewhere else, in some country other than America, although in that age, especially, I wouldn't bank on it.

But this was all long ago and far away. And even reporters with a strong taste for history soon find themselves asking, yes, but what about now? My interest in the American dream eventually led me to a more pressing question: Where is the American dream today?

So it was that, about two years ago, I started talking to a couple of producers at the *CBS Evening News* about developing a new running feature for the broadcast. The idea was to discover what, if anything, the dream means to today's Americans. What's more, we wanted to know if Americans were realizing their dreams. And if they were, how?

We wanted to find people who seemed to be living the dream or on the path to achieving it, sought to get their stories and perspectives on the most primal, powerful piece of America's mythic appeal. We sent letters to the various CBS News bureaus and our affiliates across the country, asking the people there to let us know about Americans who might fit the bill. We also kept an eye out ourselves for the people in the news, because one of our aims in putting together the series was to maintain a topical approach—to look for the American dream peering out at us from behind the headlines.

The suggestions poured in. And the news, as always, kept happening, revealing the special people who make the most out of being in a certain place at a critical time. It was, in fact, one of the year's most tragic and disturbing news stories that gave us our first subject, a Los Angeles trauma surgeon named Clarence Sutton. Dr. Sutton had grown up poor on the mean streets of South Central Los Angeles. No one in his family had gone to college, let alone medical school, but, as he put it, "All I knew was, that if I studied hard, I could potentially get out of life what I wanted." The fulfillment of his dream put him in Providence Holy Cross Medical Center on August 10, 1999, where he saved the life of five-year-old Benjamin Kadish, one of the victims of the Jewish day care center shooting that shocked the nation that summer.

The series ran for more than a year, giving us a whole video scrapbook full of people living the dream in their own ways. These were snapshots of the dream in action, as varied and kaleidoscopic as America itself. They were also, it became clear, portraits in hard work, persistence, and generosity—traits that more often than not lived side by side in the same person.

There was, for example, the story of Delores Davis, a woman who had once been homeless. When we meet her, she had made it her life's mission to provide shelter to every homeless person in Beaumont, Texas. Firm in her conviction that "homelessness is not a sin and it is not a disease," she had recently taken over three abandoned buildings, including a notorious crack house, and was in the process of renovating them for her charges.

And then there was another doctor, Ken Williams, who had experienced what it was like to grow up black in Mississippi during the height of the Civil Rights movement. The prejudice he witnessed as a child not only drove him to pursue a career in medicine but impelled him to make his mark in his home state. We learned about Dr. Williams because he had succeeded so far, despite being told by blacks and whites alike that "a black physician couldn't make it" in the town of Holly Springs, Mississippi. Dr. Williams established his first practice in a trailer, caring for black, Hispanic, and white patients. He sought to make a statement, and he has. But he has done so much more—including putting himself in debt in order to reopen the only hospital within fifty miles of Holly Springs after financial troubles closed its doors.

If you sense a common thread running through these stories, you're no doubt correct. The American dream affords us opportunity and the freedom to seize it. It has also created, in my experience, some of the most generous people anywhere in the world. So we kept an especially sharp eye out for Americans who had not only found their own dreams but were making the dreams of their fellow citizens possible as well. These are the folks who are living exemplars of John D. Rockefeller's words that "Every right implies a responsibility, every opportunity, an obligation, every possession, a duty."

It may sound circular, but we also recognized that, despite all the historical context, sometimes the American dream is simply, well, what Americans dream of. We knew that any effort to shine a light on the American dream would inevitably come up against the limits of our own ability to define the dream. In this country—and this was, in a sense, the central point of the project—it is probably more appropriate to talk of American *dreams,* millions of them. With this in mind, we aimed to get our subjects to speak for themselves as much as possible.

This approach lent itself naturally to people who were what you might call "characters"—folks who had an interesting story to tell and who could tell it well. The person who positively leaps to mind as I write this is a man named J. R. Tate, the subject of a piece we called "Appalachian Hiker." One day in his impoverished youth, he told us, "My dad called me in and said, 'Son, this is all the money I have in the world right now, sixty-five dollars.' He said, 'Take it, and go as far as you can.'" It wasn't what his father had in mind, but he joined the Marine Corps, where his "very competitive" nature took him to the rank of lieutenant colonel. A good career's work, to be sure, but, he says, "I really didn't have any good firm dreams until I retired." Until, that is, he became transfixed by a dream of hiking the Appalachian Trail. Once his footsteps had carried him to the end, he said, "It was like I had a film over my eyes and the film was lifted . . . the hard-boiled edge was gone, I was so tolerant of others." He left us with the words "I am blessed, I am truly blessed and I am so thankful I have the ability to recognize this."

People like J. R. brought to mind the Walt Whitman line "I hear America singing, the varied carols I hear . . ." There is no typical American, and there is surely no such thing as a typical American dream.

I have a great belief in the power of television to tell a story. The ability to join words with sound and pictures and to reach millions of people on a given night makes it a tremendously rewarding medium in which to work, and a good and effective way, I thought, to explore this question of the American dream. Likewise, the American dream pieces I did for my daily commentary on CBS radio served as a very useful "notebook" for working out a lot of ideas on the subject.

But both of these forums, for all that they offer, present the intractable problem of time. There just isn't enough of it in an *Evening News* broadcast, much less a minute-and-a-half radio piece, to present these people and their dreams in a way that does them full justice, with nuances and unpredictable edges intact. What's more, these pieces for television and radio left little room to explore how each of our subjects' dreams may have fit into the larger currents of the American dream. While the people we met in the course of the series more than proved to us that it is tough indeed to speak of the dream in general terms, looking for that point of connection between an individual aspiration and some established strain of our national character was one of the things that made the enterprise as rewarding for the mind as it was for the spirit and the heart.

The answer was to explore the subject further in a book—the book you now hold in your hands. This isn't intended to be anything approaching the last word on the American dream—far from it—but is my hope that it will in some small way get people talking and thinking about the dream themselves. Maybe it will inspire you to see your own situation as part of the dream's continuum. At the very least, I think you will find the stories themselves to be inspirational. I know I have.

All but one of the people whose American dreams I have collected here are new to this book. (Enrique Camarena, Jr., son of a DEA agent whose brutal murder made international headlines, is one person from the *Evening News* series whom I could not resist revisiting.) Here are teachers and stockbrokers, writers and farmers, detectives and house cleaners, and even a politician or two.

Here, too, are folks for whom the American dream first took root on native soil, and those who crossed oceans and national boundaries to find it. The dream's call resonates far beyond our borders, perhaps most of all in the words "Give me your tired, your poor, your huddled masses yearning to breathe free." I believe nothing could be more fitting than to keep an eye peeled for the immigrant perspective when searching for the American dream.

Like their television predecessors, the people between these covers are a diverse lot. Their lives are no less varied, and from them I have learned much about not only the American dream, but America itself. Without wishing to pigeonhole anybody or their dreams, I've tried to group the stories I have gathered here into a number of loose categories: For some, the American dream is one of freedom; for others, it is of fortune, or family, or service to one's fellows. Some place greatest emphasis on the pursuit of happiness, or of keeping alive the innovative spirit that once led us to create "A New Order Under God." For so many of these people, though, an argument could be made for their inclusion in a chapter other than the one in which I've placed them.

Even the most straightforward American dreams here, the modern Horatio Alger, rags-to-riches stories, show the complexity of the dream. Riches are realized, and then used to give something back. Family plays a hand almost everywhere. The value of liberty, of education, of following one's own definition of the dream is felt throughout these pages. Yet all of these people feel there is something that binds together the disparate elements of their lives. They sense the dream's presence, and importance, and feel that America has made their own dreams possible.

This commonality, this interconnectedness between our own dreams and a national ethos of aspiration may be the dream's most important contribution to the America of today and tomorrow. I remember a time when, for example, if the president spoke, his words would be carried live by all the major networks—and the vast majority of Americans would tune in to watch. Now the coverage, live or otherwise, is no longer a given and the evidence is that the American people are tuning out our national dialogue.

The reasons are well documented and hardly surprising: we are, on the whole, busier than ever, with more distractions competing for our time and attention than have ever faced any culture in human history. Daily we perform a precarious juggling act between job and family, with many of us finding scant time for social interaction or a civic life. Even our dwindling leisure time has become Balkanized, with the Internet custom-tailoring a world of information and entertainment to our narrowest, most specific niche interests. Though understandable, it is nonetheless a troubling trend.

And it is a trend that intersects with another in America, that of our changing national demographic. Immigration from all corners of the globe and the vaunted "melting pot"'s fall from favor have remade us to a tangible degree. Those who honor and value the tradition of America as a nation of immigrants understand that we are enriched by this new cultural mosaic. But I think that we should also understand the challenge it poses, as we search for the common ground of democratic consensus.

The American dream provides the best common ground on which to build the American future. As an idea, it is inherently inclusive, and it has the power to strike a chord in all of us. It defines us as a people, even as we add to its meaning with each new chapter in our national experience and our individual actions. Here, then, is the result of my quest to discover the American dream as your neighbors are creating it today—I hope that you receive it well. And I wish all of you the best in bringing your own dreams to fruition.

DAN RATHER
January 2001

SWEET LIBERTY
THE DREAM OF FREEDOM

*Freedom has its life in the hearts, the actions, the spirit of men
and so it must be daily earned and refreshed—else like a flower
cut from its life-giving roots, it will wither and die.*
                                        —Dwight D. Eisenhower

I NEVER doubted that any discussion of the American dream would
rightly begin with freedom, and that the word would echo throughout.
Freedom, after all, is America's bedrock. As a people, we demand it—
often and unabashedly. We don't, however, seem to spend a lot of time
thinking about just what it is. Perhaps this is a measure of our good fortune. Freedom seems, like the truths our founders seized upon, to be
self-evident. It is most often defined by its opposite: the absence of
bonds. But what is freedom in an affirmative sense? Trying to wrap your
mind around this Big Idea of American thought and history can be a bit
like trying to lasso the wind.

As I talked to the folks whom you'll meet in the pages that follow, the
abstract concept of freedom began to take solid shape. It was a form
recognizable to any American, distilled from that first and best articula-
tion of the original American dream: "We hold these truths to be self-
evident; that all men are created equal; that they are endowed by their
creator with certain unalienable rights; that among these are life, liberty,
and the pursuit of happiness." Freedom, it occurred to me, is equality in
action.

As such, it is America's greatest promise, and it may also be her greatest demand upon We the People. Without it, there's no America, and certainly no American dream. As the eminent midcentury American historian Henry Steele Commager once wrote, "Freedom is not a luxury that we can indulge when at last we have security and prosperity and enlightenment; it is, rather, antecedent to all of these, for without it we can have neither security nor prosperity nor enlightenment." All the material particulars, the proverbial house with the white picket fence and all that goes with it, are only possible because our founders dreamed of freedom.

It was a dream spurred by a deep and abiding sense among them that all were equal in the eyes of God. A dream of freedom from an unequal relationship with Mother England, yes, but also of freedom in a more universal sense. The most forward-thinking members of the founding generation saw America as a place where the Old World order could be remade—where all men would be liberated from government oppression, from the bondage of debt, from the hierarchies of church, state, and society that had defined life in Europe.

The founders believed greatly in equality and freedom, but their faith was fraught with error. Their decision to leave slavery intact in the new order mocked their beliefs. And "all men are created equal" was, we know too well, more than a mere turn of phrase when women were denied the vote. Here the courage of men like Jefferson and Madison came up hard against its limits. But we look back through better eyes at an era accustomed to the greatest sins against liberty. One could say that the framers dreamed of freedom, but only dreamed in black and white.

We celebrate an America born on July 4, 1776. But if we take the Declaration of Independence at its word, it is a birth with which we labor still. Because the very reasoning Jefferson used to make the case against English rule over the colonists could have been turned against the new nation itself. The American government did not rule with the consent of all it governed, and rhetoric did not begin to meet deed until Abraham Lincoln issued the Emancipation Proclamation. Lincoln had many reasons for doing this, not least of which was his belief that it would aid the Union war effort, but in this—no matter the motives—our nation was born again . . . and again when women won the vote, and again in the eradication of Jim Crow. It is reborn with each confident assertion of that which is ours because it cannot be taken away.

Marrying the founders' rhetoric with reality has never been an easy consummation. There have been times throughout our history, especially during wars hot and cold, when promise and practice moved farther apart. What I think needs to be considered, though, is that freedom is always incomplete when we look at it as nothing more than a guarantee on a piece of time-yellowed paper. It does not exist in a vacuum. Freedom is like a muscle that atrophies if it is not used; once we understand this, it becomes clear that we have a responsibility not only to consider ourselves free but to act like a free people.

This very sentiment undergirds our Constitution, a document as revolutionary in its day as the independent nation that produced it. From its opening, "We the People," it affirms the idea that our government is of us, by us, and for us. The liberties enumerated in the Bill of Rights are not handed down from above but reserved by We the People as the conditions by which we will allow ourselves to be governed.

The Fifth Amendment, as we all know from countless crime dramas, deals with the rights of a defendant. The Second Amendment fuels endless debate over what it says about our right to bear arms. The Fourth addresses the quartering of troops in private homes. These are specific assurances aimed at specific situations. The Ninth and Tenth Amendments, though crucial, do not stir the blood. But the First Amendment is general and fundamental. It stakes its appeal in universal law. It says: you are free to follow the dictates of your conscience—in worshiping the god of your choice or choosing not to worship at all, in speaking your mind, in associating with whom you please. And, especially near to my heart, you can report the story as you see it and as you know it to have happened.

These are rights that we shape with each individual action. When we exercise them with vigor, we contribute to the American atmosphere of freedom. And when we stand up for them in a court of law, we give them definition for our fellow citizens and for future generations. I wanted to tell the stories of some of the Americans who are actively using their First Amendment freedoms, who are shaping who we are today.

Do Americans dream of freedom or do we take it for granted? The people in this chapter *have* dreamed of freedom—because, at some point in their lives, they didn't have it. In Nosrat Scott's native Iran, official persecution of her Bahá'í faith kept her and her family living in fear. Margaret Pfeffer Gilleo, born and bred in the United States, ran afoul of the law with a simple bit of personal protest against the Gulf War and prevailed when her stand took her before the Supreme Court. Dereje Bereded has watched political rivalries dash the rights of Ethiopians like him to associate with Eritreans who, he insists, are practically his brothers and sisters. And Tsuyako "Sox" Kitashima, a Japanese American whose family was taken from their California home and put in an internment camp during World War II, challenged her government to own up to and atone for what had happened to hundreds of thousands of Japanese and Japanese Americans like her.

Freedom of religion, freedom of speech, freedom of assembly, freedom to petition the government. The First Amendment is more than a set of limits on state power; it is a sort of guide to living the American life, an inspirational document that encourages us to participate. The people in this chapter have answered that call. They are proud exemplars of the American dream, yet their dreams are more than American. They are reflections of the basic human yearning to breathe free.

Nosrat Solhjoo Scott

The first American dream was one of religious freedom, the Mayflower Pilgrims searching for a place where they could worship as their faith commanded. And when our Founding Fathers penned the Bill of Rights, they guaranteed that future generations of Americans would be able to worship God as they chose—or not at all—by separating church and state. It seems both remarkable and logical that this original dream was not only embodied in our rights but, indeed, took the lead.

Today's debates over prayer at football games or city-sponsored religious displays boil down to whether some individuals are being coerced or left out. Civil libertarians fight to preserve personal choice. But we tend to forget that, when the First Amendment was written, separation of church and state was also about peace. The large-scale religious wars in Europe were as fresh in the memories of the Founding Fathers as the wars in the Balkans are to all of us today. Our first lawmakers feared the potential consequence of religious intolerance joining with political and military might—that the United States would be torn apart.

Some of you reading this may well find it odd that a book about the American dream would begin with someone who is originally from a country which, for at least the past twenty years, has had a deep and lasting enmity with ours. But that's just it—so many of us are one nationality by birth, and Americans by choice. And Nosrat Scott, who fled religious persecution in her native Iran, knows well and firsthand how important is freedom, especially the protection of individual faith from the power of the state. In Iran, she knew no peace; now she sees its fruits every day in her work as president of the Interfaith Council of Greater Hollywood in Florida.

Nosrat Scott is of the Bahá'í faith. She and other Bahá'í believe all the world's major religions play a role in the evolution of humankind, directed toward the formation of a universal human family. Nosrat personally believes this will happen first here, in her adopted country. "The United States," she says, "is going to be the first true spiritual leader of the world." This is her dream.

The Bahá'í have been persecuted from their beginnings. In 1844, a Persian merchant now known to the faithful as the Báb proclaimed that God had told him to prepare the world for a divine messenger. When the Báb and his message began to attract a following, they were set upon by extremist followers of the Muslim clergy. In 1850, they killed the Báb. Thirteen years later, a surviving disciple, Bahá'u'lláh, revealed that he was the one of whom the Báb had foretold.

Bahá'u'lláh taught, to put it in simple terms, that God is too great for any one religion to fully contain. Each, however, has contributed to humankind's understanding and progress. To the Bahá'í the teachings of Abraham, Moses, the Buddha, Zoroaster, Jesus, Krishna, and Mohammed are all pieces of a vast universal puzzle. All have made equal contributions to morality and civilization, and all are studied closely by Bahá'í. In fact, when Nosrat's local hospital cannot fill a patient's request for a rabbi, they call Nosrat. If they cannot find a priest, they call Nosrat. If they cannot find a mullah, they call Nosrat. The passages all these patients need to hear are ones she knows by heart, and she shares the conviction that these are all God's words.

When Nosrat was seven, one of her Bahá'í teachers showed her class a collection of postcards. The teacher had pictures of Native Americans, Europeans, Africans, and the peoples of the Middle and Far East. "We were just kids then," Nosrat says, "laughing and looking. And when she collected those things she asked us, 'Do you know any of them?' " The children were surprised. Why should they? They were living in Yazd, in southern Iran. They hadn't seen or known much else. "We said no," Nosrat remembers. "And she said, 'They're all your brothers and sisters.' "

The lesson is one learned by all Bahá'í, and it is one they take seriously. Their faith asks them to work toward eliminating prejudice of all kinds. Women and men are equals in Bahá'í families, or as Nosrat poetically puts it, "Man and woman are two wings of the bird of humanity. If one wing is weaker, the bird cannot fly." Bahá'í are encouraged to promote their religion but to avoid proselytizing in any way that would infringe on the privacy or rights of others. Each Bahá'í is expected to obey the laws of the country in which he or she lives and to serve the needs of his or her community. They are instructed to avoid partisan politics and do not accept political appointments.

Essentially, Bahá'í do not pose a threat to any religion or to any of the more than 250 nations and territories in which they live. They are not revolutionaries. They are, however, committed to changing the world through faith and education. Because they are peaceful and unobtrusive, it can be difficult to understand why they have been singled out for persecution in Iran. Even after Nosrat explains the political and theological reasons behind the persecutions, it's hard to see it as boiling down to anything more than hatred. And that's something that's tough for fair-minded people to fully grasp.

During the nineteenth century, an estimated twenty thousand Bahá'í were killed for their faith in what is now Iran. Nosrat's great uncle was one of them. The twentieth century saw no end to the executions, denial of rights, beatings, and jailings. Since the rise of the Ayatollah Khomeini in 1978, more than two hundred Bahá'í have been executed by the state. We don't know how many have been killed by citizens acting on their own in remote regions. As of this writing, four Bahá'í are on death row in Iran for practicing their faith or for possessing Bahá'í literature. Many Bahá'í and human rights workers believe only frequent condemnation by the international community and the United Nations has prevented a much larger and systematic pogrom against the three hundred thousand Iranian Bahá'í.

Nosrat was born in 1937 in Yazd, which in 1903 was the site of a particularly vicious massacre of Bahá'í incited by a local mullah. Nosrat's father, like many Bahá'í, was denied employment because of his faith and supported his family by becoming a merchant. When the family's five daughters neared the age when they would be expected to don a chador, the traditional head-to-toe dress required by fundamentalist Islam and rejected by Bahá'í, Nosrat's father realized that raising his family in Yazd would be too dangerous. The family moved to an undeveloped section of Tehran that had been settled by Christians, Jews, Americans, and Europeans. If their new home lacked electricity and running water, Nosrat's family also hoped it would deliver them from some of the sharper edges of persecution.

This hope was not entirely fulfilled. And sometimes the challenges came from within Nosrat's own extended family. As she entered high school, her Muslim relatives openly criticized Nosrat's father for treating his daughters as the equal of his sons. To Nosrat, he had to explain that not everyone had learned the lessons of tolerance imparted by her Bahá'í teachers. When she went to school, Nosrat's father warned her that "they going to curse you, they going to run after you, they going to throw water at you, mud, whatever. You just pretend you didn't hear what they are saying, don't get angry, don't react, don't run, don't answer, just go. . . . Believe that they don't know what they're doing. Otherwise they wouldn't do it."

Her father and mother told her that this kind of hatred went just as strongly against the Koran as it did against Bahá'í teachings. Nosrat came to believe this herself as she read the Koran in school and at home. But she also saw the futility of trying to explain this to her classmates. When she was in the ninth grade, she heard two girls arguing behind her. "One was saying, 'I'm gonna kill her.' And the other one said, 'No, I won't let you, because *I'm* going to kill her.' " Nosrat sat still. She says there was nothing she could do. "If I scream something back," she remembers thinking, "they're going to come with fists. I don't know how to use fists. If I do, they're going to come with guns." At a summer vacation spot, they came for her brother with shovels and hammers. "They almost killed him. He came home with a broken ankle and a bleeding head."

Even some of their own Muslim relatives treated them like untouchables. Nosrat remembers the time an aunt visited and joined her mother for tea. Before the aunt left, she washed her hands and rinsed out her mouth. Nosrat fetched her a towel, which she refused. "She wiped her mouth with her own veil. And after she left, my mother told me, 'She's rinsing her mouth because of our tea, Bahá'í tea. Now you are giving her a Bahá'í towel?' " Nosrat finishes her story with a sad laugh.

Nosrat also recalls official persecution, often, she says, stirred up by local mullahs. Searches of Bahá'í homes were common. They would leave the copies of the Koran they found, but always took the Bahá'í books. "We hoped they read them—not that they're going to be Bahá'í, but that they'll know what we read." Her uncle was in his late eighties when he was arrested and sentenced to receive fifty lashes for allegedly possessing revolutionary materials. If not for the intervention of his Muslim son-in-law after ten lashes had fallen on his back, Nosrat believes, he would not have survived.

Determined to work and become independent, Nosrat finished high school in Tehran and went on to teachers college. This amounted to stepping into the lion's den. Being a Bahá'í was bad enough; by becoming a Bahá'í educator she opened herself to accusations that she was corrupting the youth. After she graduated, she was sent to "one of the worst schools in the south of Tehran . . . in a very fanatic area." It was also very poor. "Those kids didn't have shoes or food. I was coming home crying for my mother, and I wouldn't eat. She would say, they don't eat because they don't have. But you have to eat something." Then the head of the school board for her area asked her about a blank space on her teacher registration form.

For any sort of government job—and teaching in Iran was a government job—Iranian applicants must specify their religion. Bahá'í typically leave this question blank rather than call attention to themselves. The authorities know this, as did Nosrat's boss. " 'Okay,' he said, 'you're Bahá'í. You go there, and the fathers of these kids, they're going to kill you. They're going to come with shovels and kill you.' " He asked her to sign the form, declaring that she was a Muslim. She refused.

Nosrat believes that her evident commitment to the children and a severe teacher shortage saved her job and perhaps her life. "After two years, they realized I have the ability to do things. I always wanted to do things, to change everything for the better." Remarkably, she was made principal of a middle school with nine hundred students—a school with no electricity, no running water, broken windows and doors. "But," she says with pride, "I took care of it."

Here again, she was reminded that her life was always in danger. "I was doing all these good things, that probably no one else would do, but I was still threatened that they're going to do something, harm me." The parents of the children she taught did not know she was Bahá'í, but administrators and other teachers did, and some of them threatened to expose her. "I was not ashamed," she is quick to point out, but neither did she wish to announce the fact.

Nosrat was thirty-two when she decided she'd had enough. "It was constant," she says. "It was day and night. It was every second. At work, on the street, at home with relatives. I really got tired of it, especially because I was sure I was not doing something wrong. I was sure I didn't believe in something wrong." One of her brothers was in Germany, and she had a sister in France, but Nosrat was drawn to America. She left Iran in 1969. It was not a departure made without regret. "I don't hate Iran," she tells me, "I love it. I love all my Muslim friends and relatives. All I'm begging them is 'Open your eyes.' "

When she landed at New York's Kennedy Airport, alone and with almost no English, Nosrat sat for twelve hours wondering what to do. Finally, a kind soul directed her to the YWCA, where she stayed the night and called the Bahá'í center in New York. They picked her up and set her up with a job as a seamstress and found her an American Bahá'í roommate in Yonkers, just north of New York City. There are only five million Bahá'í worldwide, but they are a true international community. Nosrat still continues to pay back the favors done her by American Bahá'í by coming to the aid of other Bahá'í who have made it out of Iran. Recently, she says, she helped two brothers whose father was killed in Shiraz. Each had been jailed three times. They are in America now and learning English, but their mother and siblings remain in Iran.

Nosrat has a tip for all immigrants trying to learn English, one of which this reporter heartily approves: listen to the twenty-four-hour news radio stations. "They keep repeating the same things," she points out, "and they have good pronunciation. I recommend it for all newcomers!" One might think that it would be frustrating for a woman who once ran a school to wind up sewing clothes, but Nosrat took a patient approach to the long road ahead. Her thinking was, "Go to school, learn little by little. Take baby steps." That's all she could do, so she perfected it.

Once she felt comfortable with her English, Nosrat went on to earn an M.A. in economics, and started on her Ph.D. in the same subject. Her interest stems from her conviction, which she shares with many experts in international relations, that economic inequality is a fundamental obstacle to peace. But most of her learning—or more exactly, unlearning—experiences took place outside of school. It took time, for example, before she discovered that she was free to practice her faith. "When I received my first *American Bahá'í*," she says, referring to the religion's newsletter in the United States, "I sat down and said, 'God. These people are not careful. What are they doing? Why do they mail this without any envelope? That's dangerous.' " In Iran, she explains, a man on a bicycle delivered the Bahá'í papers, but only after knocking on "every door in every alley," and only after he had made absolutely sure that he was putting the paper in Bahá'í hands. "Because," she says, "we know the consequences. When I saw the difference, I couldn't believe there was so much freedom. I said 'God, these people are doing wrong things. I have to inform them not to do that!' "

Nosrat had not expected harsh persecution in America, but true freedom was beyond her comprehension. "You hear 'freedom,' " she says, "but you really don't know the limits. I thought they, for example, weren't going to kill me—they were going to beat me up, or they're going to take my book and throw it out. But this much freedom, I could not believe it. Sometimes still I don't." Her father had a similar experience—but from a merchant's perspective—when he immigrated in 1975 with Nosrat's mother. To the day he died, sadly only two years later, he was convinced that had he immigrated sooner, he would have become a wealthy man.

Even after Nosrat gained the courage to take a Bahá'í book on the subway, she had to suppress an urge to cover it with her notebook. Finally, she learned that *no one cared*. People on the subway were going about their own business. If anything, she found people who were curious, but never angry. At home, she started decorating her walls with symbols of her faith—prayers, photographs of her spiritual leaders, and even the masthead of the paper she couldn't believe was openly delivered. This is something she would never have dared to do in Iran. "I always sighed for that. Then I started having them in my house in New York. I was overdoing it even! I said, 'I'm not even going to see the walls.' "

For a time, she carried her caution to her English classes at New York University. One assignment troubled her: she was expected to give a presentation in front of the class on anything, anything she wanted: "Of course, I wanted to talk about the Bahá'í faith! But I knew I couldn't." She asked her teacher if she could. Of course she could, the teacher answered. Hadn't the teacher said "anything, anything at all"? Nosrat was thoroughly addled. "I couldn't believe that. I went to her a second time. I said, 'You mean if I'm a Bahá'í and I want to talk about Bahá'í faith, I can?' " Same answer, same disbelief on Nosrat's part. "So I went to her for the third time, because I thought maybe she doesn't understand." This time the teacher looked her in the eyes, and said, curtly, "Why do you keep asking me? You can talk about anything you want!" It may seem as if Nosrat was being dense, but this is what state oppression can do to a person. I have seen such reactions before, in people who managed to leave totalitarian states such as the former Soviet Union and Cultural Revolution–era China. For those who have known nothing but fear, freedom can perhaps be assimilated on an intellectual level, but a gut understanding of it can take much longer.

Nosrat explained to her class that during the entire time she was at university in Iran, she never once mentioned the word *Bahá'í*. Then she started to cry as she said, "And here I am, standing before you, talking about Bahá'í faith." I, personally, can think of no more ringing endorsement of America.

"I won't say anything negative about this country," Nosrat said several times. Well, what about our ongoing racial intolerance? What about what seems to be a disturbing rise in anti-Semitic attacks? They are there, there's no doubt they have happened, but Nosrat always compares the tolerance she found in this country with what she experienced in her homeland, where it seemed everyone was against her, all the time. Here, she says, she can openly fight intolerance. In Iran, she could only hide and hope.

Even during the Iran hostage crisis, when Nosrat was living in conservative Orange County, California, she found acceptance. She'd moved to California in 1977 to escape the cold New York winters, but after extremists captured the American embassy in Tehran, she could see that things were getting "really hot" for Southern California's Iranian immigrants. She called her mother, who had settled in Florida, to tell her she was going to visit her neighbors. She "wanted them to know . . . I'm not that type." Nosrat went to their doors and said, "I don't want you to be scared of me." Only one person on her block was concerned enough to ask exactly how different she was. "I'm so different," she replied, "that if I was there they would kill me." And she told all of them "that I believe in peace."

Nosrat was happy with multiethnic Southern California and found plenty of work teaching Persian at various colleges. But in 1984, shortly after she married an American Bahá'í from Birmingham, Alabama, she realized other communities could benefit more from her dedicated volunteer work. Nosrat, who was helping to organize race unity celebrations that she hoped would take place across the country, says her husband told her "that if one city on this earth needs a race unity celebration, it's Birmingham." They moved there the same year they married, and Nosrat saw her efforts pay off in a successful event. She even got a proclamation of support from Governor George Wallace.

Two years later, the job market took them to Florida, where they settled into a comfortable life of steady work and dedicated service. But when her mother fell ill, she turned her attentions to her family. For two years, she took time off from work to care for her ailing mother. After Nosrat's mother passed away in 1998, Nosrat's husband helped her dreams come true. They had learned how to survive on one paycheck, he explained to her, and they could continue to do so. Her efforts could now be totally devoted to unpaid volunteer work. "This was always my dream," Nosrat continues, "and he said, 'Now you're going to have your dream life!' " Nosrat has since volunteered at the local hospital, worked with Iranian immigrants, and helped organize unity events with the city. But the work that speaks most directly to her past and her beliefs is with the Interfaith Council of Greater Hollywood.

She went to the council with a few proposals for educating children and bringing in representatives from more diverse faiths. "I wanted to pick it up, or pull it up, to the stars," is how she puts it. In six months, the council made her its vice president of programming. She organized meetings that included leaders of the Native American, Jewish, Christian, Muslim, and Bahá'í communities as a way of "opening eyes and softening hearts."

She paid special attention to the Muslim community, which was then keeping a low profile. "Because of all these negative publicities about Muslims," she explains, "they were not really attending. They were probably not comfortable." To a local Muslim leader from the Caribbean she said, "Don't only come yourself, bring others. Let them *see* Muslims. Let them see that 'Muslim' does not mean 'war.' " When Nosrat was made president of the Interfaith Council the following year, she asked this man to serve as vice president. Her other vice president is a rabbi.

Nosrat then reached out to Buddhists and Hindus, and now she's casting a net for Zoroastrians and Sikhs—"Anybody," she says. "Why not?" Each faith, in Nosrat's view, believes in the same God, and all have the same goals. By pooling their community services, they can reach more people in need. By praying together, they can deepen their respect for other faiths and see their own in a new light.

Nosrat's life continues to resonate with the lesson she learned so long ago from her Bahá'í teacher back in Iran, when she showed her class those pictures of faraway people. "I'm seeing more of my sisters and brothers," she says, "learning about them, and with them. And this is the beauty of life." Her Interfaith Council has been visited by Archbishop Desmond Tutu and the Dalai Lama. Her neighbors in Pembroke Pines, Florida, are from Greece, Japan, South America, and the Caribbean. Her local school district claims to have students from more than 150 countries. *E pluribus unum* isn't just something Nosrat has read on the back of a quarter; it's her conviction and her way of life.

When Nosrat first read the First Amendment in classes she took for her citizenship exam, it was another occasion for tears. Those words— "Congress shall make no law respecting an establishment of religion, or prohibiting the free exercise thereof"—might not seem to carry much emotional weight, but Nosrat saw them not only as an embrace of humanity and a call for peace, but also as a political reflection of God's law: accept one another, love one another. We Americans, in our history, may not have always followed this higher law, but we have enshrined the idea that any religion or ethnic group will have a chance to call this country home . . . as Nosrat did when she learned how high her faith could fly in America. Home is more to her than simply where she lives. "Home," she says, "is where you are free."

Margaret Pfeffer Gilleo

The vigor with which we Americans still debate freedom of speech, two hundred years after the First Amendment was penned, testifies to the necessity of this guarantee. Freedom of speech means that almost all Americans will at some point have to endure speech and actions they find offensive. It has given us tasteless bumper stickers and "shock jock" DJs, Nazi marches and Klan rallies, not to mention court rulings protecting the "expressions" of exotic dancers. And it makes America a country worth living in.

Somewhere between the heights of Martin Luther King Jr.'s oratory and the least common denominator, anyone can become involved in public discourse with something as simple as a lapel pin or, in Margaret Gilleo's case, a lawn sign.

You may remember Margaret Gilleo. She's the woman whose quiet protest against the Gulf War took her to the Supreme Court. She unexpectedly became a champion of free speech while championing her lifelong cause of world peace. Now her fight with city hall has shaped legal precedent, resulting in a court ruling that bears her name and expands the First Amendment rights of every American.

Growing up in St. Louis during World War II, five-year-old Margaret dutifully put her family's empty tin cans out on the curb for the war effort. "I remember thinking," she recalls, "why was the war in Europe, and not in the United States?" When it occurred to her that it *could* come to the United States, "I just decided at that point that I was against war," she says. "That it was a terrible thing, and that I would do what I could to try to stop it." It was a loss of innocence that, for her, was "a defining moment."

By the time Margaret was in her twenties, her work for peace had also become an investment in the futures of her three young children. She worked behind the scenes to protest the war in Vietnam, gathering signatures and helping to raise awareness through meetings. Legal channels were Margaret's preferred method of operation; unlike some of her fellow protestors, because of her children she drew the line at risking arrest. Margaret believed, and still believes, in "the process in this country for legitimate protest."

That faith was shaken in 1968, when Margaret became an active supporter of antiwar candidate Eugene McCarthy's bid to gain the Democratic presidential nomination. "That was my first plunge into politics," she says, "and it was not a happy one." Margaret worked close to home to enroll like-minded people in the party and urge them to attend an open meeting where they could vote on a slate of delegates to go to the township's Democratic convention. She was not working outside her home at the time, and so she made hundreds of phone calls. She thought that she had made a difference. "The night of the meeting," she recalls, "we got there, and we had a *big* turnout. And we thought, 'We've got it made!' " She was surprised to find out that the folks who were running the meeting weren't interested in taking a vote. "So the committee-woman stood up," she continues, "and said, 'I have over six hundred proxy ballots here, our slate is elected, meeting adjourned.' " The party members who had shown up at the meeting never got a chance to have their say, and no one ever saw the proxy ballots. Margaret and her group weren't even sure if this counted as playing by the rules.

Margaret adds that she and her fellow McCarthy followers showed up at the county convention to protest but were thrown out. She was dumbfounded, and even worse, she says with a laugh, she had to hear her staunchly Republican father gloat: "He was kind of delighted to see that. He said, 'Well, that's what happens with Democrats.' "

Her disillusion transformed into "horror" and "shock" as Margaret watched the events unfold inside and outside the 1968 Democratic National Convention. Like so many who were there and watching on television screens across the country, she "couldn't believe this was America." Her respect for the law left her deeply offended by the actions of the police. "We can disagree," she says, "but there are *processes.*"

Margaret spent the next decade or so working for environmental causes and, in keeping with the times, got an M.B.A. and worked on Wall Street in the late 1980s. She soon left that world, though, because the market's unresponsiveness to her concerns for social and environmental justice left her cold. As she puts it, "I didn't like the cutthroat attitude . . . and the total lack of ethical content." In 1989, Margaret, then widowed, returned to the St. Louis area.

A real estate agent friend took Margaret to see a house in Ladue, a close-in suburb of nine thousand, while warning her liberal acquaintance that it was "a very conservative area." Margaret loved the house and the town's verdant streets, and wasn't put off by the warning. After all, she wasn't planning to incite anything.

"I remember the day I moved in, I just sat in the yard for about an hour and stared at the trees," she recalls. Margaret threw herself back into the life of her community, serving on the St. Louis Catholic Archdiocese Commission on Human Rights, and eventually rising to chair its Environmental Concerns Committee. Then, in July 1990, Iraq invaded Kuwait.

A group of about thirty formed an ad hoc committee, calling itself the St. Louis Forum for Peace in the Persian Gulf. "Every day," Margaret remembers, "we'd see fifty thousand more troops going to the Gulf, and a small group of us began to get really worried . . . We started having early morning meetings, and we thought the first thing is to get people really aware of what's going on." At the time, polls were showing the country evenly split on whether the United States should go to war or not. That would change, but this small, idealistic group thought they should try to tilt the balance toward peace.

Margaret and her group soon found themselves at odds with the overwhelming tide of public sentiment. Even after ten years of Persian Gulf stalemate, most Americans today would disagree with Margaret's assertion that the war was wrong. But our speech freedoms are meant to protect unpopular views. Expressions of prevailing opinion and the wishes of the government need no protection. Margaret's expression, in the form of a small lawn sign, did.

Against a red, white, and blue background, the sign read SAY NO TO WAR IN THE PERSIAN GULF, CALL CONGRESS NOW. True to Margaret's stubborn belief in working within the system, it advocated democratic participation, not revolution. Margaret put the sign on her front lawn. The next morning, it was gone.

The next sign was free; the man who'd sold her the first one laughed when she explained what happened, says Margaret, "That made my average cost two dollars per sign." She borrowed a hammer from a neighbor and pounded the stake holding the sign deep into the ground, thinking that might deter any thieves. Three days later, Margaret found the sign lying on her lawn after being pulled from the ground. She felt it was her civic duty to call the police.

The two policemen who came to her door had some news for Margaret: she was breaking the law by having the sign on her lawn. Ladue's city ordinance allowed FOR SALE signs and banners that announced birthdays, anniversaries, and the like, but not a sign of protest. The law even made an exception for cases of "unnecessary hardship," but to this day, Margaret doesn't know what they meant by that: "Nobody had ever defined that. Nobody had ever asked them before. I joked about it, because this is an affluent community, and asked, what do they mean, I take in laundry or something like that? But nobody knew."

Margaret drove down to city hall to look at this ordinance for herself. She wondered out loud if this law could somehow be against the First Amendment and was told, "No, dear, it's been tested." Then the "very pleasant" lady behind a counter asked her what the sign said. "I told her," Margaret remembers, "and I could see this sort of electric shock." The woman excused herself and got her a copy of the ordinance.

The exception for "unnecessary hardship" required a permit and a ten-dollar fee. Margaret highlighted this passage and took it back the next day, explaining that she would like a permit because war is an unnecessary hardship. Then she got what they call the runaround. The person she needed to talk to was away from the office. After three days, Margaret insisted that they give her someone else to speak to.

They directed her to the chief of police, who, according to Margaret, was very friendly, but after she explained to him the content of the sign he was also very firm. He said she couldn't do that in Ladue. He recommended that she go to the city council meeting to present her request. Margaret decided to push forward: "At this point I thought, 'I'm getting into something big. This is no longer just a little local thing. This is getting to be a bit hairy.' "

Margaret went to the city council meeting flanked by her friends and armed with advice. She'd learned that municipalities could regulate signs as far as time, place, and manner were concerned. That is, they could determine how large the sign was, how long it could stay up, and, for example, how far back from the road one could put it. But in Margaret's mind, while they could regulate her protest, they could not prohibit it.

As involved citizens and any reporter who's worked the city government beat might have been able to predict, the city council meeting was, as Margaret puts it, "interminable." Margaret sat through all the business of potholes and driveway extension variances until they opened up the meeting to citizens' requests. Margaret asked the six council members and the mayor for permission to pay ten dollars for a permit to post her sign for one month. One of them asked what the sign said, and she told them. "I remember one man laughing and one man looking just horrified. They talked about it a bit and they said something like, 'Do we want to put holes in an ordinance which has served the city well? Ladue will get to look like junk city.' " This is the argument that the city would use all the way to the Supreme Court.

Two of Margaret's friends got up and also asked for permits. Then two lawyers, also Ladue residents—one of whom worked with the American Civil Liberties Union—stood up and argued for these citizens' First Amendment rights. The mayor and the council chewed it over for a while and decided to put their request to a vote. The result? "They voted seven to nothing against me."

Margaret's suspicion that she had started something big was borne out right away. Somebody, and Margaret insists that it wasn't her, called the *St. Louis Post-Dispatch,* which sent a reporter to interview her and a photographer to her home to take a picture of her sign. Expecting to find a small article in the Metro section, Margaret opened the paper the next day, "and there was this big picture of me on the third page with [a headline] that said 'Ladue Denies Permits for Yard Signs.' " Margaret remembers this as a "very crazy" day, punctuated by a call from her mother. "She said, 'That was a cute picture in the paper.' I said, 'Oh, well thank you,' and she said, 'Now you're *not* going to do any more?!' It was sort of half a question and half a command."

In fact, Margaret had herself decided that things had gone far enough. She had, after all, accomplished her original intention beyond all expectations—the picture in the paper of her holding her sign showed all who saw it that public opinion over the storm then still brewing in the Persian Gulf was not monolithic. There were those who believed that the best way to support our troops was to bring them home.

But one of the lawyers who had spoken at the city council meeting told Margaret that she *needed* to take her complaint to the ACLU. A few of her friends agreed. She called the ACLU and found out that the organization would handle the legal expenses if they accepted her case. Margaret would, however, have to give a deposition and appear in court. She knew that the cost to her life would be something else. She considered the possibility that "people would get angry with me, people would not speak to me, I might lose friends over this." But her conscience would not be silenced. With a woman she calls her spiritual advisor, she discussed "my conviction about war, how as a child I had this thought that war was wrong, but as I grew up I believed it became a serious moral issue." What it came down to, she says, was her conviction "that war in general was immoral."

Nevertheless, Margaret was still very nervous when it came time to sign on with the ACLU. For her and her cause, it seemed a point of no return. She was deposed on Christmas Eve, 1990; on December 26, they went into court for their hearing. The city had prepared videos to show what a beautiful town Ladue is, and how their ordinance was the only thing preventing a rash of lawn signs that would ruin it. They argued that lawn signs would invade the privacy of other residents, and that visitors would drive in to see them. Margaret's lawyers came prepared with pictures of permitted signs, such as banners that wished a happy birthday or announced an anniversary.

The hearing lasted four hours, and then Margaret went skiing in Yellowstone. That's where her lawyers reached her to say that she had won, that the judge had called Ladue's law unconstitutional "on its face." When Margaret got back, she put up a new sign.

By that time, the war had broken out, and she chose to adapt her message. She and other members of her group put small signs in their bedroom windows, FOR PEACE IN THE GULF, with a small white candle next to it. "Our thought was, okay, whatever side you're on, whether you're for it or against it, you'll want peace. You'll want it to end." Margaret felt the same way about her fight with city hall, but it wasn't over.

"So they wrote this new ordinance that was, as my lawyer put it, even more obnoxious than the original one." This one attempted to get around the exemption for FOR SALE signs and birthday greetings with a complete ban on all signage on front lawns. They even banned signs in windows, like the one Margaret had in place.

The judge's opinion on this new ordinance was terse, explaining simply to see her previous opinion. Later in the spring, the city took it to the Eighth Circuit Court of Appeals. Margaret didn't have to testify this time but watched her lawyers argue the case before a three-judge panel. They ruled unanimously, upholding the previous decision. "I thought, end of story," Margaret says. "And then my lawyer said to me that it might not be the end, because they have until a certain date to appeal to the Supreme Court." This possibility seemed very remote to her—even if they did appeal, she reckoned, why would the Supreme Court take such a case? "It's just one little sign, one person, one unimportant municipality," was how she looked at it at the time.

But the town did appeal, and the Court was interested. In Margaret's case, the Justices saw an opportunity to flesh out legal understanding of the First Amendment's free speech clause. The highest court in the land heard opening arguments in *City of Ladue v. Gilleo*, 512 U.S. 43 (1994) on February 23, 1994.

Margaret admits that she has a hard time conveying the thrill of watching your own case come up before the Supreme Court. She had expected to be bored by a string of "legalese," but she found the questioning full of "high drama and high comedy." She also thought the questions directed at her lawyer were so tough that her side might not prevail. But in June of 1994, the Court ruled unanimously that "the ordinance violates a Ladue resident's right to free speech." In other words, Margaret had prevailed. The majority, in their written opinion, even called her little eight-by-ten-inch sign an "important and distinct medium of expression of political, religious, or personal messages."

Although Margaret had not sought her day in the court of last resort, she found herself immensely satisfied with the vindication the Court's decision represented. "I really did see the ideals of this country working," she says, adding that her experience showed her that an individual could get respect from the system. Margaret took time off, after the decision, to share the civics lesson she had gained with local schools. In some other countries, she would tell the students, someone who spoke out against the government could be jailed. In this country, they are protected at the highest points in the government they are criticizing.

Even before Margaret went to the Supreme Court, a reporter had asked her to pose holding her sign while thrusting a clenched fist in the air. Margaret demurred, saying, "That's not my style." But the case had left her with a high profile that many in her area thought could be parlayed into politics. So she sought the Democratic nomination for Congress in her district, "an experience," she says, "which I hated."

The beginning stages were exciting, Margaret adds, but "what I found out was that what people care most about is how much money you can raise . . . people aren't interested in any kind of nuanced opinions." Margaret also couldn't fully support the Democratic pro-choice plank. "One of the most difficult things for me, as a Catholic, is the abortion issue. So I found myself an advisor at St. Louis University who was a Catholic priest, and we spent hours to develop a different approach that wouldn't be either pro-life or pro-choice." Margaret wanted to work on the "causes" of abortion, to investigate how a society that confronts poverty while providing educational opportunity might provide a middle way. But she feels that voters and party members were simply interested in whether she was on one side or the other.

When she realized that she was losing the primary, her attitude was, "good." Margaret learned that while she believes in the system and will always work with and within it, her dreams don't necessarily include becoming a part of it. In the years since her foray into politics, she's gone back to school to study "the theology of the natural world," a way to bring her spiritual life into her environmental activism. She's now an adjunct professor at Maryville University of St. Louis.

Margaret Gilleo might not have turned her Supreme Court case into political gold, but she did find an outpouring of support in the form of letters from around the country. She was in the habit of placing a quick phone call to the writer—those letters really did mean a lot to her. One day she called a man who, as it turned out, had quit his job with a defense contractor following a crisis of conscience. And, like Margaret, he'd also worked for the St. Louis Economic Conversion Project, which sought a post–cold war transition to a peacetime economy. The two agreed to have lunch. Now they are married. Margaret and her husband joke about "the most elaborate and expensive personal ad anybody ever wrote," with her husband saying, according to Margaret, that "it only took Saddam Hussein, George Bush, the mayor and city council of Ladue, the ACLU, four federal judges, and nine Supreme Court justices to introduce us. But we did meet."

Margaret says she's seen a few more lawn signs in Ladue since her court case. They tend to spring up during an election year, she says, send their message for a couple of weeks, then disappear. She points out the irony that most of the signs are opposed to her own political views, and her husband jokes about "what Margaret hath wrought." She still gets along with her neighbors, and says she even has a cordial, mutually respectful relationship with the mayor. She doesn't think the signs have ruined the town's aesthetics—after all, the city is still allowed to draft *reasonable* regulations covering these expressions. Besides, Margaret Gilleo knows that the American dream can't always be picket-fence neat. "Democracy's messy," she concludes. "It's not easy to listen to everybody."

Dereje Bereded

Not long before he was interviewed for this book, Ethiopian graduate student Dereje Bereded ran into a fellow student, an Eritrean, outside the Howard University Dental School they both attend in Washington, D.C. As Dereje explains, the conversation took a quick serious turn. "You guys keep deporting us," the Eritrean accused, referring to the latest in a series of mass deportations of Eritreans from Ethiopia. Dereje, who supports neither the current government of Ethiopia nor that of Eritrea, shot back to her that the same thing had happened nine years ago to Ethiopians living in Eritrea. Still, he says, "I laughed at it," regarding the encounter as more political than personal. Ten minutes later, though, Dereje was told that the young woman's mother had been deported. "At midnight, a day before. She doesn't know where her mom is."

That missing mother joined the tens of thousands of Eritreans who have been deported from Ethiopia in recent years. And Dereje personally knows some of the tens of thousands of Ethiopians who have been forced to leave Eritrea. Both sides were expelling people because of their national heritage, even if these folks have never set foot in their "home" country. Both sides were breaking up families and deporting children and infants, simply because one or another parent may have had roots on the wrong side of a disputed border.

Eritrea gained independence from Ethiopia in 1993, at the end of thirty years of war that, like so many conflicts in Africa, had its roots in colonialism. When a sympathetic regime came to power soon afterward in Ethiopia, it seemed possible for a time that the two countries would become strong international partners. Ethiopia and Eritrea, after all, share a common history and ethnicity. Their people speak the same language. For a brief period in the 1990s, the nations forged strong trade relations and fostered common interests. Intermarriage was common. But that all came tumbling down in the spring of 1998, when a border dispute put an end to the era of good feelings.

In the United States, freedom of association goes hand in hand with freedom of the press and the right to petition the government. Our associations give us the strength of numbers to work for our dreams, the quintessential example being the exhortations of Martin Luther King Jr. on the national Mall before one of the largest peaceful assemblies ever seen in that time. He had a dream, he told us, a dream few at the time dared to voice. But freedom of assembly and association also nourishes our "small" dreams, our pursuit of happiness, be it in our small pleasures—a Little League team, a sewing circle, a friendly card game, a backyard cookout—or in life choices like joining a church, adopting a child, or entering into a marriage. In American dreams, freedom of assembly and association play a quiet role in our daily lives. In Dereje's life in America, it has allowed him to organize a small, nonpolitical group that he says would not have been possible in his homeland.

Ethiopia professes to grant freedom of speech, freedom of assembly, and other basic human rights. But as in many developing nations, these rights all too often become mere currency in a bid for stability. In Ethiopia, dozens of political parties sprung up after the fall of the Marxist government in 1991. The majority of those parties now strongly oppose the policies of the ruling Ethiopian People's Revolutionary Democratic Front (EPRDF), and so are barred from participating in the political process. These politics have a way of filtering down to the personal, as Dereje has seen.

"We are a forgiving people, but now it's extreme," he says. "The hatred is in everyone's imagination right now." He has just returned from a stay in Ethiopia, and with the memory of the visit fresh in his mind says that the government plays "an extremely strong role" in fostering division. If you're the government, he explains, and want to hold on to power, "You have to make people fight each other. You have to make sure people don't live together. And that's exactly what happened." It wasn't always like this, he adds, but he also allows that politicians have turned some of the old tribal rivalries to their advantage.

Ethiopians are, as Dereje says, a forgiving people. But even when individuals manage to put aside their regional and tribal differences in day-to-day life, they cannot help but become caught up in the Eritrean and Ethiopian governments' efforts to expel each other's people. Concentration camps sprang up on both sides of the border, filled by arrests and emptied out by forced marches through rough terrain and across the often-flooded Mereb River, which separates the two countries. The report of the U.N. High Commission on Refugees puts the number of refugees at 345,000, enough for several journalists covering the region to call it "Africa's Kosovo."

It is an apt but imperfect comparison because in this case there is almost no ethnic difference between the deporters and the deported. The background of each country's leader, Dereje insists, "tells you everything." Referring to the pair several times as "*those* guys," he points out that "the president of Eritrea is more Ethiopian than the prime minister of Ethiopia. The prime minister of Ethiopia is half Eritrean and half Ethiopian. The president of Eritrea is almost like three-fourths Ethiopian and one-fourth Eritrean. I'm talking about the president of Eritrea! So that will tell you everything about those countries. Definitely one people, one bloodline. You're talking about almost close brothers."

But those in power have made the two peoples out to be distant cousins locked in a blood feud. Three months before Dereje took his yearly summer trip to Ethiopia, an Eritrean friend of Ethiopian heritage saw her family deported from Eritrea. To Dereje, it was a confirmation of what he had seen and heard in the news. "Even if a child's mother is Eritrean," he says, "because his dad is Ethiopian, they're kicked out without anything. Just thrown out of the country. These are people like you and me, they have televisions, telephones, they're wonderful people, they're educated people, but they throw them out. Some of them, they still live, nine years later, in the shelters, on the street! Some of them live in caves. Nine years later!"

Another friend at Howard, an Ethiopian of Eritrean ancestry, saw her entire family deported to Eritrea. Now, she told Dereje, nearly thirty of them live under a single roof in Asmara, the capital. Dereje's friend struggles to maintain her studies while she holds down the two jobs that enable her to send money back home. "Some of my family married Eritreans," Dereje says. "I'm expecting them to be deported very soon." In the large Ethiopian and Eritrean community in Washington, D.C., everyone watches the news from home, and, Dereje says, "It is like every Ethiopian is affected by this."

Dereje came to the United States nine years ago, before the current troubles flared up. His family was established in southern Ethiopia, their biggest ongoing issue being the fact that they chose to live outside their tribe. They emigrated from northern Ethiopia, crossing provincial lines drawn according to the assumption that some ancient tribes would not want to live together. He says these days some of his friends find it difficult to get work, enroll in school, or secure housing, simply because their parents or grandparents came from another place. The time Dereje has spent in the United States has amplified the absurdity of this attitude in his mind. It's as if, he explains, people were to find themselves excluded because they had moved to, say, Washington from Minnesota. He places the blame on the present government of Ethiopia.

Since coming to the United States, Dereje has reveled in his freedom of movement. He's paid for his education—a bachelor's in biomedical sciences from the University of Minnesota and the degree in dentistry that he earned in May 2001—with a combination of student loans and hard work. The hardest work he remembers well. "I worked for seven months in a slaughterhouse in South Dakota. It was extremely difficult for someone from my [relatively comfortable] background coming to the United States and working in a slaughterhouse. Very dirty. Extremely dirty job." But, he adds, the work paid well and kept him in school. "I had a dream," he says, "so to continue that dream I have to work hard." Dereje also waited tables and worked in a supermarket, while his loans piled up.

But even after his dental school payments and the money he sent home, Dereje had something left over to start a small business. During a summer at home, about two years ago, he witnessed an outbreak of malaria. Dereje knew he could do something about it. The small investment he made at the time has given rise to a general clinic, and he was hoping to open a second one. For the present, Dereje is exporting cheap, and sometimes slightly used but much-needed, medical equipment that he finds on the Internet. His clinic charges on a sliding scale based on ability to pay. During times of drought, many services are free. "When the rich guys come you charge them more, and make it even. I think this is kind of morally fair to do it that way," he says. And just as his clinic won't turn away a patient based on his inability to pay, it won't turn away anyone based on that patient's friends or associates.

Like Nosrat Scott, Dereje does not see America as flawless but says, with intensity in his gaze, that "it makes you stronger, all of these problems." Racism, for example, is something this African immigrant is not blind to. He has seen it in South Dakota ("almost 99.9 percent white people") and in Washington, D.C. ("the opposite"). But in each place, he could see a way to get through. "There's problems in every society, but here in the United States, you can manage. You can pass those obstacles." The fact that government is prohibited from interfering in our associations, he points out, makes passing those obstacles a matter of personal choice, not of politics.

After living in the Midwest, Dereje was happy to join the large Ethiopian and Eritrean communities of Washington, D.C. But at Howard University, he found himself dissatisfied by the level and degree of contact between Eritreans and Ethiopians. With his faith that, in this land, we can work together to forge solutions, Dereje founded the Ethiopian/Eritrean Student Society at Howard University in the spring of 2000. It was a time when the conflict in the horn of Africa was at a fever pitch, when the forced deportations and revelations of concentration camps were reaching their peak. He saw the society as a place where students from the region could celebrate their common heritage while debating their political differences out in the open.

"It's a cultural show," Dereje says when asked to describe the club's purpose. "There are dialogues, lunch breaks. We come together here, watch some videos about our heroes, make fun of our politics. It's mostly just socializing. It keeps us together." All are aware of the hardships and even horrors suffered by those they left behind, but those in the student association seek the common ground and try to meet one another there. "Now we are in exile," Dereje says, "but we almost have an identical child life." The "cultural show," he concludes, is something "to keep us close together and to comfort one another in bad times, good times."

With unity the goal, the club's emphasis on social and cultural exchange is no doubt a good idea. But those in the society are well informed, and everyone has a stake in the situation in Africa, so politics inevitably enters into their meetings. Whenever this happens, Dereje says, his group of forty students—about thirty Ethiopians and ten Eritreans—divides into three groups: the Ethiopians who support the Ethiopian government, the Eritreans who support the Eritrean government, and those who believe both governments are in the wrong. Dereje counts himself in this last group.

Although members are deeply immersed in their lives as students in a large American university, Dereje says they cannot ignore what is happening back home and can't help but argue about it. "There is no way to be distant," he says. "We are from that area, and there is no way to be distanced from politics. We talk about politics all the time, but what happens here is, we're not influenced by government. The government is not affecting our lives. We're in the United States, so there is no deep animosity. If you go to Ethiopia or Eritrea, you don't even see dialogue between those three groups, because one of those groups has the power."

In the horn of Africa, Dereje continues, one must endure daily slights against one's ethnicity, large and small. The hatred builds, and he believes people play right into the hands of governments who seek to divide them. You can be arrested or deported for associating with someone of the wrong nationality or tribe, but free association is also less likely to take place when members of another group have made life harder for you. "Here," Dereje says of the students in the society, "we are worried about, we talk about our families, our country, but not ourselves. We are outside of a whole lot of things when we are here. So we are free to talk. There is no hatred—not *that* much deep hatred. But when you go to Eritrea, or when you go to Ethiopia, it's extremely, extremely difficult because they don't even talk to each other. They *hate* extremely."

Dereje admits that not all is harmonious in the Student Society. They even argued at the beginning over what to call the club. Laughing, he describes how the loyal Eritreans wanted their country's name to appear first, while the loyal Ethiopians, who don't recognize Eritrea as a separate nation, couldn't accept any mention of their rivals' country. Neither group could accept one student's compromise of "East African Student Association." Dereje, who finds this sort of bickering absurd, says that the name is still disputed from time to time, a constant distraction from the real mission of their association.

The organization's social work remains, by necessity, decidedly non-political. "We give to starvation causes," the founder explains. "We work on AIDS, and a whole lot of things, but when it comes to government, we don't support or help the government. But we help the people." For the most part, though, the students are exercising their right of assembly in order to enjoy one another's company. "We have fun together, we party together, we date one another," Dereje says. As for politics, "We make a lot of comments. We can joke about it or have serious discussions about it. But in the end, we are the same, the same people."

A short time after he was interviewed, Ethiopia and Eritrea took steps to turn a shaky cease-fire into a permanent peace agreement. This development didn't convince Dereje, who thinks it doesn't address the animosity he believes was created by the two governments. "They need to be gone," he says. With luck and restraint on both sides, though, the peace does allow citizens of both countries to reacquaint themselves with those neighbors on the other side who have not been deported or killed. It's only a glimmer, but it is a hope. And perhaps when Howard's Ethiopian and Eritrean students return, they will remember the perspectives they gained from friends in a land where they could get together as they pleased.

The American melting pot—an often noble but sometimes problematic ideal—has changed a great deal over the years. Our immigrants were once cut off from their homelands by the long transatlantic crossing and the tenuous lines of communication. Now they can be home in hours and send E-mail home in seconds. Dereje himself returns to Ethiopia every year, and he is torn between "longing for Ethiopia," as he puts it, and the knowledge that he is freer, with more opportunity, in America. Increased contact with home might mean that today's immigrants will remain outside of the American mainstream, or that the mainstream itself will fracture into many streams. Some alarmists believe these outlying subcultures will lead to culture wars on a national scale, that the center will not hold. That special, not common, interests will carry the day.

But our governing document has provided an antidote to any corrosive effects of isolation and alienation. We can join with any ethnic, political, or religious group we choose—to build a dialogue, to address a political agenda, or with no other end in mind than to enjoy one another's company. If we have the nerve, this right invites us to associate with people who believe and behave very differently from ourselves. I would like to think of this as an integral part of the American dream, one which acknowledges that, as Dereje repeated again and again, "We are the same people." He may have been speaking of Ethiopians and Eritreans, but his words also resonate with a precept central to what this country is all about.

Tsuyako "Sox" Kitashima

When all else fails, Americans have the right, as the last phrase of the First Amendment tells us, "to petition the government for a redress of grievances." This last right granted by the First Amendment serves as a safety valve for the entire Constitution. It ensures our freedom by saying that if We the People feel we have been wronged, we have every right to take it up with our representatives.

Tsuyako Kitashima, who says everyone knows her as "Sox," lived through one of the greatest injustices perpetrated by the federal government in the twentieth century, to the imprisonment of 120,000 Japanese and Japanese Americans in the early months of the United States' entry into World War II. I'm including this shameful chapter of our history in this collection of stories about American dreams because 120,000 dreams could have been washed away by disillusion during those years. But the intense loyalty of the West Coast Japanese-American community prevented this from happening.

They volunteered for military service, enlisting straight out of the camps. They returned to find their property confiscated or destroyed, and they quietly started over. And some, like Sox, would come to believe that the best way to be a loyal American was to point out that crimes were committed by the government and use legal channels to petition the government for reparation and redress.

At eighty-two years old, Sox is short of stature, silver-haired, and unbelievably energetic. The story she has to tell is one she's told many times before, in schools and community centers, in her effort to keep history alive, no matter how painful. When she speaks about her experiences, it's impossible to detect any anger or resentment. Although she occasionally laughs as she remembers the camps, her overall tone is serious and matter-of-fact. It is the tone of a woman who knows that her efforts helped move the mightiest nation in the world to look back and apologize.

While the attack on Pearl Harbor came as a total surprise to most Americans, our government was already preparing for a possible war with Japan and growing suspicious of Japanese Americans. In October 1941, special representative of the State Department Curtis B. Munson was sent to the West Coast and Hawaii to gather information about potential security threats from this population. His highly secret report was submitted in November 1941.

Munson gathered information from the military services, and logged the opinions of "business, employees, universities, fellow white workers, students, fish packers, lettuce packers, farmers, religious groups, etc.," according to the now-available report. Although he did not "mix indiscriminately" with the Japanese-American population, he did manage interviews with "select Japanese" in all age groups. What he found was a large group of people trying their hardest to live the American dream.

Of the first-generation Japanese, or Issei, Munson wrote: "They have made [the United States] their home. They have brought up their children here, their wealth accumulated by hard labor is here, and many would have become American citizens had they been allowed to do so." Of the second-generation, or Nisei, he wrote: "in spite of discrimination against them and a certain amount of insults accumulated through the years from irresponsible elements, [they] show a pathetic eagerness to be Americans." As Munson's interviewers came back from the field, he wrote, "The story was all the same. There is no Japanese 'problem' on the Coast."

Sox's family was a living example of Munson's findings. Her father had come to America in 1905, and struggled with language and cultural barriers to run a restaurant that catered to American tastes. His wife came over in 1906, and shortly afterward, their restaurant was destroyed by the San Francisco earthquake. Sox's father would have started over, as much of San Francisco did, but he was beaten badly and repeatedly threatened by a local gang after he refused their protection.

"So," Sox continues, "he went into the country to raise strawberries, and that's where most of my life was. My parents worked hard and long hours to see the children get their proper education. It didn't matter if Sunday was just another day of hard work." Sox was born in Hayward, California, in 1918, the fourth of six children.

The Naturalization Act of 1906—as interpreted by the Supreme Court in 1922 in *Takao Ozawa v. U.S.*—said that Sox's parents could not become citizens. That meant they could not own land. Prior to Sox's birth, they moved from town to town until they leased a farm in Centerville, California, from a woman who kindly said they could stay as long as they wanted. They built a house and grew strawberries while sending their children to school.

The small farming community accepted Sox's family, and she remembers only one person—her postman—who ever gave her trouble. Sox's father, who died in 1940, generously gave his strawberries to friends and neighbors, and his children played with the children of the Portuguese immigrants who had settled in the area. It wasn't an easy life, but it could easily be called an American dream. It turned out to be a very delicate one.

The Fourth Amendment was supposed to protect dreams like these: "The right of the people to be secure in their persons, houses, papers, and effects, against unreasonable searches and seizures, shall not be violated." But on February 19, 1942, Executive Order 9066, issued by President Roosevelt in the face of the findings of Munson and against the advice of the FBI and the Office of Naval Intelligence, granted broad powers to the military to ignore the rights of all West Coast residents and citizens of Japanese descent.

From that day on, the family lived in fear. Sox's mother thought she would be deported. The FBI immediately started rounding up leaders in the Japanese-American community, often picking them up off the street without passing word on to their families. The police started shining a spotlight into Sox's home late at night, almost every night. Meanwhile, they were being told by the military to prepare for an "evacuation." They were told it was for their own protection.

"However," Sox remembers, "in one instance that I know, this lady who had two small children, her husband was taken away. He was out in the field somewhere, and the FBI stayed in the house and waited for the husband to come back. While waiting around, they knocked all the pictures off the wall, took the Buddha shrine outside and smashed it to pieces, and tore up all the mattresses. I realized what they were saying [about protecting us] was not true. It was not necessary to do something like that."

After this incident, Sox's mother solemnly gathered every piece of clothing, piece of paper, picture, and religious article that had anything to do with Japan, piled it up in the backyard, and set it all on fire. Pictures of her son in Japanese clothes, letters from home, and the family's shrine were all sacrificed in her attempt to prove her loyalty to the United States. "We were doing everything to not be a suspect of any kind," Sox says. "We would just try to keep busy and not do anything that would indicate any problems."

That proved to be impossible—they were already suspects simply because of their heritage. Sox's brother worked at a car dealership and would bring home discarded pieces of metal that he would use to repair mufflers. The FBI came to their door one day and asked if he was collecting metal to send to Japan. After they got sick of the spotlights in the window, Sox's family covered them with blankets. This only increased visits from the authorities. One night, the family was up late in preparation for the evacuation when their Portuguese neighbors came to bid them farewell. "There was a knock on the door . . . and the little boy went to open the door, and there were these policemen there who said, 'What are you people gathering for?' " Their visitors spoke up on their behalf, but Sox's family was deeply shaken. "Those were the kind of things that they would come and do, they would always keep you very worried about what's going to happen next." In America, where your home is supposed to be your castle and how and with whom you spend your time your own business, this was deeply offensive behavior from the state. Even in wartime.

On May 9, 1942, a "really saddened" Sox said good-bye to her home and the few neighbors who came out to see them and other Japanese families off. The lady who leased Sox's family her land had them all over for breakfast and then drove them to the schoolyard that was to serve as their point of departure. Sox remembers that this good woman was the only person who came inside the schoolyard to say good-bye to them. A young man who owned a place that sold hamburgers also came to the school, but he said his farewells from outside the school fence. "They," says Sox, "were the only two people."

At first she was disappointed and angry with the others whom she considered her friends. But on her way to the Tanforan racetrack in San Bruno, near San Francisco, which was to be their first stop en route to the camps, her anger softened. She remembers thinking, "Well, you know, I can't blame them, because somebody might get upset about them, calling them 'Jap lovers' and things like that . . . that's why they can't come and see us off."

Sox adds that many who didn't show up wrote her letters when she was released from the camp, saying, "When you come to Centerville, don't forget to look us up." But the family would never return to the farm they had cultivated for almost ten years. Their house was demolished to make way for additional farming.

Each prisoner was allowed to bring only what he or she could carry. Sox packed her life into two suitcases. Military police searched Sox and her suitcases as soon as she entered the Tanforan Assembly Center. As her tightly packed belongings spilled out of her cases, her brave front began to crack.

It crumbled further when they served her a lunch of discolored cold cuts, overcooked Swiss chard, and moldy bread. "I was humiliated," she remembers. "Just an hour before that I was eating in this wonderful dining room in a rancher's home. And here . . . we had to stick out our cups and our tin plates to accept this kind of food. I refused to eat it. And I wasn't even thinking about when I was going to get my next meal."

Tanforan had been a horse-racing venue. Now the prisoners were packed in like cattle. Sox's family—four grown children and their mother—unpacked their belongings in a nine-by-twenty-foot horse stall that had been lightly swept and whitewashed. The cramped space smelled of manure, and horsehair still littered the floor. Holes in the walls afforded little privacy. "You could hear everything . . . couples arguing, children crying, and sick people coughing away, and you got a terrible, terrible idea of what was going to happen to you." After she saw the latrines, she thought that "whoever was assigned this job to humiliate us did a *grand* job. Every which way you turned, there was a humiliation, a degradation."

Army personnel gave her a sack, showed her a pile of straw, and told her to make a mattress. The night brought confusion. "I remember sleeping on that straw," she says, "and thinking to myself, 'I can't believe I'm in America. That America would do this to us.' "

Sox and most of the internees were at Tanforan for four months while the authorities prepared permanent camps throughout the western states. When they announced that the Tanforan group was ready to be relocated to Topaz, Utah, a rumor spread quickly around the camp: "[People were saying] the government is trying to take us all inland and they're going to drop a bomb and get rid of us all at one time. Of course, I did not tell my mother, because why upset her with something like that? If it's gonna happen, it's gonna happen."

When she saw the newly constructed barracks at Topaz, she realized that the government wouldn't go through all this trouble just to bomb the Japanese Americans out of existence. The camp was vast, holding more than eight thousand prisoners, and ringed with barbed wire and guard towers. The guns and the wire were pointed inward, eliminating any lingering beliefs anyone might have harbored about having been evacuated for their own protection. Sox's family was again crammed into a single room.

Sox volunteered to be assistant "block manager," which meant that she was responsible for administering to the needs of two hundred people in twelve barracks. It was Sox to whom her fellow internees came to talk about the humiliations they faced daily: the toilets without doors, the meager supply of coal to keep them warm, the unfamiliar and often just plain disgusting food. The job, though, was something to stave off the numbing boredom of camp life, and Sox maintains that it "kept me sane."

Sanity was at a premium; all around her, rumors and speculation continued to fly. One day, a terrible incident made any rumor seem possible. A grandfather and grandson were playing catch and the ball fell on the wrong side of the fence. "So the grandfather got on his stomach and was trying to retrieve it and the guard yelled 'Halt!' but he was kind of deaf and he didn't hear it, and he probably didn't even know what it meant. So they shot him."

The internees took it mostly in silence. "It was useless to even try to make an issue of it, because you couldn't win in those days." But despite the brutality, debasement, and complete loss of freedom, Japanese Americans volunteered in droves when the draft came and the military allowed them to serve.

"Of course the mothers got really upset about that," Sox remembers. They knew that their property had been sold or confiscated, that if their sons were killed, they would be destitute if they ever got out of the camps. "The sons would beg their mothers," Sox continues, " 'Mom, we can't stay here forever, and we have to prove our loyalty in some way.' . . . It was a very, very trying time. We had many meetings to see if as a group we could come to some kind of conclusion . . . and it was terrible. Crying people and people who were heated up about it. It was a terrible period." Those who did serve served with distinction. The all-Japanese-American 442nd Regimental Combat Team was placed in some of the most dangerous battles of the European theater, and came back as one of the most decorated regiments of the war.

Sox left the camp in September 1945. She had become engaged to a man she met in the camp, and they married in Salt Lake City. But V-J celebrations were under way and, she says, "I was afraid to stay there, so we came right back. And people were surprised that I came back. . . . But I was happy to be in, because who knows what happens, some people go crazy and maybe throw a bottle at me or something." She went back to the camp, which remained open as its occupants cautiously sent family members out to find housing and jobs. Upon her return, she found that her work as assistant block manager had gotten her a letter of recommendation to work for the War Relocation Authority—which had organized the evacuation—in San Francisco. She was just glad to have a job.

Sox would work for the government for the rest of her professional life. She took the civil service exam, and got a job with the Veterans Administration in San Francisco, from which she retired in May of 1981. And by that time she had decided that three and a half decades of silence was enough.

Her husband had died of cancer in 1975, and to "get rid of the loneliness," she got involved in community service. That's when she came into contact with some younger Japanese Americans. "It wasn't until 1979," Sox says, "when the third generation gave us a shot in the arm and said, 'I can't understand why you people didn't stay together, and stay put and not leave your home.' Well, we explained to them that we had no choice and when the Western Defense Command is behind us and got the bayonet sort of in our back, and saying you gotta march into a camp, we have to march!" Well, they replied, the survivors of the camps should at least try to get an apology from the government. So Sox and others formed the National Coalition for Redress and Reparation.

The organization started with no money, no resources, not even an office. When Sox moved into Japantown in San Francisco, she rented a three-bedroom apartment so they could run the operation out of her home. The small group reached into their own pockets to fund a letter-writing campaign, starting with Japanese Americans in Congress.

It would take almost ten years before Sox's group would see their labor bear fruit, but their work caught the attention of President Carter almost immediately. Before he left office, he organized a nine-member commission to hear the testimony of those who had been imprisoned. The commission visited San Francisco in August 1981, where they held hearings that brought out emotions buried by decades of daily life and fear of making waves. Sox saw this fear throughout her campaign: "They would say they didn't want to sign a letter to the president because they might be put in jail and such crazy things like that. And I would tell them that I would go in your place to jail if that happens. I know there's no law saying you can't write to the president!"

Ms. Kitashima went to Washington in 1981. "We didn't know what we were supposed to do," she remembers. "In fact, we were kind of gingerly knocking on the doors to see who was going to open the door and greet us." As she continues, one is reminded that, for those who address it head-on, the system can actually be quite responsive: "The congresspeople were very good when we would go there. They would see all of us in the elevator and say, 'What are you people here for?' And we'd say, 'We're trying to get the support of Congress on our problem.' And they were very helpful to us." She can only think of one time her group was turned away at a congressman's door.

Even so, it took three tries to get a bill passed for reparation and redress, despite the support of congressmen such as Senator Daniel Inouye, the late Senator Sparky Matsunaga, Representative Norman Mineta from San Jose, and Representative Robert Matsui of Sacramento. "Each time the bill got to Congress, it was recess time and it died. . . . It took ten long years of ups and downs, but we never gave up. I'm so proud we stuck together."

Sox and her group did not limit their lobbying campaign to Congress. She and a core of ten committed workers and as many as a hundred volunteers canvassed and sent out tens of thousands of letters to fellow Americans. Sox herself mailed more than twenty-five thousand letters before she lost count. Each missive encouraged the recipient to do as they were doing—write to Congress. In the streets, Sox and her group set up tables and asked passersby to sign form letters for Congress. The effort proved to have an educational value, over and above the political, as people who didn't know about the camps learned of the injustice for the first time. And they got mad: "They said, 'Well, give us that paper, we'll sign it!' "

Sox tells her story with great stoicism. Until, that is, she gets to the part where she watched President Reagan sign the Civil Liberties Act of 1988 into law. "It was a moment I will never forget," she says softly through trembling lips. "To be in front of a president of the United States and to see that all that negative feeling we had was being wiped away. It was a great moment. One of *the* great moments."

The Civil Liberties Act provided each surviving former prisoner twenty thousand dollars and a presidential letter of apology. Sox says that the letter was much more important than the money. She gave most of her share away, starting with a gift to her grandson of ten thousand dollars for college. Too young to read the cashier's check, Sox tells with a laugh, he thought it was a gift of one dollar. Sox also donated a large sum to a legal group that had given her encouragement and advice during her campaign. "But I don't know where the rest of it went," she says with a smile.

Sox gave me a copy of the letter signed by President George H. W. Bush that was sent to each former prisoner. The letterhead reads, simply, "The White House" and the text is to the point: "A monetary sum and words alone cannot restore the years or erase painful memories. Neither can they fully convey our nation's resolve to rectify the injustice and to uphold the rights of individuals. We can never fully right the wrongs of the past, but we can take a clear stand for justice and recognize that serious injustices were done to Japanese Americans during World War II. In enacting a law calling for restitution and offering a sincere apology, your fellow Americans have, in a very real sense, renewed their traditional commitment to the ideals of freedom, equality, and justice. You and your family have our best wishes for the future."

"The Constitution was just a piece of paper in those days," Sox says, referring to the era in which she and a nation grew up. "It was only meant for certain people." On one level, of course, the Constitution is always "just a piece of paper." Those who first organized a government of We the People put it in writing that, having vested their God-given rights in the hands of our elected representatives, we would not have them taken from us. From the beginning, it has been flesh-and-blood Americans who have breathed life into that parchment. We fulfill its promise by exercising the freedoms enumerated there. And the appeals of those citizens who challenge government trespass on these rights, along with the judges who rule on them, define the shape of justice for their age.

By knowing, using, and holding fast to their First Amendment rights, the folks in this chapter have done their part to keep the dream of freedom alive for all of us. In doing so, they have renewed their own connections to the principles that, for them, make America a special place.

Does Sox consider herself a patriot? "Oh, yes! I have never stepped into Japan. I feel this is my country. I got my education here, made good friends. I had the opportunity to go to Congress and do all this. I can't see myself giving up this country. This is my country."

ENTERPRISE
DREAMS OF WORK AND WEALTH

America has been another name for opportunity.
—Frederick J. Turner

*I*N America, so the immigrant dream is spun, the streets are paved with gold. It's the mythic depiction of America as the land of opportunity that has drawn millions to our shores and across our borders. For good and bad, America is the citadel of capitalism, the place where fortunes are made and where so many come to try and make theirs, too.

It has been so almost from the beginning. People for whom land ownership simply wasn't possible in Europe came to the New World to make their way relatively unfettered by the boundaries of class. A few hundred years later, America is still a place where your station when you are born does not automatically determine your life's course. Much of the rest of the world has caught up with this way of thinking, but we, though so new upon the face of the earth, were first. The freedom to speak, to practice one's religion freely, to peaceably assemble—all of these are at the very core of the American dream. So is the freedom to go beyond the circumstances of your birth.

This is the value of money. Some folks think it's impolite to talk about it. I note that these tend to be the people for whom it has never been an issue. But to those who have gone without, to those who go without today, dreams of fortune aren't crass—they are visions of a better life, and often the first step toward it.

What is disturbing, what is crass, is the accumulation of wealth for its own sake. True, love of money has been the root of all evil in every nation in every age. But when Alexis de Tocqueville wrote, among his many observations on the new American nation, that he knew of no country "where the love of money has taken a stronger hold on the affections of men," he likely did so with reason. De Tocqueville was writing in 1835 and his words, unfortunately, resonate well into the present. This is how the world sees us, and how we see our lesser selves in our more honest moments.

The many Americans from all walks whom I've met in my work and life, though, lead me to believe that the reason is not that Americans are more venal than their counterparts around the globe but that dreams of wealth are more possible and therefore more widespread here. They become excessive to the degree that Americans are human in their weaknesses.

For those of us who grew up during the Depression, there was certainly no shame in trying to make more money than you had. You likely had very little, and everybody learned to work harder in those days—it was your only hope of getting by. My father was, to put it bluntly, a ditch digger. There was more to the job than that—laying in pipe for the newly growing oil industry, and all the skills that came with that—but "ditch digger" gets to the heart of just how demanding and close to the earth was his work. Nevertheless, it was a badge of honor to always have work, and folks like my father wore their end-of-the-day exhaustion with pride.

As tired as my father's work made him, he always made time in the evening for the correspondence courses that were his road to self-improvement. While the sun was up, he would dig the ditches; once the sun went down, he would go to work on digging his way out of the ditch. He studied electricity and electric motors, and his work paid off when he moved up to the job of lineman. It was still backbreaking labor, but it was done above ground and it paid better. Some years later, he and a friend even started their own business repairing electric motors. The eventual failure of this venture took a lot out of my father, but I remain thankful that this man who had worked so hard and so long for others at least got his shot at the American dream.

There were others in my town, entrepreneurs who were better able to put their drive and determination together with good business sense and know-how, who were more successful at becoming their own bosses. Some even made it quite big over time. We hear a great deal about how the surest way to success is to do what you love, and there's much to this. But to those who came out of the Depression, any gainful work was work well loved. And many who had stuck with and built up their furniture stores, their funeral parlors, their nurseries during the lean years found their sterling work ethics rewarded by riches when times got better.

Today, by most measures, times are good indeed. And taken as a whole, wealth in this country is not only increasing but shifting. Even though the first flush of dot-com mania has run its course, we are hearing less about family fortunes, and more about ground-zero start-ups. The underlying and social reasons for this shift are too numerous to delve into here, but what is really surprising is the degree to which it has been guided by groups that had been excluded (or had excluded themselves) from the traditional corporate environment. Generation X, women, minorities, and immigrants have been frequently slandered as unsuited for the jungle rules of business. Now they are symbols of a new American entrepreneurial spirit.

So if the wealthy are starting to look like everyone else, part of that may be due to the fact that the upper classes are edging slowly closer to reflecting society as a whole. Mark well, the gulf between rich and poor is great and growing, and the billionaires club is still the near-exclusive province of white, middle-aged men. But we've never had as many successful and wealthy young people, women, and minorities as we do now. And with this change in who has money, we get a new perspective on what role money plays in the American dream.

The people you'll meet in the following pages aren't the wealthiest Americans I could find. But I've never believed in measuring one's worth by the size of his or her bank account. I prefer to look at distance traveled. Or as former slave Booker T. Washington put it long ago, "Success is to be measured not so much by the position that one has reached in life as by the obstacles which he has overcome while trying to succeed." These are people who have traveled far in pursuit of their dreams. For Internet entrepreneur Trung Dung, the voyage was literally one of thousands of miles. For Chris Gardner, the physical journey was not long but the cultural one was formidable—his first step to success was to convince himself that an African-American man could succeed as a stockbroker. And on Delores Kesler's path to success, she had to negotiate obstacles familiar to too many women.

I also wanted to hear the stories of people who haven't forgotten where they came from. I hate to see someone succeed in grand fashion but completely lose touch with themselves and their roots along the way. In part, it's because I know of very few people who have simply pulled themselves up by their bootstraps. In my experience, you just can't do it alone. So when I see someone who makes him or herself out to be the embodiment of the "self-made" man or woman, I begin to wonder: whom are they forgetting and why?

None of the people here have forgotten. They know that to whom much is given, much is expected. And they expect a lot from themselves. Perhaps the most encouraging thing I found is that the people in this chapter is that they seem to truly *enjoy* giving back. Stockbroker Chris Gardner doesn't hide his affection for the material trappings of his wealth but insists that being able to give back is by far "the coolest thing" about having money.

Granted, these aren't people who set out to become philanthropists. They wanted to make money. Maybe not as much money as they ended up making, but if they made more than originally planned, well, that was okay with them. And as their wealth grew, they became, I believe, even more aware of the bitter inequalities that have always existed in our country. Those who find their fortune, more than those who are born into wealth, seem to me to retain an acute sense of just what money can *do*. Money, after all, is not an end in itself. What matters is not that you make it but what you do with it once you've made it. At its best, the American dream of fortune is kept alive by those who seem to understand the words of the great American thinker Ralph Waldo Emerson, who wrote that "money, which represents the prose in life, and which is hardly mentioned in parlors without an apology, is, in its effects . . . as beautiful as roses."

Just ask anyone who's done without it.

Delores Pass Kesler

"My dream was never to have a million dollars," says multimillionaire entrepreneur Delores Kesler, "or five million dollars. That was never the dream. . . . The money is almost—and I know someone will say this can't be true—but it's almost coincidental." Really? How is it that millions of dollars can be called coincidental? Does that kind of wealth just happen?

In some ways, the answer is yes. That doesn't discount the value of hard work, careful planning, and having the right idea at the right time. Every successful business starts with these elements. But something else—call it the invisible hand, the free market, the American way, or whatever you will—sets those elements in motion and rewards renewed effort with momentum. That's how the contributions of a single person or a small group can become an unstoppable force.

Talk to successful entrepreneurs, and chances are you will hear them say that the company they founded took on, at some point, "a life of its own." Delores uses this phrase frequently. It happens when the company grows to support more than its founder, when it enters the life of the community, when growth and change become the rule. And when this happens, yes, the money can become coincidental. In Delores's case, the amount of money involved became almost incomprehensible.

Delores used a $10,000 loan in 1977 to found a temporary staffing agency in Jacksonville, Florida. When she retired from the board of directors of AccuStaff in 1997, the company she had formed through a series of mergers had projected revenues of $2 billion. Delores admits that figures like these are "unreal." And adds that when "you realize you have so many employees that you can't see them or touch them, and they're strung out all over the world," it enters the territory of the "totally unreal."

Reality, for Delores, remains the place where she started. In a relaxed, but far from slow, Florida accent, she describes a conversation with her father that led to her first encounter with a checkbook. She was thirteen and wanted ten dollars to attend a 4-H camp. "He said, 'There is no money.' I can remember the conversation well. I said, 'What do you mean? We don't have ten dollars?' At that point, he gave me the checkbook and gave me a stack of bills, and he said, 'If you can make all this work out, then you can have ten dollars.' I started writing checks, and soon ran out of money." It was a rude awakening, but from that day on she managed the checkbook.

The family led a precarious middle-class life on a Jacksonville poultry farm. Delores's father worked for the phone company while dreaming of success as an entrepreneur. The farm was just one of several business ventures that brought him more debt than success. Delores was very close to her father and was deeply affected by his struggles, especially his struggle with alcoholism.

His drinking may have started because of failed business ventures, or his businesses may have failed because of his drinking. Delores isn't sure. She is, however, sure that failure was something he never wanted for himself or his family. When he gathered them together to apologize, and to swear that he'd never drink again, Delores "saw how sincere he was." Her "heart went out to him" because she realized that he was up against "something larger than him."

Our mentors can be deeply flawed and still be powerful motivators. Forty years later, Delores still sees her father's face when he told her, "You can do anything you want to do." Every time she would ask, "Can I do this?" she remembers, he was there to answer "Darling, you can do anything you want to do." Those things stay with you, as Delores will attest.

Her father's positive message was one that Delores needed to hear. She entered the workforce in the early 1960s, when the ceiling for women was very low, and they didn't even bother to make it out of glass. Her dreams, when she got married a year out of high school, were of "a white picket fence, a wonderful home, smiling children, an apron." The death of her father, the birth of her first child, and her divorce all happened by the time she was twenty-two, shattering this simple dream and bringing on a flood of responsibilities.

"I really had to get committed to how I was going to live the type of life I wanted and wanted for my children," Delores realized. Her family—her mother, her younger brother, her child—relied to a large extent on her belief that she could do whatever she wanted to do. Delores started as a secretary with a heavy equipment dealer, and despite a series of promotions, found the deck stacked against her: "I was in the sales training department, training people to sell, but I was not allowed to go out and sell. I was a little frustrated with that. . . . I could see people around me making two, three, four times what I was making, and they were doing it using the skills I knew I could utilize because I had taught them."

Delores thought she could get around this inequality by furthering her education but was told point-blank that the company's tuition reimbursement program was for men only. Her supervisor offered a creative solution: they sent an application to the Chicago headquarters for "D. Pass," and no one asked any questions.

She was now free to fill every corner of her life. She worked full-time, went to school at night, and raised her children at home. "Time," she says, "was almost a blur. I didn't even have time to think." Thousands of women like Delores were discovering, at about the same time, that they had to work twice as hard as their male colleagues for much less pay and recognition. That they were still expected to be the primary homemaker when the day was done. This is not the way things should be in a country that claims equal opportunity for all, but sometimes barriers create a determination in people that can't be stopped.

When Delores founded Conval-Aide Medical Staffing in 1977, female entrepreneurs were a rarity. By 1999, women-owned businesses accounted for 38 percent of all American firms. These companies employed more people in this country alone than all the Fortune 500 companies did internationally. And, according to the National Foundation of Women Business Owners, women-owned businesses are more likely to remain in operation than the average U.S. firm, despite the fact that women-owned businesses continue to have less access to capital.

Delores has a theory about this: "Women don't have as many options. I think quite often women hit that glass ceiling, either low or high within their organization, and have moved out on their own because they don't have a choice." Seeing their dreams stopped short within corporate America, women have sought them elsewhere. They have proven themselves to be very, very good at it.

In 1977, Delores, remarried and with a second child, went out to look for a bank that would give her a $50,000 loan to start Conval-Aide. Nine banks said no. They didn't know what a staffing company was or, if they did, could not see a woman running one. One loan officer openly wondered what would happen to the loan if she had another child. Then, at the tenth bank she approached, Delores found a high-school classmate who told her that no bank was going to loan her fifty grand. So she asked what he could loan without seeking higher approval. Ten thousand was the answer, "and he knew he had said the wrong thing." She insisted on the ten thousand and set up an office with a telephone, a card table, and a folding chair. Six months later, she had paid back the loan.

Delores obviously enjoys looking back at her company's history. There's an excitement in her voice as this trim, blond sixty-year-old explains how *her* company took on a life of its own. Indeed, her timing had been perfect. She got in when temporary staffing was in its embry-onic stages, and gave bankers and customers a thorough education on what it was all about. To a large extent, she got to make up the rules as she went along. By the late 1980s, she had her home market pretty well locked up and started moving into new ones. "At that point," she remembers, "I really began to sit down and say, okay, this could be bigger than just something that would support me here right now."

As Delores's business grew, it became more and more a part of its larger community. Besides the jobs she offered, she also required employees to devote time to community service. Local charities, selected by employees, received a portion of the company's bottom line. Delores one day woke up to the fact that her company was earning $50 million a year, and a large portion of that was going back into the community of Jacksonville, Florida. If the company continued to grow, it could give back even more.

At the time, there were only three staffing companies operating on a national scale, and the demand for temporary workers kept expanding. There was room for another national firm, and Delores decided to step into that space. She set her sights on three other regional staffing ser-vices, eventually convincing them that they should consolidate and then go public. "My dream continued to grow, and my employees, and all of my stakeholders, all got caught up in that dream." By going public, Delores effectively pushed her child out into the world, creating several instant millionaires within the company at the same time. People who had struggled and worked all their lives suddenly could, without bor-rowing or skimping, send their kids to college, buy homes, and even give back something. "An awful lot of people benefited from what started with a ten-thousand-dollar loan," Delores says with a glow.

After Delores's vision of a publicly traded company was complete, she began to see a new life course: "Once I had taken the company public in '94, my goal was, in three to five years, maximum, to move out of there and be in a foundation." She had, she says, enjoyed working with charities so much that her vision now was not just to give, but to create services that weren't there before. The millions she made may be coincidental, even incidental, to her—but they aren't to others in need.

"Retirement" to Delores means she gives about twenty-five to thirty hours a week, rather than ninety to a hundred. She refuses to call what she does these days "work," except in the loosest sense of the word. Through her partnership in a venture capital firm, she completes a cycle in her life by supporting new entrepreneurial ventures. Through her family foundation, she focuses on making a difference in young lives through education, mentoring, and children's programs. Since it was never her goal to make millions, her commitment is now to make those "coincidental" millions work for others.

This chapter was written to examine the role of wealth in the American dream, but people like Delores only help to confuse the issue. It would be so simple to be able to say that greed, pure and plain, was behind their dreams. But so many Americans, once they make their millions, start giving them away. They thrive on it. It becomes, at some point, the most tangible justification for all the hard work they've put in.

A fortune has the potential to isolate its owner. Unless you love humanity, riches will ensure you a life separate from others. While dreams of fortune are ingrained in our national consciousness, so too are images of Howard Hughes dying paranoid and alone, of Charles Foster Kane's dying plea for the lost youth symbolized by "Rosebud."

Once you or your company is worth more than you could easily spend, the only purpose more money serves is to keep score. The money itself becomes meaningless unless it is put to good use. Delores admits that she cannot conceive of a million dollars, but she does know what it means. In 1997, she gave that much to the University of North Florida to provide scholarships to students from Raines High School in Jacksonville. She cried before an audience of thousands when the principal thanked her. She told them that they didn't know how good it felt to be able to give that money away. And she met the first twenty scholarship recipients. Those children are a real measure of a million dollars. For Delores, their futures provide a concrete, meaningful way to keep score.

Trung Dung

The term "Internet millionaire" fast became a cliché in a society obsessed with the "new economy." Internet millionaires were for a time our hottest business heroes, their youthful image and cutting-edge, casual glamour fueling countless American dreams of avarice. But, like all stereotypes, this one obscured the individuals behind it. In San Francisco, a virtual stone's throw from Silicon Valley, there's an Internet millionaire named Trung Dung (pronounced "Young"), who doesn't at all fit the mold of the Brioni jacket–wearing man-child eternally at play.

Thirty years ago, when Saigon fell and the book closed on America's longest war, Trung Dung was an eight-year-old boy living in Vietnam. The images of those final days, of the last helicopters evacuating Americans and South Vietnamese dependents, are deeply etched into our national consciousness. Trung Dung and his family were not on one of those helicopters.

Trung's family had lived in relative stability in wartime Vietnam. His father had been a politician before the war and had served as an officer in the South Vietnamese army. Once the new regime took over in the south, however, Trung's world crumbled around him. His father was sent to a labor camp. All of the family's property was confiscated. And Trung, his mother, grandmother, and two sisters were left to fend for themselves as pariahs in the new communist state.

There was no work for the wife of a former enemy, but there was the underground economy. Trung's mother bought simple goods, such as clothing and appliances, in Saigon and sold them for a small profit in the family's hometown of Phan Thiet. In Phan Thiet, she in turn bought fish sauce for a fraction of the "official" price in Saigon and was able to sell it there; and so this former housewife gradually became a merchant. "These were very heavy things and the transportation was by bus," Trung remembers. "It was a very tough life for her, and so, being the only son in the house, I had to step up from early on to help out."

This only son was only in the fifth grade, but he still found ways to contribute. Trung caught fish after classes and sold them in the evenings. At school he sold fruit to his classmates in between classes on Marxist theory. As he got older, he built and repaired bikes with scavenged parts. Trung's small enterprises were thoroughly illegal in the new Vietnam . . . and crucial to his family's survival.

Trung's family was able to get by with a combination of hard work and ingenuity, but Trung wanted something more. He dreamed of pursuing higher education. Looking around him, he began to see that he would not be able to reach his dream in his homeland. "By '78, the height of the boat people escaping Vietnam, we realized that I can never get into school, into university, because of my background," Trung recalls. His father was still in a labor camp, and there was no sign that he would ever be released. "The only way to have a future was to get out."

The family directed its efforts toward saving for Trung's escape. If he could establish himself somewhere else, they thought, maybe the rest of the family could join him later.

In 1982, the day finally came. After selling all their furniture, jewelry, trinkets, extra clothes, and everything else not already confiscated by the government, Trung's family had five ounces of gold—enough to pay a smuggler to take him down the Tien Giang branch of the Mekong River and across the sea to a friendly country. Trung's mother sent him off with a tenth of an ounce of gold—about fifty dollars—to start a new life, and he joined a group in a shack by the river to wait for a boat that never came.

"The boat never showed up, and the local police came in the morning," Trung remembers. "They took me in for a day and questioned me about who was organizing all this stuff. I told them I ran away from home and just saw these people waiting. I didn't want to implicate my mother. They gave me a few slaps and released me."

Today Trung laughs about his unexpected homecoming, but at the time it was deadly serious. "I went back to school and went back home—normal, but now we [had] lost everything." Everything, that is, but the dream of a better life for Trung. A year later, they found a more reliable boat at a cheaper price. The few belongings they hadn't sold for the first attempt they exchanged for gold. And again Trung waited by the river.

The boat left on schedule, but only ten minutes into the voyage, a patrol boat appeared as if from nowhere and opened fire. "They were shooting because they didn't want anyone to jump into the river.

We had to lie on the deck. It was really traumatic." To make matters worse, Trung realized as shots whizzed over his head that he wouldn't get off as easy as he had the first time. "This time I was fifteen, and so they put me in this hard-core jail, where all the hard-core criminals live, and I stayed there for a month. That was a very interesting experience in itself."

By the time he got out, Trung found that his mother had worked her way into the underworld of refugee smugglers. She was now a middle-man, connecting families with boat owners. It was an incredibly risky business, as Trung's own experiences had shown. And when such arrangements go wrong, it's generally the middleman who gets caught holding the bag.

Trung's mother wasn't profiting from the risk, though. Her commissions went toward getting another place on another boat for her son. As Trung says now, with considerable gratitude, "She put her life on the line for me."

Her efforts finally paid off in 1984. Trung's third try seemed to be a charm, as he successfully boarded a boat that took him and about forty other escaping Vietnamese to an Indonesian offshore drilling rig, and from there officials took the group to a refugee camp. He was out, and he knew why: "My mother had absolute confidence in me, and I cannot even imagine what she went through. Imagine a housewife raising three young kids in a very hostile environment and then [having] to take care of the grandmother and a husband in jail. How she managed to do all that and make sure we are in school and do well in school. . . . And she's personally responsible for me getting out here. It's mind-boggling to me. I have no idea how she did it."

Once he was out, it was as if the baton had passed to Trung. Responsibility for carving out a place for his family in a new country was entirely on his seventeen-year-old shoulders. Luckily, he wasn't alone. One day, as he bided his time in the refugee camp, his elder sister stepped off a boat of new arrivals. Their mother was still at work.

It took a year for Trung and his sister to gain admittance to the United States as children of former allies. Trung says they picked Louisiana because of the climate—reminiscent of home—but something went wrong down the bureaucratic line. "When I got off the plane," Trung remembers, "I realized I was in Boston." No matter. Trung knew that there were schools in Boston as well, and that's where he went, just days after his arrival.

Trung had learned some English in Vietnam and in the camp, but not enough to join a class of his contemporaries. A high school counselor told him that he would need to take two to three years of classes to earn a diploma. This was unacceptable. "I knew my mother was in pretty bad shape, so I asked around and a counselor at the University of Massachusetts said he could help me get admitted if I took the GED." He did and passed by the slimmest of margins: "Pure luck. I think I did well enough on the math and science part to pass."

Trung started to learn, slowly, that he could safely raise his expectations in his adopted country. He could work. He could get scholarships and student loans. He could become a college student. Although his situation was bleak—he shared an apartment with other immigrants who slept three to a room and worked as a janitor in a hospital and a dishwasher in a restaurant in order to send money home—he sensed opportunity in the air and breathed deeply. "I took twice the normal load of classes, too. I don't know how I did it, but at the same time there was so much to do."

Just months earlier, Trung had seen a computer for the first time in the refugee camp. He even remembers the model—an old Apple II. He had never even used a pocket calculator before he took his first computer class at the University of Massachusetts at Boston, but he knew as soon as he dove in that his future would be in programming.

Why was this former refugee from an undeveloped country drawn so strongly to computer science? This was, remember, well before the Internet boom. Perhaps it was a matter of control. Programming gave Trung absolute control over a complex and expensive machine—a stark contrast to the helplessness he had felt in a childhood where others determined his fate. But beyond that, he says, programming gave him a way to express himself clearly and unambiguously. In computers, Trung found a bridge across the language barrier. As he puts it, "The way people program is to articulate, as if to a young child. It's very simple stuff, but you can accomplish very complex things. That's why I enjoy it."

Trung graduated in 1988 at the top of his class. In three years he had taken every undergraduate and almost every graduate course in computer science that the university had to offer. He had fulfilled his child-hood dream . . . and he was immediately presented with a serious choice.

"I was offered a job and also offered a chance to study for the Ph.D. program at Boston University. A Ph.D. was an unimaginable dream, because when I was in school, people who had the Ph.D. were like gods to me, beyond what I could even think of." A job, on the other hand, would have allowed Trung to send more money home. His mother and his father, still in prison, both wrote Trung urging him to take the scholarship. The slightly better life the extra money would have afforded them was not as important to his mother and father as the opportunity before their son.

Trung's parents didn't realize it at the time, but a better life was just around the corner. In 1990, as relations between the United States and Vietnam warmed, Trung's father was released from prison and the entire family was allowed to immigrate to the United States. A joyous reunion was in the making. "When I left the country, my younger sister was a lit-tle girl. Now she was almost twenty. And my father, I didn't even remember what he looked like. It was wonderful. It was the first time since 1975 that the whole family [was] together in one place. For the first few days all we did was talk."

The son they had sent abroad was already a success in his parents' eyes, but the addition of three new family members into Trung's small, run-down Dorchester apartment forced him to reconsider academic life. Just short of completing his thesis, Trung left the Ph.D. program and joined a promising e-commerce company. Before long, he had saved enough to buy his family a house.

Trung's goals were still very modest. He could see his life moving for-ward methodically, in the risk-free, traditional manner favored by his father. But with the emergence of the Internet as a popular medium, Trung again found himself at a crossroads. Should he enter the high-risk, high-return world of start-ups and IPOs or stay on the steady career path that would guarantee his family's well-being?

By day, Trung dutifully performed his role as company man. But in the evenings, he played with a piece of revolutionary programming. The idea came while he was building a contact list of refugees for a local Vietnamese temple's Web site. After he got tired of searching for common Vietnamese names, cutting them from various sites, and pasting them onto the list, he automated the process. This meant that a visitor to the temple's Web site could run a complicated search with a few simple clicks, without leaving the Web site.

This technology, now common, had commercial applications that Trung could see even before "e-commerce" was a household word. Businesses don't want viewers to leave their Web site. Trung's application pulls information from other sources and organizes it in a user-friendly manner so they don't have to. That makes it extremely valuable.

But the company Trung worked for, Open Market, couldn't see that far ahead: "It was way too early. The Internet was too young for that kind of idea." Besides, this start-up didn't seem to need it. Their initial public offering in early 1996 was an early success, and Trung's stock options soared to a value of over one million dollars.

This should have been a happy time, but fate had dealt the household a heavy blow. Trung's mother was dying of cancer. "I guess a lot of the hardworking years caught up to her," he says. Her illness brought the family closer together, and Trung spent countless hours by her bed, where he told her about his idea. "She was in a lot of pain. So I kept talking to take her mind away from the pain. I talked to her about all these dreams, about the difficulty I was having persuading the Open Market people to try to adopt my idea. And maybe I should go out on my own and pursue my idea. She was always very supportive, but at the time I didn't believe I could do it."

The day Trung's mother passed away, he knew that he had to start his own company. It really didn't matter that he was leaving a million dollars in stock options behind. "I considered having a hundred thousand dollars very, very rich. But the more I talked to my mother the more she said go and do it. So I made up my mind that I had to do it. All I could think about was that idea."

A former classmate put Trung in touch with a prominent venture capitalist who found him a business partner in technology pioneer Mark Pine. Their instant rapport led to a partnership, with Mark as CEO and Trung as chief technology officer. Trung flew to California and lived in Mark's pool house while he expanded on his initial idea. After four rounds of financing, they raised $35 million. OnDisplay went public in December 1999, pushing the value of Trung's share over $100 million. Trung gave his sisters stock worth more than $20 million each.

What did $100 million mean to a man who used to fish for a living? "It's ridiculous. But I think having the money is great because my sisters and father and relatives don't have to worry." His older sister used to be an accountant who took temporary and contract assignments. Trung says, with a smile, that she's in retirement now. His younger sister recently finished optometry school and relocated to the Bay Area to be closer to her brother. And his father couldn't be more pleased. He's director of a federally funded program for Southeast Asian refugees, and will more than likely continue to do social work after his coming retirement.

With the family taken care of, Trung's attention turned to his company: "After the first few weeks of becoming public, I checked the stocks every day to see what's going on. To me right now it's more meaningful to survive, to be one of the companies that survives." Being so focused on survival doesn't give Trung much time to be extravagant. He's working fifteen-hour days, six days a week, and tutoring Vietnamese-American youth on Sundays. He did find the time to fall in love with and marry a medical student from Vietnam. They even squeezed in a honeymoon. But the couple returned to the same modest apartment in southwest San Francisco that she had lived in before she married a multimillionaire.

Every Tet (the Vietnamese New Year) Trung looks back on the year past. This year, he says he'll be asking himself, "How did this happen?" He knows that he owes a great deal to his mother, his teachers, his financial backers, and his team. But most of his fortune, he believes, is due to something larger: "When I look back," he says, his open gaze reflecting the distance of his journey, "what I see is opportunity."

That's what Trung sees when he looks forward as well. Even if it all came crashing down tomorrow, he says he would "take a few days to suffer" and then go on. "The important thing is how do you recover from the mishaps. There's always more opportunity. There's never a lack of opportunity. That's what I love about this country. So many opportunities."

Chris Gardner

The message that Delores Kesler's father gave her, that "you can do it" push, is one that is amplified and multiplied almost beyond measure in the American mass media. Such optimism is a basic part of the American outlook, one that is reflected back to us in our movies, our television programs and plays, and in the rhetoric of our candidates for political office.

But just as a politician's appeals to America's can-do spirit can amount to so much sugar to help the government's medicine go down, our cultural sunniness can carry a dark side for some in our society. Subtle messages have the capacity to tell certain of us that our goals are out of reach. The young Chris Gardner never thought he could be wealthy. No one had ever actually told him otherwise, but he had only seen other African Americans achieve wealth through sports and entertainment. "It never really crystallized in my mind that I could [have money]," he says. "I wasn't a good athlete. I couldn't sing, I couldn't dance."

The right person sent Chris a very personal piece of encouragement, and sometimes—as we saw with Delores—that can make a big difference. Chris's mother was a schoolteacher who raised him on her own. One day, while Chris was watching a college basketball game, he exclaimed, to no one in particular, that one tall and talented player was going to make a million dollars. "My mom was right over there ironing, and she said, 'Son, you know what? If you want to, one day you can make a million dollars.'

"I believe everything my mom ever told me. If she said I could make a million dollars, damn it, I could do it. But until I *heard her say it*"— Chris raises his voice for these last four words, and claps his hands for emphasis after each passes his lips. He pauses before finishing the thought—"I never thought I could."

Chris Gardner, one learns quickly, makes certain points with force. His deep voice will start to boom, his hands will come together for punctuation, and his eyes will lock in. It only lasts for a second before he leans back, assured that he has made his point. Then, in these more relaxed moments, he'll casually swear or refer to folks as "cats." Somehow, this hipster habit doesn't clash with his taste in clothes—all refinement, no flash—or his fashionably shaved head.

He's made his millions, he isn't ashamed to say. He wanted to make money, he found out how it was done, and he worked for it. His success means that the public schoolchildren he speaks to actually listen, and he tries to make sure they get the same message his mother gave him. To his inspirational talks, however, Chris Gardner adds one big qualification: he is not a role model. No one, he emphasizes, should try to do it the way he did.

When Chris graduated from high school, he had two vague goals: to someday become a doctor and to see the world. If he joined the navy medical corps, he thought, he could do both. Instead, the experience convinced him that he did not want to become a doctor, and the farthest corner of the world he saw was North Carolina. But he did prove himself to be a valuable researcher to an up-and-coming cardiac surgeon, with whom he took an offer to work in San Francisco after his discharge.

Four years later, 1978, Chris had a son with his common-law wife and mounting expenses convinced him that he was ready to "start making some money." The best option he could see was selling scientific and medical supplies. If he worked hard enough, if he sold enough test tubes and Erlenmeyer flasks, he could make maybe $80,000 a year. With this, he thought, he could provide for his family, and start building a nest egg. He didn't love his job but thought that his choices were limited by his past experience and by his decision not to attend college. This route at least promised eventual comfort.

"So one day, I was going out to my car with a catalog, a box of free supplies and gidgets and gadgets and all that, and I see this guy looking for a parking place. Sharpest guy I'd ever seen in my life, driving this gorgeous red Ferrari. . . . I asked him two questions: What do you do? How do you do that? Turns out he was a stockbroker. Turns out this guy is making eighty thousand a month." Chris has a good laugh at this point, and continues. "I'm not a math major, but I kind of figured it out." If Chris was working for the money, he might as well work where the money was.

The typical way to become a stockbroker is to go to college, intern during the summer, and make the connections needed to gain entry. That's the message Chris Gardner gives to the high school students he meets. He tells them to remember that his is not the best way, as he discovered when he started looking for a job with a brokerage firm. For ten months, he interviewed without success. "I didn't fit the profile," he explains. "I don't think race had anything to do with it. I just did not fit the profile. I didn't go to college, I didn't come from money, I wasn't connected. So it's like, who's going to do business with you?"

It was easier to persevere in the beginning of this process, when Chris still had a sales job and a career change carried minimal risk. All he needed was a chance. Finally, someone said, as Chris puts it, " 'Look, guy, we'll give you a shot.' " As it turned out, however, Chris continues, "The day I show up, the guy who said he'd give me a shot had been canned. Nobody knew who I was or why I was there. Meanwhile, I'd quit my other job. I thought I was going to be a big-time kick-ass stockbroker."

Instead, he became a house painter, a yard worker, a laborer on odd jobs who still dreamed of becoming a stockbroker. Months later, as he completed a series of promising interviews at Dean Witter, tension at home was on the rise, and one day it finally broke. Chris came home to find his common-law wife and their son gone without a word. "Took everything but the dust," he says. Out on the stoop of their house in Berkeley, he tried to figure out his next move. Just a few yards away, a policeman was typing his license plate number into a computer.

Chris had twelve hundred dollars' worth of unpaid parking tickets, which sent him to jail for the first time in his life. He describes the experience with words that echo with the young litterer's experience on the "Group W" bench in Arlo Guthrie's "Alice's Restaurant": "They put me in a jail cell . . . with three cats—a murderer, a rapist, and an arsonist. And I'm in for parking tickets." The judge gave him a choice that, because of his empty pockets, was no choice at all: pay now or do ten days in Santa Rita. Chris was forced to do the ten days, no big deal in itself, except for one nagging thought: "Problem was, I'd finally got myself a position. I had one final interview with the man who could say yea or nay at Dean Witter. . . . The day before I was to get out was the day the interview was scheduled."

Put yourself in the position of a job interviewer. An applicant you've never met calls to reschedule his appointment because (and he's very evasive about this) "something came up." The next day, at six-thirty in the morning, he shows up in paint-splattered bell-bottom jeans and sneakers and tells you that his wife left him on the same day he was arrested for parking tickets, that he just got out of jail today and came straight here. Plus, he's got no college degree and no experience in your field. So. Is he the person for the job?

Chris Gardner found perhaps the only man in America who would answer this question in the affirmative. "I told him the whole story," Chris says. "I told him the truth; I could not think of a lie bizarre enough." He explained to his interviewer that "today is the biggest day of my life," adding, "I must admit that I'm underdressed for the occasion." That's how he got into the training program at Dean Witter in San Francisco. By telling the truth.

That initial foot in the door was still a long way off from Chris's visions of making eighty grand a month. He had to pay his dues before he could enter the club. Miscellaneous errands—fetching coffee, ordering lunch, setting up rooms for meetings—were the order of the day. The compensation package the brokerage had given Chris was designed to allow him just enough to get by while he studied for the brokers' exam. But with the promise of riches down the road, Chris had no doubt that he was on his way.

In quiet moments, he wondered where his son was. He was tormented by the thought that this child would grow up, as he had, without knowing his father. Then, out of nowhere, came a knock at the door of Chris's room in an Oakland boardinghouse. It was his ex, there with their eighteen-month-old boy. It was his turn, she told him, to care for their son. Chris couldn't refuse: "I had to break a cycle in my life. . . . So there was no doubt in my mind. There was no hesitancy whatsoever."

This, however, changed everything. Chris and his son were immediately homeless simply because the boardinghouse didn't allow children. The money for first and last month's rent wasn't there, and Chris found that his options for affordable temporary housing—boarding homes or trucker hotels—just weren't safe. Chris's circle of friends could offer only limited help. On many nights, the father and son's only shelter was in the locked bathroom of the subway station, where Chris's son learned to play a game called "Shhhhh!"

Chris was living between two worlds. During the evening, he scrambled to arrange for tomorrow's day care, to find food and a warm place to sleep. During the day, he was learning how to trade millions of dollars of other people's money, taking his cues from wealthy bosses in corner offices. "And nobody knew," he says. "Nobody knew that when I left, I was going to pick up my son, and I didn't know how we were going to eat that night. That I didn't have enough money to take the train."

But Chris was there to learn, not to seek sympathy. He did know, however, that he would need help. In his search for secure housing, he learned of the Glide Memorial United Methodist Church's new shelter for homeless single mothers. He met with the program's founder, the Reverend Cecil Williams, and explained that while he was not a mother, he was a single parent and was indeed homeless. "And more importantly," he continues, "I had a job. I had an opportunity. I just needed someplace to stay so I could get myself together and get an apartment." Williams told him he and his son could become tenants.

The shelter, in the heart of San Francisco's Tenderloin district, had strict rules to encourage tenants to seek employment. No arrivals before six in the evening, everybody out every morning by eight. Tenants never got the same room twice; any personal effects left in the rooms in the morning wouldn't be there in the evening. So every morning, the hard-pressed regulars of the Tenderloin were treated to the curious sight of Chris Gardner, dressed in a suit and pushing a stroller, as he made his way to the subway station carrying a duffel bag full of clothes, an umbrella, a briefcase, a spare suit on a hanger, and "the biggest bag of Pampers in the world."

The smallest things can make huge differences in the lives of families on the edge. Chris remembers with fondness his son's efforts to make life easier for them after they finally got an apartment in Oakland. Their new home was affordable and relatively safe, but now Chris had a complicated, U-shaped commute by train to get his son to day care each day: north, through Oakland, across the bay, south through San Francisco to the end of the line at Daly City, and then back to San Francisco for work. In the evenings, it was the same thing in reverse. There was a day care center right next to an Oakland station, but it only took children who had been potty trained. Chris's son was just over two years old.

As his boy watched him clean their apartment, he wanted to help. "Children want to help you when they're tots. I explained to him, 'The way you help poppa is, whenever you think you want to go to the bathroom, just do like this.' Two weeks . . . and I was able to say 'Yeah, he's potty trained.' I can't tell you the load that took off me."

Again, it's the little things that can make a difference. Chris soon found out that their apartment was in the middle of a center for prostitution. The women who worked there would smile at the boy in the stroller, and looked forward to seeing him pass through each night. "They started trying to give him candy. I didn't let him have candy until he was five years old. So instead, they started giving him five-dollar bills. And if it weren't for those ladies of the evening giving that boy five-dollar bills, there would have been some days I wouldn't have been able to feed him."

Chris finally became a broker. He still wasn't making eighty thousand dollars a month, a sum to which he by then had attached an almost mystical importance, but he thought he knew how to do it. He would be the first one at work in the morning, and the last one to leave. He would work the phones all day. Two hundred cold calls, two hundred pitches. He felt he was slowly making progress, but only a big break would take him into the big leagues.

That break came in the form of a job offer from Bear Stearns. "This was the perfect place for me," Chris says, "because it was built by guys like me." His new firm gave him access to brokers with experience, gave him mentors, and inspired him to start building his fortune.

He was gaining material comfort but learned that even at this stage, the road to riches had plenty of potholes. Chris was highly recommended to a Texas oil millionaire who loved to play the market and quickly became Chris's biggest account. They had never met face-to-face, and every time Chris called him up, this particular Texan would break the ice with a racist joke. Then he would turn around and place an order that would put thousands of dollars in commissions directly into Chris's pocket.

As a young broker in a ruthless business, Chris decided this was not the time or place to make a stand. He managed to convince himself that it was just business, and some day, further down the road, he would be in a position to pick and choose his customers. A lecture on race relations would, he realized, be lost on this customer anyway. He swallowed hard, made money, and waited for the right moment to turn the tables.

In the end, he got to keep both the money and his pride. The client called to announce that he was going to be in San Francisco, and wanted to stop by to meet this broker who had been making him so much money. Chris decided that the best way to change the Texan's thinking about African Americans was to show him how successful one could be. Chris's manager was out of town that day and his luxurious corner office was vacant. "I go over, I take his name tag down, I put mine up. I take these pictures of his two white kids, I put them in a drawer. And when this guy walks in the door, I whip around in my chair, stick out my hand, and say 'Pleased to meet you.' You could see the blood just drain from his face."

They didn't speak about the racist jokes, but Chris soon learned that he may well have changed this man's thinking. He closed all his accounts with other brokers and gave them all to Chris, who managed all this customer's trades until the day he died. Needless to say, the jokes stopped after their face-to-face meeting in that corner office. "He had to see that 'This guy is good. This guy is making me money.' " Chris continues, "You put money in somebody's pocket, and suddenly, pigment is not a problem."

Chris made a personal choice by not confronting this racist client. No one should have to face a choice like this, but in the real world, achieving the American dream often means accepting the most unsavory compromises and trade-offs. Only individually can we judge if it was all worth it. Was suffering through racist jokes worth it for Chris Gardner? He, personally, has few doubts that it was. Others may feel differently, for their own good reasons.

Today, Chris runs his own brokerage, Gardner, Rich & Company, in Chicago. He makes sure his employees, two of whom started as interns when they were high school sophomores, attend college and buy homes. And he writes big checks to the American Federation of Teachers, to honor his mother and the teachers who inspired him as a child. He has also donated money to the homeless shelter that gave him and his son a place to stay at such a crucial time, and has invited the shelter's founder to his office to show him what his charity made possible.

Like so many others in this book, Chris found that his original goal—

$80,000 a month—wasn't set high enough. But he did make sure to buy that red Ferrari, the car that inspired him to become a broker in the first place. Chris's car once belonged to Michael Jordan, which in Chicago during the Bulls' heyday was more than enough to turn heads. Chris put his imprint on it with a license plate that reads NOT MJ. "I love that car," Chris says, "but now that I can afford stuff like that, I don't have time for it." While having the car was a nice way to satisfy the impetus that gave his career its start, Chris now knows that money buys more than things. And that one thing it doesn't buy is time.

Chris talks of an uncle who was, he says, full of earthy aphorisms. There's one in particular that might apply to why Chris started down the road to fortune. Living in this country, he told a young Chris Gardner, is like eating a sandwich made out of a certain, uh, unappetizing substance which we won't call by name here. The more bread you have, the less of this undesirable filling you have to eat. It's an aphorism that could speak to any group put at a disadvantage by any society, in any country. Asked dead-on about the American dream, however, Chris answers, "I think it comes down to having options. To having something to say about what's going to happen to my life." Chris cautions that he doesn't want to "sound like a jerk," but for him, in this country, "it comes down to dough."

Michael A. Cruz

The fortunate Americans in this chapter take education seriously. Even those who never went to college were adamant, when I talked to them, about getting a message to young readers: you can't expect wealth unless you have a degree, no matter how hard you work.

Some readers will remember a popular and optimistic board game called The Game of LIFE, the one where players would drive little plastic convertibles on a road to the American dream. The old version of the LIFE board offered players only one strategic choice, right at the beginning: go to college or go straight into business. The business route was shorter, while the college route offered the potential of a higher salary. But both routes were legitimate paths to wealth.

That game has been completely revamped to reflect what all the people in this chapter know is true: you don't *have* to go to college to build a fortune, but if you don't you'd better have plenty of talent and at least as much luck. The folks in this chapter have an almost religious fervor about the value of higher education. They give to educational institutions, they teach and mentor others, and they continue to learn. They believe firmly that college credits pay off in real dollars and in ways less easily measured.

Nowhere is the correlation between schooling and monetary success more direct and evident than at the nation's top M.B.A. programs. A degree from Harvard Business School, the Kellogg School, or Stanford's Graduate School of Business can truly be as good as cash. The American dream of enterprise is very much alive at these institutions; it gives them, in fact, their impetus.

That's where you could find Michael Cruz, who, at twenty-seven, was finishing his second year at Stanford's Graduate School of Business, and serving on the board of directors of Lenders for Community Development, a small bank in San Jose. Michael went to Yale for his undergraduate degree, interned at Merrill Lynch, and did mergers-and-acquisitions work for Bankers Trust and then James Wolfenson, an M&A "boutique" run by the president of the World Bank. Michael's résumé amounts to a ticket to all the fortunes the American dream has to offer.

It's curious, then, to hear what's on Michael's mind: "One of the things Stanford doesn't teach you is about how separate you are from the American mainstream in a lot of ways. I think if you are constantly exposed to the top tier of experiences, your perspective gets a little bit distorted. Not all of America runs on Microsoft, the whole economy isn't made up of dot coms." Michael's first experience with a business venture helps explain his perspective.

When Michael was in fifth grade, he started joining his parents on the evening outings that kept him and his two older siblings—a brother and sister—in Catholic school. His father worked in a nuclear weapons plant outside Amarillo, Texas. His mother worked for the police department. They lived in what Michael calls a "relatively safe" lower-middle class neighborhood. They were comfortable on that scale, but there just wasn't any money left for a college fund, much less the additional bills from Catholic school.

Some entrepreneurial adventures are born of big dreams. Others are, to borrow a term from the so-called new economy, more "mission critical." Michael's mother and father set up a small cleaning service not for the thrill of being their own bosses, but just to get the kids through school. When they got home from their day jobs, the entire family would head out to one of their few contracts—a factory or an office building. Michael would go from office to office, emptying trash cans, cleaning out ashtrays. Mom would be doing windows while dad buffed the floors.

"I think we learned very early on that this was a family affair, and that while we weren't the wealthiest people, we definitely had each other." There was even room for fun, and the whole experience brought the family closer together than if they had spent the evening in front of the TV. "It was a good time," Michael says now. "It wasn't all bad. I used to mimic my dad in the way he used to put a rag in his back pocket and put window cleaning stuff in his front pockets." Michael holds many memories from this formative experience, like the time "my sister tried to help my dad out buffing the floor, and the machine went wild on her." Although it was work, as Michael puts it, "We were together. I would much rather have had it be that way than me at home by myself knowing that my family was out there."

Getting home late at night, tired, looking forward only to another day of work followed by another night cleaning wasn't easy on Michael's parents. But it made Michael work that much harder at school, which rewarded his father more than he knew: "I found out much later on that when I would bring my grades home he would actually take them to work to show off to his buddies." Late at night, while the rest of the family was in bed, Michael would listen to his father explain the importance of family, hard work, and education. During one of these talks, he asked his youngest son what he wanted to be. Michael said he wanted to work at the factory with him: "I said, 'That way you and I can go to work together and mom can pack our lunches.' I thought that was the greatest idea, and I distinctly remember him getting upset with me and saying, 'No. You need to do something better.'"

Michael was thirteen years old when he lost his best friend. "On my father's birthday," Michael remembers, "he went to his medical checkup. I still recall him sitting down at the kitchen table talking to my mom about it. And myself, kind of off in the background hearing about it, but not really knowing. And going to the encyclopedia to see what leukemia was. And being really scared." Michael's father died within a year.

His older brother and sister had already left home, so the cleaning business hadn't been a necessary supplement for years. It was just Michael and his mother, but his father remained, and still remains, a central figure in his life. When his and Michael's hard work paid off with Michael's acceptance to Yale, he was at first afraid of leaving Texas, of paying the high tuition, and of being on his own after relying on his family for so much. But his father's wish that he have "something better" led Michael to swallow his apprehensions.

The Ivy League isn't just an athletic league or even a mere network of schools; it's a culture. Some of the kids Michael encountered at Yale had been born and bred in that culture. Michael obviously had not been. His background and upbringing automatically separated him from a good chunk of his classmates. He admits now, somewhat sheepishly, that he cried himself to sleep at night when he first arrived. By the time he had made social inroads, he found his back to the wall financially. The financial aid director advised him to take a year off. Michael found that idea unacceptable.

There was a lot of money floating around Yale. Why couldn't a poor kid from Texas work his way into some of it? One of Michael's classmates was running a small dry cleaning service for pocket money—about $750 a semester—but had tired of putting in the extra hours. Michael, sensing an opportunity, stepped in. "It was something of a flashback to what I was doing a long time ago," he says. Once again, a small-scale business venture had come to the rescue of his education.

With a fellow student's investment, Michael turned the university-affiliated dry cleaning service into a full-service laundry business. College students have problems with the concept of laundry, as anyone who's seen the inside of a dorm room knows. Michael went directly to the parents with a mailing that told them the last thing their budding scholars needed to worry about was dirty clothes. "Business just boomed. . . . By the end of my senior year, we had over a quarter of the Yale student population on our contract. It became very much a status symbol to have this done because you were too busy with debates and drama and everything else."

As he achieved this small success—he was able to pay his tuition—Michael found his outlook changing. First, he decided he would go into business rather than law. Second, he saw himself as less disadvantaged. He came to realize that opportunity wasn't just something that happened to the well-off. So when he set his sights on a business career, he set his sights as high as he had for his college education. Michael papered Wall Street with his résumé until he got an internship at Merrill Lynch.

From the outside, his progress from that first internship seems common enough. Hundreds, if not thousands, of Ivy League graduates flock to New York every summer to begin building their fortunes. Michael's talent and work ethic made him stand out from the crowd, and earned him promotions that were typically reserved for much older employees, usually those with M.B.A.'s. But something else makes him outstanding in terms of our discussion of the American dream. He knew every step of the way that no matter how far he climbed, his success depended on his ability to keep his feet on the ground.

The first time Michael returned to Amarillo from Yale for summer break, his girlfriend told him point-blank that he had become an arrogant jerk. His family and friends, in more gentle terms, let him know that he couldn't "get too far out there." He might be at Yale, he realized, but he would always be from Amarillo. He would always be the son of a factory worker, a man he deeply loved and respected.

Perspective is a balancing act. It's not easy to keep in mind both where you are from and where you want to go. Michael nipped a budding arrogance, but when he got to New York, he learned the downside of knowing where you are from: "My first week in New York was the same kind of thing as when I got to Yale. There was this homesickness, that kind of queasy feeling in your stomach; you are not at home, but you know you're going to be there for a while." This transplanted Texan, who made New York City his home, can certainly relate.

Working a hundred hours a week won't make that feeling go away, Michael found. The solution was to focus on someone else. "I think a lot of the times when we start feeling sorry for ourselves, if we can move that outward and look at someone else, then it makes our problems seem a little smaller." Through his church, Michael founded an SAT prep program for inner-city students to help him focus on someone else. He ended up tutoring between 250 and 300 kids during his time in New

York, kids who never could have afforded the expensive SAT prep courses. "A lot of times, during the tough days at work, that's what kept me going. Knowing that at the end of the day, it's not about how much money you make, and it's not about how high up you go. . . . It's about what kind of impact you make."

Careers often reach a point where immediate demands obscure long-term vision. For some, there's no better way to clarify and reestablish goals than graduate school. Michael saw that he had a desire to step back, "look among the clouds," and learn about what other people did, and Stanford Graduate School of Business was the place. It's a small program, with fewer than four hundred students, but they come from all walks of life. Michael says he's been able to interact with engineers, bankers, lawyers, and even doctors with future plans as diverse as their backgrounds.

However, Michael is now in a place and time when the Internet economy provides a powerful gravitational pull on business students. There are billions of dollars in venture capital just down the road from Stanford, so Michael has had to seriously consider whether he wants to be an entrepreneur or an employee. That experience of focusing on someone else has given him an answer.

Michael started consulting for Lenders for Community Development, a San Jose community development bank, when he started business school. The following summer, he was asked to join the board of directors. The bank was started by a Stanford business school graduate and focuses on business ventures in low-income areas. "Very small scale," Michael says. "Loans anywhere from ten thousand to fifty thousand dollars. Small loans in terms of what I was used to—two-hundred-million-dollar acquisitions and things like that."

What's the difference between completing a multimillion-dollar acquisition and making a ten-thousand-dollar loan? For Michael, the smaller scale can bring greater personal satisfaction: "It's probably more rewarding in terms of being able to go to someone's house and say, 'You've been approved for the loan.' Seeing their faces light up. Sitting in their living room. Even the little kids are excited, but they don't know what they're excited about, just that mommy and daddy are really happy. . . . It's very real in terms of people's needs, not just 'We're looking to have a synergy across Latin America, blah, blah, blah.' "

Michael remembers a street cleaning company owner who came to the bank wondering if the time was right to grow the business with the purchase of another street sweeper. He remembers a hair salon owner who was looking to add five hundred square feet, in the hope that the extra income could send her kid to college. "That's where you see the bulk of this economy's coming from," he says. "It's from the mom-and-pops and the bodegas on the corner, where they've taken out a second mortgage to run a little deli or a little janitorial service. . . . It's the people who don't have a college education who say, 'I think I make a great hoagie,' or 'I make a great pizza.' That's the beauty of the American dream, where people really have their backs to the wall and say, 'You know what? I believe in myself so much that I'm willing to do this.' "

Michael's not there yet. Months before graduation, he wasn't exactly sure where he would go after grad school, but he knew that he wouldn't become an entrepreneur. For one thing, he says, it's not all that risky for a Stanford M.B.A. to start a company. If it failed, he could just get a job and move on. Instead, he feels drawn toward firms that invest in established and expanding businesses. For now, he simply wants to be close to risk takers, while actively helping them risk wisely.

This next step will take him closer to his real dream. Down the road, he'd like to be able to set aside a few million dollars (he's confident he will one day have that much to set aside) for an equity fund for Hispanic entrepreneurs. And keeping it on a small scale is fine: "I want to really be involved with the businesses, making sure they grow and prosper the way I believe they can. I think that would be an amazing way to spend a portion of my career—watching businesses grow, and being along for the ride."

As we close this chapter on American dreams of enterprise, it should be clear that we have given wide berth to the role of greed. This is by design. We've had a long time to rethink that late 1980s mantra "Greed is good." Some would say that we've learned to phrase this credo with more tact; I believe that, by and large, we have rejected it.

Something drives this economy forward, though. But I don't think it's necessarily greed. It's defiance. The people we have looked at in this chapter all openly rebelled against their circumstances. Through their actions, to themselves and others, they said, "This is *not* the way it has to be."

Now, someone making that statement could be called greedy if they had a sense of entitlement. If they also said, "I deserve more, I'm going to get what's coming to me." But with the people here, it's quite the opposite. Each person in this chapter accepted the risks associated with their defiance. They didn't feel they were owed anything. And even though most of us would agree that everyone deserves a chance, none of our subjects in this chapter felt that anyone "owed" them a chance.

These are success stories. The stories of failure are more plentiful. And yet our nation is made better by every risk taken. The moment of initial vision, which can take place long before dreams of wealth enter the picture, is pure inspiration. It reminds us that we are a free people—free to succeed or fail on our own terms.

THE PURSUIT OF HAPPINESS
THE DREAM ITSELF

It is neither wealth nor splendor, but tranquility and occupation, which give happiness.

—Thomas Jefferson

HERE'S an undeniable poetry to how Thomas Jefferson laid out the justification for our democratic republic. The phrase "life, liberty and the pursuit of happiness" has a natural rhythm and lilt to it. And it contains the word *happiness;* in a government document, that in and of itself seems a great victory, a cause for celebration. The political philosophy that guided our founding managed to transcend the prosaic.

When you think about it, the pursuit of happiness could stand in for the other two rights the Declaration of Independence deemed unalienable: If you are allowed to pursue happiness, you are by implication alive and free. Free, most of all, to determine for yourself just what it is that happiness means for you.

After all, what could be more subjective, more uniquely open to individual interpretation than happiness? What is happiness? It is the condition of being happy. What makes you happy? That which brings you happiness. It is a completely circular proposition, depending entirely on your point of view. A morning spent knee-deep in a trout stream makes me happy; for others it might elicit nothing but chilly boredom.

This subjective quality gives the words much of their appeal, not to mention their strength. The pursuit of happiness invests us with independent thought and action, and says that no one—certainly no government—can take them from us. Recognizing that we are free to live our life as we see fit is not only essential to the American dream; one could say that it is the dream itself.

Students of history point out that Jefferson's language owes a great deal to that used by the political philosopher John Locke, who proclaimed the right to "life, liberty and property." On the surface, Locke's "property" seems a pale and uninspired right, a rather too-materialistic vision of human existence. And in terms of language alone, there's no question that Jefferson's phrase is more evocative: Locke grants us stuff, Jefferson the stuff of dreams. Still, by "property," he is understood to have intended more than simple real estate, or wealth, or the human beings for whom the Declaration and the Constitution meant continued slavery. Property signified what we could accumulate on this earth, but it also encompassed our ideas, our emotions, our desires . . . all that is ours because it belongs to no one else.

It has been said that Jefferson settled on "happiness" because classical thought held that it is the only good we pursue for its own sake—the end goal, in fact, of all human pursuit. For some, like the folks we met in the first chapter, the immediate pursuit is of fortune. But none of them would say that money buys happiness outright. Delores Kesler became happy when she saw what money could do. Michael Cruz derives happiness from the intellectual challenge of moving around millions of other people's money. And Chris Gardner, the most outspoken champion of the dollar in this book, believes happiness comes through the options that money can give you.

These people's lives reflect the truth to which Franklin Delano Roosevelt gave voice in his first inaugural address, that "Happiness lies not in the mere possession of money; it lies in the joy of achievement, in the thrill of creative effort." We know all too well, though, that not every creative effort and not all achievement brings monetary rewards. With no disrespect intended toward those dreams that bear financial fruit, I wanted to devote a chapter in this book to those for whom the American dream is distinctly about pleasures that can't be measured in dollars. Folks for whom happiness is not the final result of a life's pursuit, but its central aim.

This is admittedly a somewhat arbitrary proposition: more, perhaps, than with the other chapters in this book, the pursuit of happiness invites all American dreamers. Nevertheless, the people here seem to me to have a special hold on a personal vision of success. They have pursued happiness as an end in itself.

For Deborah Cline, an urban farmer in my home state of Texas, the pleasure found in a bite of a tomato grown with her own hands, care, and sweat has come to match the satisfaction she gained from getting off food stamps. The small patch of earth that feeds her family and then some has proved fertile ground for her version of happiness. Jesús Serrato's climb from the poverty he knew as a child in Mexico left him with a deeper appreciation than most for the American dream of home ownership. For him, happiness was found in the long journey from the makeshift hovel of his youth to the spacious home he designed, built, and now lives in with his family. This is the meat and marrow of his dream; the opportunity his work gives him to design homes that thousands of Americans call their own is so much gravy.

For Corporal Ryan Clark, happiness has always come in serving the United States of America. It's an ethos of elegant simplicity, but hardly an easy one to live up to. Corporal Clark has done so with distinction, in feats of heroism with the Los Angeles Police Department and in his renewed commitment to the U.S. Army. For those who follow such patriotic dreams, the demands are many and the financial rewards few. But folks like Corporal Clark understand that material comfort means little alongside doing what you love for the country you adore.

And then there are those, like Stacy and Mark Green, who follow the path of Henry David Thoreau, America's prophet of simplicity. Their move to small-town Washington may not carry quite the drama of Thoreau's removal to Walden Pond, but it was clearly undertaken in the same spirit. They found that a choice between remaining in their high-stress, high-income lives and cultivating their relationships with each other and with their children was really no choice at all. Ever since they found the courage to bring their lives in line with their true priorities, they have not looked back.

It's an equation with which all the people here are familiar. They have heard the call to follow their dreams and their dreams alone, and they have heeded it. They live their lives in response to conscious choices they have made, with evident relish. Here are everyday Americans who find compensation not in power, or wealth, or the arbitrary prestige of title but in the comforts of home, the strength of family ties, and the satisfaction that comes from working for something that is bigger than oneself. In choosing to pursue only happiness, it seems that happiness has captured them.

Deborah Cline

The small farm has long stood as an almost mythic symbol of the simple, productive, self-sufficient—even idyllic—American life. In actuality, it was a back-breakingly difficult way to make a living. And if you ask today's small farmers, those who've managed to hold on to their farms, they'll tell you that it still is. It's work hard enough to be called labor—two syllables.

Nevertheless, there's an understandable urge to romanticize the process of working a piece of land and actually getting to sink your teeth into the fruit of your labors. For some, this way of life truly counts as an American dream. It's a way of life steadily being supplanted by "factory farming," but small farms are still around. The U.S. Department of Agriculture, in fact, classifies 94 percent of all farms as "small." But these farms take in only 41 percent of all farm receipts, and the pie is getting smaller—total farm revenue for the year 2000 was expected to drop 12 percent from the 1990–1999 average. A large corporation can ride out such downturns, but a family-owned farm has almost no chance.

Against this dark backdrop, however, there is a glimmer of hope. Some small farmers are discovering that while they can't compete head-to-head against big-time agribusiness, they can do some things better than the factory farms, like grow crops for niche markets. Exotic produce, gourmet vegetables, and organically grown foods are in demand and don't fit into the business plans of the corporate giants. Even further down the scale, there's a small movement afoot toward organic micro-farming. That's where you'll find Deborah Cline, whose life was changed by a community gardening project in Lubbock, Texas. Before that, Deborah says, her only gardening experience had been "watching houseplants die."

Growing up with a father in the air force meant that Deborah moved around a lot as a child. In the early 1960s, when she was nine or ten, her father was transferred to Thailand. Later the family followed him to a post in the Philippines. As Deborah's father neared retirement, however, her mother moved the family back to El Paso, the city of Deborah's birth. Awaiting her husband's return, Deborah's mother instead received a letter from her husband informing her that he would not be coming back.

Overseas, the family had lived a sheltered life, with maid service and the support of a close-knit military community. Now, as Deborah started high school, her mother started working for the first time in her life, waiting tables at Denny's. Deborah says that they received no support from her father overseas.

Her family was already teetering on the edge of complete fiscal collapse when Deborah's mother was in a car accident that put her out of work. She was still legally married, so she couldn't go on welfare. Her husband was still abroad, so she couldn't force him to support his children. "We were just kind of caught in a loop," Deborah summarizes. At fifteen, she was the oldest child. So she dropped out of school to fill her mother's shoes.

She waited the same tables at the same restaurant for the same meager wage. She did her job and her duty, but it wasn't always easy to smile for the customers: "It was a very angry point in my life," she remembers. "I was extremely mad at the government, extremely mad at my father, and very rebellious." She admits to feeling "a sense of accomplishment" in providing for her younger brothers and sisters but still could not shake what she calls the "anger" at having been put in that position.

By the time her mother was back on her feet, they were so far behind in paying their bills that Deborah could take no breaks. She and her mother now worked different shifts at the same Denny's, and when Deborah wasn't working, she was taking care of her three siblings.

When asked where she saw her life going at that time, Deborah has a ready answer: "No place. In a rut. With not much chance of escape. You know, you barely make enough to pay the bills, and every time you'd think you were getting a little bit ahead, something would come up. . . . There was no way to get out of it." Adding to Deborah's sense of helplessness, was the sense that "you can't escape it when you're too young to survive on your own. . . . And then you don't really want to get out, because what are you going to do if you leave? And then there's less for the ones left behind. It's a very depressing state. Children shouldn't be under that type of pressure, and yet so many are."

It didn't take long for Deborah to start running with "the wrong crowd," as she puts it. Sometimes added responsibility can have a salutary effect on a young person, but Deborah's experience was one of too much responsibility and not enough hope. "You also start thinking you're older than you really are," Deborah adds. "You grow up fast, but you're really not grown up inside. Yet you think you are because you're doing all this." Deborah's mother might have been busy, but she wasn't unaware of what was going on. As soon as she got an opportunity, she moved the family out of El Paso to the tiny New Mexico town of Carrizozo to, as Deborah says, "get us away from the drug and hoodlum environment."

All of her brothers and sisters attended and eventually graduated from high school in Carrizozo, but Deborah says she "just didn't go back" to school. Instead, she left home and moved in with a man she'd met there, thinking she'd live out her life in this town of "five hundred people, dogs, and cats," working as a cook or waitress and raising her newborn daughter.

After she split up with her daughter's father, she got into a job program and worked for the local sheriff's department. At the same time, her mother remarried, to a man who became "a wonderful father" to the children still living at home. For a while, all seemed to be getting back on their collective feet. Deborah got a job in Lubbock training to become a bookkeeper, but she left for a union job as an apprentice bricklayer. After four years of relative stability, she married in 1980. Her husband joined the navy, and for the next three years, it was traveling again for Deborah. When he was discharged, the couple returned to Lubbock and had two children.

Life outside the military wasn't so easy. Deborah's husband lost his job, and intense financial pressure put a strain on their marriage that led to their separation in 1987. That's when Deborah was forced to file for food stamps, a time she calls "the down point of my whole life . . . it was just like being back in El Paso. You can never make enough to get off it. So you're basically in that same loop, without any place to escape to."

If anything, the fact that the government was involved made her situation worse. Most people who are on public assistance are ashamed of the fact, but that doesn't stop the agencies behind the checks from rubbing it in, Deborah says. "You have to go in every month, and they make you feel like you're doing nothing. You're categorized as being a lazy bum, unwilling to work. Just being in their offices, the questions they ask, the way they check up on you . . ." Deborah pauses, revisiting it all in her mind before she completes her thought, "It makes you feel like a criminal."

In the middle of all this, Deborah's eldest daughter took extra courses and graduated high school early. She moved back to Carrizozo with her grandparents. "She needed a break and I couldn't think of anything better than for her to get out of it," Deborah explains. But Deborah was still stretched to make ends meet for her children. Even once she and her husband reconciled, she was out of work and still taking food stamps.

Deborah found out about the South Plains Food Bank after she and her husband moved to the neighborhood: "The little old lady next door told me that they had a program where you could get help with groceries if you were in a lower income bracket. It was right down the street." The process was simple and accepting, especially when compared with the public assistance bureaucracy that Deborah had been through. You filled out a form, and if you needed groceries, they gave them to you. But what surprised Deborah more was the fact that the food bank was run mostly by volunteers. "Well, I didn't have a job," she continues, "so I started just going over there and helping out as a volunteer. Eventually, they gave me a part-time job when a position came open—a paid position." Deborah was now putting in eight-hour days—half volunteer, half paid. And she was still getting some donated food.

Deborah was finally able to get off food stamps altogether when the food bank helped her get her commercial truck driving license and hired her full-time. They also trained her as a supervisor for the new dehydration plant they had built, which for Deborah was a big step. Her pay went up, and she got a real "sense of pride about what I was doing." When the plant closed, Deborah went part-time at the food bank and part-time at a local smoke shop. But her passion, she learned, wasn't driving trucks or sorting cans. It was in the garden.

When Deborah first started volunteering, the South Plains Food Bank primarily worked with donated canned food and fresh vegetables. But things really picked up when they started a community garden program on some vacant lots that had been donated, to which the city agreed to supply free water. The food bank would help needy individuals set up garden plots and grow their own food. Deborah got a plot herself. After a couple of years she was among the many food bank gardeners who found that she was able to grow more than her family needed. Some of her surplus went back to the food bank, some to a market the food bank had set up so families could supplement their income while cutting back on their grocery bills.

Deborah sold shares of her plot to five people: one's the executive director of the food bank, another is their grant writer. Both are too busy with the office to get out into the fields, but they love fresh produce. The other three shares belong to people who heard of Deborah through word of mouth. Deborah uses their money to pay for plants and supplies, and pays them back in food. Each week, she personally delivers a harvest. During a good season, even a sixth of her crop is too much for the families to eat themselves, and Deborah's shareholders can make a little money selling the excess at work.

Now there's always plenty of good food at the Cline residence. Deborah says she's learned how to stagger her crops so she can bring home fresh-picked produce year-round. She talks about tips she's picked up at the food bank and over the Internet on how to keep her garden pest- and pesticide-free. She meets with other gardeners to exchange healthy recipes. Having raised her children on what food she could afford on a small paycheck and a government supplement, she can definitely see and feel the difference: "I hated saying, 'Well, I'm sorry, you're having beans and potatoes again because that's all I've got.' That was the most heartbreaking thing in my life. To not be able to feed them like I felt they should be fed."

Her two youngest kids, both college bound, don't take many trips to the doctor these days, and look visibly healthier, Deborah says. There's a lot of pride in her statement, but she adds that pride isn't the only feeling she gets from her garden: "It's a lot of work, but there's a *peacefulness*. There's a sense of accomplishment at the end of the day when I kick back and my garden looks gorgeous." And since her garden is chemical-free, she continues, "When I pick a tomato off the vine, I can just stand right there and eat it." The same thing will go for the grapes that she planted for the first time in the season before she was interviewed: "This year we put up our first trellises and our first grape arbor, and, I mean, it gives you a sense of amazement to see the vines climbing over them. Now it looks like someplace you'd actually like to go sit out and relax in."

For most, bringing home work means bringing home stress. When Deborah brings work home, it carries that same sense of calm. "My husband is seeing that I'm getting a little carried away," she says, laughing. "I have three gardens in my yard, growing along my fence. One little plot out front, two little plots in the back." She's been trying new things, like asparagus and strawberries, that are expensive in stores. With another laugh, she says, "I just haven't gotten to the mushrooms yet."

Mushrooms are one of the few things Deborah picks up in the store. Lettuce doesn't last long, so she might buy an occasional head. She used to buy a few canned goods, but now that she knows how to preserve her crops in jars or by running them through a dehydrator, all she really buys is meat. One of the plots she helps out on is full of fruit trees, and then there's fresh honey from the beehives. Her Waldorf salad ingredients, pecans and all, are the result of her own joyful toil. And since everything's been carefully cultivated, she says, she knows the difference and could never go back to store-bought produce.

"You have more blemishes than what you would have in the store. They're not genetically engineered to be perfectly round or have the perfect skin. But when you bite into a tomato—the *flavor*,"—she sighs, "is incredible. I used to not know that tomatoes had any taste. I have lemon cucumbers that have a sweet, lemony flavor. You know, the cucumbers in the store kind of just have the same flavor and it's not a strong flavor. When I pick up a banana melon, that cantaloupe smell is just . . . it's such a sweet, clean, fresh smell."

As her eloquent description of the simple pleasures of growing your own food makes clear, Deborah almost bubbles over with enthusiasm about the effect the South Plains Food Bank has had on Lubbock. Everyone who has a piece of the thirty-three lots developed by the program shares food—someone may have had a bad year, but others will make up the difference. They lend one another a hand on projects big and small, exchange tips, and provide encouragement. When Deborah was on public assistance, she felt alone. That feeling is gone: "You know you're not the only one struggling. You've got all these other people who are struggling too, but you're all gaining from the experience. You're steadily moving up."

Help for the program comes from all quarters. Churches, schools, sororities and other groups from Texas A&M, the Rotary Club, nonviolent offenders completing community service requirements, the city of Lubbock, and corporate donors like John Deere, Case, Water Master, and Bioflora have all pitched in. "The whole community in Lubbock has really jumped behind these programs," Deborah says, "the businesses, churches, everybody. You meet people and get to know them, instead of being just strangers passing by."

Deborah sees a moving effect on the children who come to work there. Some of them are as young as six, out on a field trip. They come by the busload. Some are at-risk teens. They come via social service organizations. "They know their work is important," Deborah says, "because they deliver the vegetables too. They take it and they see the families that they are helping. And they're able to take vegetables home to their own families. They're seeing the results of what they've done. . . . They start out a little hesitant, because it's hot out in that sun, and swinging a hoe is hard. But when they look back and see how that squash can grow . . . they *know* they've done great."

Deborah earns about eight dollars an hour in her part-time job at the smoke shop, plus whatever she can make selling extra vegetables. But there's no question she's rich: she's in control of her life and also part of something larger than her. What's the biggest difference between her life ten years ago, before the food bank, and her life since? Deborah answers without hesitation: "I don't feel like I have anybody controlling me or watching over me or dictating what I do. I don't belong to the state anymore. And they're no longer keeping me stuck on that level of not being able to better myself. I *have* bettered myself, and I feel *proud* of what I've accomplished."

And what about that strain of the American dream bent on building fortunes? "I really don't think that Americans all want to be filthy rich," Deborah says. "I think everybody would just like to be in a position where they can pay their bills, make sure their kids have shoes. And not have pressure. Not have the high pressure." Deborah has managed to banish the "high pressures" from her life. Her work is actually relaxing and spiritually fulfilling, and she has few wants she can't meet. She speaks of how, just the other day, her kids wanted to go see a movie—so she picked an extra twenty tomatoes. It's an anecdote that succinctly captures the self-sufficiency that Deborah has recovered, and that she brings to the American dream. If she wants something, she plucks it off the vine.

Jesús Serrato

When economic news turns to home ownership and housing starts, chances are you'll hear the latest figures put in terms of the American dream. As in, "With real estate prices going up, is the American dream moving out of reach for young couples?"—the kind of question you see in magazine headlines, the sort I've had occasion to ask any number of times on the *Evening News*. Owning one's own home is, like becoming one's own boss or coming to this country to escape oppression, something that's considered synonymous with the pursuit of happiness. It's one aspect of the dream that is even considered quantifiable.

But when Jesús Serrato and his family came to America, home ownership was far from their minds. Considering the poverty they had known in Mexico, Jesús says, "We never even *thought* about buying a house." Like so many who come to this country, the Serratos were simply looking to make a better life for themselves. And? "Fortunately, we've been able to do that and more," says Jesús, who is now architectural director for a major builder. Jesús, his wife, and their children now live in Rolling Meadows, Illinois, in a house that Jesús designed and built himself. Whenever Jesús remembers the shelter in which he grew up, he is filled with wonder at the beautiful house in which he now raises his children.

The Serratos' house in Santiago Maragotillo, a small town in the Mexican state of Guanajuato, Jesús says, was pretty standard for the area— one room, stone walls, dirt floor. The roof was fashioned from spare terra-cotta tile supported by sticks. "It would get cold at night because, of course, there's holes all over the place," Jesús remembers. "And you would definitely know when morning was and when dark was because you could see right through the spaces." Jesús' mother cooked their food on an open fire, and not even the ashes went to waste. Jesús tells of how his family would mix them with dirt and water to make a material not unlike cement, which they would then spread on the floor to keep the dust from flying around. "It wasn't as hard as cement," he says, "it was just something to block the dirt with."

Jesús' father worked the fields. There were times when he would be away as long as four months at a stretch while he followed the crops. In the fall, he'd work the corn harvest at home. His typical salary was five dollars a day; that's how he'd lived since he left the second grade to help his parents survive. It was the only life father and family knew, and it was one they accepted. As Jesús points out, "You don't always see the bad times. You're just going to enjoy the good times as they are handed to you. I mean, you could see that some people are well off, and you feel a little bit of jealousy and you ask yourself, 'How come they have that and I don't?' But then, once you get a little bit older, you start to realize, hey, that's how life is. Some people have certain things and some people don't."

They didn't have much, but neither was their existence bleak. There was a creek nearby to fish in, and open spaces. They were a close family—they had to be, with, at that time, three children and two parents sharing a ten-by-ten-foot room. But for the sake of the children, Jesús' parents knew they would have to find a new way to get by, one that wouldn't involve long months away from home for starvation wages. When Jesús was seven, his family moved to Mexico City, where his two brothers were born. The city had factories where Jesús' father could work, and people who needed his mother's laundry and ironing services. But there was no creek, nor any fields to play in, and the living situation was worse than what they had known in the country.

"I remember the room," Jesús says, chuckling. "That just doesn't go away. It was a little tiny room, even smaller than ten by ten. It was just kind of adobe walls, but they were so old that all the adobe material was starting to come down." The roof was made of long sheets of tar paper, so when the sun beat down on them, it got unbearably hot. Home improvement took place whenever Jesús' dad came home with sheets of plastic from the factory, which he nailed up on the walls to keep the room from getting too dusty.

His father also made a bed out of materials he found in a Dumpster. "Actually," Jesús says, "it was my first bunk bed!" It was about three feet tall; father and Jesús' youngest brother would sleep up top, "and the four of us, my two sisters and my older brother, we just laid underneath. Raised up off the floor, but that's where we would sleep." As Jesús speaks, his wife and kids step in to say "bye" before they head off to visit his mother, who lives nearby. He smiles at the interruption, reminded of why the tight conditions in Mexico City were bearable. "At least we were together," he says, "and that was the only thing that mattered. For us, family is a big thing. My wife and kids just left now to go have dinner at my mom's. They call, you know, at least three times a week . . . and say, 'Hey look, we're making chili rellenos,' or whatever, so of course we go!"

Family mattered; so did opportunities for the Serrato children. After about six years in Mexico City, Jesús' father and mother realized that the capital just did not offer enough for them. It was a difficult decision, but they came to believe that building a life north of the border would be worth the sacrifice of a few years apart. Such a life would not be much easier, but it held promise.

Jesús did not need to be convinced. Compared with the family's life in the country, Mexico City seemed rough and ugly. "We didn't know anybody out there," he remembers, "so we were on our own. And because it was a bigger city, you have a lot more of 'Welcome to the real world. Everybody for themselves.' " Particularly disturbing to Jesús was the way kids around him were dealing with the hardscrabble urban environment: "Back then you didn't have the cocaine and all that stuff that goes on now, but they used to do the rubber cement, inhaling the rubber cement. You could see kids, six, seven years old, actually doing this." Jesús' reaction was, "No way, man, I'm not sticking around here."

Moving to America was a complicated operation. Jesús' father went first to Palatine, Illinois, to earn money and find a place to live. He soon sent for his wife and youngest son, leaving Jesús, the eldest of the children, with his two younger sisters and younger brother. They moved back to Santiago Maragotillo to stay with their grandmother, and responsibility for the younger children fell to Jesús. "I was like the guy in charge or something," he says. "I always tried to make sure that my sisters and brothers were not getting into some of the stuff I would see around."

The children survived on money sent back from Illinois, where Jesús' father had found work in a bakery, and on whatever earnings Jesús could eke out of the cornfields. Sometimes he would help cut up the corn stalks for animal feed, a job he remembers as "the toughest thing I had to do, because when it's dried up, it's like sharp knives." The solution was to start at nightfall, and hope the dew would soften the stalks. Of course, that meant that Jesús would be up until midnight or later, praying he could get enough sleep before school the next day and thinking, he says, that "there's *got* to be a better way to make a living."

Four years after Jesús' father left and two years after his mother had gone to join him in America, they finally sent for the rest of their children. Jesús took his brother and sisters by bus to Ciudad Juárez, across the border from El Paso, where they met up with "a friend of a friend of a friend of a friend" of the Serratos who would serve as *coyote*. They crossed the Rio Grande by cover of night.

"After it happened, I heard of many people dying from underwater currents that would take them away," Jesús says. But at the time, they felt they were in good hands. "I remember taking our clothes and putting them over our heads and just walking the river. Once you cross the river, there's a little fence, and they have a channel. In that channel the water's a lot faster." The smugglers had a cable rigged just below the water, which gave the small party a handhold across the treacherous waters. The water was high on the night they crossed, and Jesús' little brother and sister had to be carried on the guides' shoulders. Jesús held tight to his other sister's hand to keep her from going under. "And once we got over the channel," Jesús sighs, "then we were in the United States."

They dressed and were picked up by a waiting truck. They spent the night in a strange house in a new country, and in the morning were put on a plane to Chicago. On the other end of the plane ride was a long-awaited reunion: "When we got there, my mom broke down in tears, and then all of us did."

The Serratos were thrilled to be reunited, but life for a family of illegals was harrowing at times. "We were living in fear for probably the first year," Jesús recalls. "You see a tow truck, and everybody would hide." Jesús seems to find this last hilarious and stops speaking to keep laughing. Of course—tow trucks have flashing lights. "Anything that had lights on," Jesús continues, "you just don't know. Of course, people who had been there longer knew and would make fun of you. They would say, 'Hey, look, *La Migra*.' "—the INS. After almost ten years of worry and hiding, the Serratos jumped at the 1986 amnesty program that preceded a crackdown on illegal immigration along the Mexican border. They had been in the country more than long enough to qualify and breathed a collective sigh of relief when they got their residency cards.

But the fear of being picked up and separated yet again from his family didn't stop Jesús and his brother and sisters from attending school. Jesús was a year behind because of all the moving around, but he managed to make the grade nonetheless. His dishwashing job helped his family but didn't interfere with the schoolwork. His ESL classes were the only ones he could fully understand at first, but that didn't keep him from graduating in the top third of his class.

Jesús' new high school was "huge." Of four thousand students, maybe forty or fifty were Hispanic. Jesús watched as his classmates from Mexico, Guatemala, and El Salvador struggled for acceptance, which sometimes meant denying their heritage. "I mean, you couldn't even count on your own peers to help you out. I knew a lot of people who came at the same time that I did, and two years later, they would refuse to speak Spanish, or even admit they were from Mexico." They even suggested to Jesús that he change his name: "They'd say, 'Why don't you call yourself Jasper?' Well, I'm like, 'It's my name. I can't change that.' I believe in myself and trust that people will respect me for that. In some cases, it doesn't work out, some people still look down on you. But that's their own opinion."

There are many ways to cope; by working hard at school, Jesús chose to make himself into someone that others would have a hard time looking down on. Without knowing exactly where his studies would take him, he signed up for as many drafting and math courses as he could. In fact, Jesús had been interested in building design long before he knew the word *architecture*. In Mexico, he'd watched his uncle, a bricklayer, build small square houses that met modest needs. Although, or maybe because, his own family couldn't afford one of these more structurally sound homes, Jesús saw a beauty in this trade: "That got me to thinking, 'Hey, that's cool. You can draw and build something and people *live* in them.'" He knew, he says, that he "just wanted to do something, *build* something." When he went to junior college, he found they had an architectural technology degree. Right away, he said to himself, "I can do that."

Jesús did it well enough to become the student others asked for help. After he got his associate's degree, he interviewed for a draftsman's job he had seen in the paper. There he discovered that college had given him a network in addition to an education. The interviewer told Jesús that he had come "highly recommended." His response was, "Highly recommended? By whom?" Then they walked into another room "and there's this guy who went to school with me. He remembered me from taking a class together."

The interviewer asked Jesús to do a quick rendering and hired him on the spot before he'd even finished. Already his dreams were coming true: "It was great—I can draw this thing, I'm getting paid for it, and I can go out there and look at this stuff being built." Jesús was being watched by the management of his firm, who promoted him to submanager, and by others in the tight-knit industry. Without ever looking for a new job, Jesús got better offers at other companies through people who'd seen his work. Since that first job he's never had to scour the classifieds.

In 1990, Jesús accepted an offer to work for the national construction company Kimball Hill. His first position involved checking the work of freelance architects against Kimball Hill's requirements. Eventually someone questioned why he was spending so much time redoing the work of others. So Jesús started drafting the original designs himself, using outside architects to add the technical details. "That saved us megabucks," Jesús says proudly, "because in any architectural firm, you make your money in the design part. This way saves us money, and we get a lot more control over what we want."

Kimball Hill has been building homes since 1939. They work in eleven markets nationwide and develop a wide variety of product lines to meet local needs. One of the most satisfying parts of the job, Jesús says, comes when he meets people who have bought a home he designed. It's then that he's reminded that his work is a big part of people's lives. When he sees a new home going up in Rolling Meadows, Illinois, where his family moved eight years ago, and can say "that's mine," he knows he's a part of the life of the community as well.

Jesús lets his customers' needs drive his designs, but there's a big part of himself in them as well. How families live is foremost in his mind. "When I design a house I think about how I would live in it, but try to keep in mind how other people live. We all want to spend time with our families, so we try to get the family room, the kitchen, the dining room all to relate. That's how people live now." He also seems to understand everyone's desire to have their home be their castle. "No matter how small a house or what price range," Jesús says, "we try to make it look like a million-dollar home."

The first home Jesús got with his family—he was married in 1989 and has two children, ages six and ten—was a far cry from a million-dollar home. "It was just a little Cape Cod . . . that was enough for me and my wife and my daughter." They lived there for three years before they started thinking about a larger family and a quieter neighborhood. "So that's when I decided," Jesús says, "well, I'm in the business, why don't we design something?"

Drawing up the plans for what would be his family's home had an effect on Jesús. "I'm not the type of person who's showy," he says. "I try to keep it low profile. But somehow, with the house I have right now, I went overboard. We have much more space than what we need." Jesús laughs, adding that even if they can't use all the space, it's probably a solid investment.

Jesús found a neglected, wedge-shaped lot near a soccer field, a community center, a municipal swimming pool, and shopping. The presence of a Catholic church across the street closed the deal in this family's minds. It took six months for Jesús to gain approval from the city; a number of planners thought the house was just too big. Jesús finally convinced them and now says he sees larger houses and additions going up all over the neighborhood. "Now I'm like, 'See, I'm helping the city, getting the level of living up!' Everybody's starting to see that people are not leaving the town, they're staying. They like the area and they're willing to add to it." According to Jesús, new people he meets in the neighborhood usually say, " 'Oh, the big house? That's yours? We love that house. It's beautiful.' "

And how does it compare with that first house in Mexico? Jesús says you could probably fit ten inside the one he designed and built. It's something he and his mom talk about sometimes as they walk through the door of his dream home. It still brings tears to her eyes.

The house is the most visible symbol of how far Jesús has come, but he's also seen success throughout his immediate family. His father has left the backbreaking work in the fields far behind and now works as a baker in the little restaurant and bakery where he started as a dishwasher. One sister manages a travel agency, another a dry cleaners. His brother works for a major insurance company. "All of us are doing quite well," Jesús sums up, "thanks to our parents . . . for giving us a lot more than they got."

Everybody in his family, Jesús says, has bought a home. A house is the largest purchase most Americans will ever make; for the Serratos, a house means more than that. "It's a good ego trip for me," Jesús says with a smile. "I've done it on my own, and I've survived, and it will only get better from here." He has traveled far enough, in miles and experience, to be allowed more than a measure of pride in his journey. "I know that I have my home," he says, "and whatever happens, there's always something for me to go home to."

Ryan William Clark

The American dream, no matter what its manifestation, has always rested on the shoulders of the men and women who wear our country's uniform. We owe so much to them, but those who dedicate their lives to military service are almost guaranteed to know little more than a modest lifestyle. Much the same is true of our police. For them—and fortunately for us—the pride they take in their duties and in doing for others is reward enough.

Corporal Ryan Clark has done more than his share, but he isn't done yet. After two years in the United States Army and four with the Los Angeles Police Department, he's returned to the army, where he plans to spend the rest of his career. Ryan's service with the LAPD, though relatively brief, was highly distinguished. In May 1997, he saved the lives of two fellow officers, at great risk to his own. The "Top Cop" award he received at the White House for his bravery hasn't brought him riches, but it has reaffirmed his belief in the intrinsic value of what he does.

For as long as he can remember, all Ryan wanted was to join the army and become a police officer. He has pictures of himself at age five wearing a replica army uniform. When he was ten, he hung his American flag on his wall. Growing up in Moorpark, California, he served with the Ventura County Sheriff Explorers all through high school. There was simply no question in his mind where his life would lead.

All along, he also knew what he would be leaving behind. Ryan's father was a successful financial officer who worked in downtown Los Angeles and easily maintained an upper-middle-class lifestyle for his family. But for Ryan, "There was no way I'd ever want to wear a suit and tie to work every day." It's not that he thought his father's life was boring, he says, "but it just wasn't what I wanted." His goal, he tells me, "was never to be a rich man . . . as far as moneywise."

Ryan focused instead on America's patriotic heritage. Our national holidays stirred him in strong ways. "The Fourth of July wasn't something that was really celebrated in Los Angeles," he says. "It was just a day off work. But for me, there was always a lot more to it." When he was in the sixth grade, he remembers, the city put up a veterans' memorial in downtown Moorpark. "That was something. Me and my friend, we walked down—it was about three, four miles away. It seemed like forever for a little kid, but we got down there. Just seeing that thing, the names on it. It had a lot of significance for me."

A trip to the nation's capital solidified dreams that had started with the John Wayne and William Holden films Ryan had watched as a boy. "I went to Arlington [National Cemetery] and saw the tribute that America pays to its veterans, and saw how respectful it was. I wanted to be part of an organization that had so much tradition. I wanted to be a part of a tradition, a heritage. That trip to D.C., to Arlington, did have a pretty big impact."

At the Catholic high school Ryan attended in Ventura, California, no one tried to take Ryan off his single-minded career goals: "I don't think the guidance counselor ever talked to me, because it was for sure. He's going into the army, and he's going to be a police officer. There was no margin for something else, no other possibility for him." Ryan hung out with kids who had similar ideals, avoided the parties, and stuck with the sheriff's Explorer program. He wore his patriotism on his sleeve, and flew a flag off the back of his Jeep. His peers, far from deriding him, offered support. Six of his buddies, he says, also went into the army.

Ryan entered as soon as was permissible and chose the most difficult training he could—airborne infantryman. "It was one hundred percent what I expected," he beams. "I was not let down whatsoever. And this is just right after Desert Storm, so it was at a very high tempo." Asked what impressed him most during that time, Ryan is quick to answer: "I hope everybody's military experience with the leadership has been similar to mine, because it's been truly phenomenal and overwhelming, the amount of support." When Ryan's grandfather died, his commander made sure he had time and money to get to the funeral. "He took *care* of me," he says, "sort of a surrogate father."

Ryan's commanders also gave him their trust. Ryan was and still is awed at the responsibility they placed on their soldiers at such a young age. "If I said I had taken care of something," he says, "there were no questions about it. They trusted me wholeheartedly. I felt it was nice to know that somebody didn't have to check on me." Ryan says he performed maintenance on about five million dollars' worth of weapons. He was only eighteen years old.

Ryan loved the spartan nature of army life and the way it brought him closer to his fellow soldiers. "I remember my parents came back and saw my barracks," he says, "and couldn't believe the living conditions, how horrible they were! But for me it was fantastic." The military, Ryan also discovered, is a true melting pot. His "sheltered life," as he puts it, was immediately turned around as he lived in close contact with comrades from all walks. "There was a guy who couldn't go home for Christmas because he had sent *all* his money home every month to his mom, who was sick," Ryan recalls. "Myself and three other guys gave every penny we had to him. We knew *we* were going home. We had our plane tickets. That's the first time, I think, I ever *gave*. Just 'Here. Have fun.' There were no conditions on it. It was just what people need to do for each other."

For two and a half years, Ryan gave the army all he had. He jumped out of planes in the United Arab Emirates and got to spend a few days in Spain and Portugal. At the end of his enlistment, he was sorry to leave. "But at the same time," he adds, "my career goals hadn't changed at all. I was approaching twenty-one, and that's the minimum age to be a police officer. I was ready to go straight into the police department." He also went straight into his first home, which he bought at age twenty with help from the Veterans Administration. Military service may not provide riches, but it can provide the basic building blocks of the American dream. Ryan met his wife, Laura, during the time he was with the LAPD and became increasingly confident with the security of his job and his future.

Ryan reflects for a moment on why he was drawn to the police force: "I didn't have any interest in being Don Johnson from *Miami Vice*. I think it was just the professionalism of the local law enforcement that really sparked the interest." Maybe, he speculates, it was the deputy who came to his home long ago, when his bike was stolen. "He took everything I had to say to heart," Ryan remembers. "It felt so good that this big deputy sheriff wants to do everything he can to *help* me. You know, take time out of his day of fighting crime to actually find out who took my bike. He made that extra effort, and that really influenced me."

Never one to do things halfway, Ryan took what he saw as the toughest "mission" in law enforcement. When he joined, the LAPD was barely bouncing back from the riots. Chief Darryl Gates was out, and public opinion of the department was in the depths, despite efforts to incorporate community policing. "I came from the Eighty-second Airborne division, which is a pretty famous unit," says Ryan. "Fought in many campaigns with honor. And the LAPD, I believed, I *believe* is the finest police force. You know, they have a tough, tough mission. But I wanted to go with the best."

Ryan says that he saw nothing during his four years in the department to change this view: "I don't think there was a single person who was unprofessional. I worked with some truly great officers, great servants to the public." He was aware that "with an agency eight thousand to ten thousand strong, a bad apple can slip through," but for him they were strictly the exception.

Community policing was still a new concept—or rather, a recently resurrected concept—when Ryan joined the force. The approach came naturally to him. "Maybe if I could . . . influence a little kid on the street who had *his* bike stolen," he remembers thinking, "maybe he'll be in the next generation of police officers. Growing up upper middle class, and dealing with more of the poverty-stricken areas like Pacoima, it was great to see kids who *wanted* to be police officers, who respected the law."

Sometimes these kids would sit in his patrol car, getting a chance to turn on the lights and sirens. Sometimes he'd find a kid who really needed help, like one teenager who Ryan says was involved in "ganglike activities," but wanted desperately to get out of Pacoima. After Ryan got to know him, he suggested the local recruiting office as a way to get out, get paid, maybe go to college, and of course see the world. "Unfortunately," Ryan says with a laugh, "he joined the navy, and not the army, but it was good I was able to help that one guy who wanted so desperately a brighter future for himself." One day Ryan stopped by the recruiting office and was presented with a letter from the young sailor—he had just graduated with honors from his navy training school.

Even though Ryan worked most of his four years with the LAPD in the Foothill Division—where the Rodney King incident occurred—he says he never felt under the microscope or openly distrusted. He credits his Hispanic partner, also a former army man, who "brought the language skills to the table" for a great deal of this. But most of what he accomplished, he explains, was the result of spending "the extra five minutes with people . . . that's community policing right there."

Sounds easy, but in a crowded and potentially dangerous city like Los Angeles, there's another side to the job. "I look back now with a little more maturity at the two jobs, police officer and paratrooper in a front-line combat unit, and I'll tell you what," Ryan says. "It's safer being in the military combat unit. Law enforcement is a job where you are basically going to war, for eight hours of your life, every day." Hearing his story about the events of May 27, 1997, gives this statement credibility.

Ryan was patrolling the Northridge-Chatsworth area of Los Angeles that night, which was close to his home. At about midnight, a call went out that there was an officer in trouble. By the time he and his partner arrived at the scene, fifty to sixty officers had already surrounded a warehouse that served as a studio for pornographic filmmakers. A detective from a nearby police force had been shot while serving an arrest warrant and was lying in a narrow hallway. At the far end of the hallway was the suspect, lying prone on a raised platform and armed with two high-powered handguns.

"One of the officers rolled a flashlight into the hallway," Ryan says, "and the suspect fired one round, right through the flashlight. And we said, 'Wow. This guy is still in here, and he's a good shot.' " Ryan gathered intelligence about the situation and found there was one, and only one, way to get to the injured detective. The SWAT team was over an hour away. A small group of officers decided to act. "There were about six or seven of us," he recalls, "who said, 'Hey, we're *doing* this thing, we're getting this guy out, we're not going to let him die.' "

The situation was frighteningly similar to some of the combat scenarios he had trained for during his years in the army. So Ryan helped formulate a military-style response: "We had some covering fire and four of us went down the hallway. We got all the way down to the victim, the detective, and the guy in front of me was shot, he was screaming on the ground. The guy behind me was shot, and he was screaming. It was a very dark hallway, and you just saw the smoke and the muzzle flashes, so everything's in that strobelike motion as you're moving. And the walls, on the side, were turning into powder from the bullets hitting the drywall."

Ryan grabbed one of the injured officers from the rescue team, just as he was hit two more times, and managed to drag him back down the hallway while returning fire. He then went back into the chaos of the hallway with another officer to rescue the second injured member of the rescue team. He wasn't afraid of getting shot but his feeling, he says, was one of "I was going to get shot. Stand by. Be ready. Be prepared. You're gonna get shot."

Somehow, Ryan pulled the other injured officer out of the line of fire without getting shot. They also rescued an officer who had gotten trapped in a bathroom down the hallway, and finally made it to the detective. It turned out to be the end of the rescue operation—he had been shot in the head, something the rescue team could not have known.

The immediate incident ended with the suspect dying at the scene, but for the rest of his time with the LAPD, Ryan faced stress, doubts from some of his superiors, questions over his choice of tactics, and guilt over not having been able to do more for the wounded officers. He served as a firearms instructor for his last year and a half with the LAPD, and to this day believes that if it weren't for the counseling and support of the Police Protective League, the emotions from that day would be lingering still. He also had the support of his wife and the knowledge that he had saved two lives.

The first man he pulled out had been shot a total of six times but was back on the job in a year. When Ryan was serving as a firearms instructor, blind luck brought him into close contact with this recovering officer. Ryan tells of how he came up and thanked him—"He told me he would have died for sure if I hadn't pulled him out. That was better than any medal right there. Better than any award that anybody can give you."

What gnawed at Ryan, though, was the sense that he could have been more help that day if he'd known not only how to handle a gun but how to handle gunshot wounds as well. Ryan knew that he could receive that kind of medical training if he returned to the army, but he adds that the decision to reenlist was made jointly with his wife. They were both ready to leave Los Angeles, and she considered the travel associated with military life an opportunity. "She was looking forward to it," Ryan says. "And I'm happy that she adapted very well."

Ryan remembers being honored at the White House and receiving the Medal of Valor from the LAPD as somewhat of a blur, but he says that both were very welcome. Knowing that two organizations had determined that he had done the right thing helped wash away any residual doubts. And when he found out he was a "Top Cop," Ryan was already at Fort Bragg, North Carolina, working on the medical training that he believes makes him better equipped to serve his country.

Four weeks before he was interviewed, Ryan was on a parachute jump and for the first time heard, as he puts it, "the famous call for help: 'Medic! Medic!' " He describes with excitement how he was able not only to help this injured soldier, but also comfort him. These days, his comrades call him "Doc" and get help for everything from a blister to a broken hip. He's found that his medical training offers a wide path to his ever-present goal of doing "what I can for the country, for the community I'm living in, and the people I come in contact with. . . . I don't want to take," he says, "I just want to give as much as I can."

Ryan's not taking much. "Gosh, it's almost like a priest with his vow of poverty," Ryan remarks when asked about his budget. "I guess it's like that. We know that financially we'll never be wealthy." He and Laura contribute to their daughter's educational fund, set money aside for the second child they were expecting when he told his story, and sometimes splurge on something like a used lawn mower. "That's like a big purchase for us," Ryan says, laughing.

"We get by. We get by," he continues. "It's tough at times, and we just have to do without sometimes. Purchase decisions have to be really thought out." Laura works as a supervisor at a grocery store, and she's also a volunteer firefighter. As Ryan talks about the pride she takes in this second, unpaid job, I can see how well their values are matched.

Ryan and Laura were relaxing in front of the television last July 3 in their Fayetteville, North Carolina, home when a news report announced that the American flag had been stolen from the state capitol. Laura reminded Ryan that he had a suitable replacement in the garage: a carefully folded twelve-by-twenty-foot flag. After hearing Ryan's story, I'm not at all surprised that he would have a spare extra-large Old Glory lying around the house.

"We'd already paid the bills," he remembers, "so we rolled our pennies for gas, and drove the hour and twenty minutes up to Raleigh, the state capitol." They were received by news cameras and photographers when they presented the flag as a donation. The governor later sent Ryan a letter of thanks. None of the attention was necessary, of course. To Ryan's way of thinking, if you know you can help, it is your duty to do so.

The bonus came in seeing his flag flying over the state capitol. That flag—any American flag—means everything to Ryan. "Maybe it sounds a little corny," he says, shrugging, "but the Star-Spangled Banner, the Land of the Free, Home of the Brave—that always had significant meaning to me. That's what I wanted to be a part of representing." Ryan takes a deep breath before explaining why: "I think the best thing that's ever happened to me was being born in America."

Stacy and Mark Green

There are two ways to a simple, secure, and happy American life. Jesús Serrato and Deborah Cline got there from the point of extreme financial insecurity. Stacy and Mark Green started from a point of complete financial security but chose to make do with less when they discovered that Mark's career brought disconnection from family, sanity, and community.

Stacy and Mark lived out the American dream of escape. In the beginning, the New World itself served as a haven for European forebears, then the frontier beckoned, and now we still have more than our share of wide-open spaces to entice us. Free as we are to move about as we wish, many answer the call. And Emerson and Thoreau are always there to remind the rest of us that maybe we should, as well.

Stacy Green describes her father as an exemplar of the American dream. Raised on a farm in Kansas, he made it to college and became a part of the aerospace industry that helped Southern California's economy soar in the 1960s and 1970s. "Watching that was wonderful," Stacy says of her childhood. "He achieved all of his dreams and he was very successful and we had a very nice life."

Her nice life was spent in Newport Beach, California, the crown jewel of Orange County. Although the city has long had an element of wealth, during the 1980s the money took over. The small-craft harbor, the bluffs, the pristine beaches, and the fact that it was close but not *too* close to Los Angeles attracted people with means. It's now one of the richest communities in the country.

Mark Green's father was a career Marine Corps drill instructor, so he moved with his family from San Diego to Hawaii to Santa Ana, the seat of Orange County just inland from Newport Beach. Mark says growing up with a drill instructor has left him "still fairly regimented," but as he entered college, his childhood ambition to work in law enforcement shifted to an interest in business administration.

Stacy, meanwhile, only remembers dreaming of having her own apartment and, she says, "living the Newport Beach life because that's what I knew." It was a life informed by her proximity, growing up, to a mecca of consumerism known as Fashion Island and classmates who received new BMWs as sweet sixteen presents. She was immersed in this lifestyle but says she never fully embraced it. She moved toward the writing life, majoring in journalism at the University of Southern California. After she graduated, she accepted a job back in Orange County as a sales rep with a business-to-business firm that sold copiers and fax machines. That's where she met Mark.

Mark was operations manager of the firm and moving up fast. The business was still small, but everyone there seemed to know that it had great potential for growth. They seemed to feel the same way about Mark, as they put him through his last two years of college at a private university. Both Stacy and Mark use words like *dynamic, fun,* and *wonderful* to describe what the company was like. Once they got engaged, however, the stresses of working together and planning their lives together didn't mix, and Stacy left the company in 1990.

Even before she left, however, changes were being made that would catapult Mark's career. The company had been bought by a holding company and injected with capital. It turned out to be a wise investment on their part. Mark says that in two years, their revenues tripled. This caught the eye of a major industry player, who, according to Mark, aggressively moved to buy the company.

"And so the company changed an awful lot," Mark continues. "In about the last year before I left the company, it really became headhunting season" and "the business model had changed a lot." There was a lot Mark was unhappy with, even though he had received a "significant" promotion to where he was "the focal point for twenty-five thousand customers, from a support standpoint."

Life had changed at home as well. Stacy and Mark bought a condo in a development south of Newport Beach, about thirty miles from work in Huntington Beach. They had one child, and another on the way when Mark's promotion brought him increased hours and a long commute, several days a week, to an outlying branch of the company. "We were miserable," Stacy remembers. "I was home with this baby and he was working twelve hours a day plus commuting. Sometimes it would take him two hours to get home." They rented out their condo and rented a house in Costa Mesa, a bedroom community adjacent to both Newport and Huntington. This arrangement cost them about three hundred dollars a month, but the small amount of time it saved seemed worth the price. They agree now that it was their first step.

Mark's salary had tripled in just four years, but his frustration level was also on the rise. Mind-numbing hours and death march commutes aside, he was becoming deeply disturbed with a business ethic that, as he puts it, paid "huge bonuses out to sales managers who weren't even making quota and laying off staff people who were doing their jobs." He watched the new ownership cut a quarter of his staff in the four departments he supervised, all while new accounts were coming in. Mark's job was to deal with customers, and those customers were becoming ever more underserved and hostile.

Stacy, meanwhile, was doing advertising and marketing work from their home, and watching Mark's job take its toll. "Our lives were just overwhelmingly stressful," she says, "totally dominated by Mark's job. It took everything he had, not just the hours, but all his energy." What might have been weekend family time became a chance for Stacy to take the kids out of the house so Mark could have downtime instead. "So every Thursday, he'd come home and say, 'Do we have any plans? No? Good. Don't make any. I don't want to do anything.'" Mark objects that maybe it wasn't *that* bad but contributes an example of how multitasked family life had become: "My job was to bathe the kids every night, so I'd throw the kids in the bath and read the whole time they were bathing. So it wasn't like we were having any time together."

Mark had four weeks' vacation allotted him every year but was rarely able to take it. He had a 401(k) with 100 percent matching, but sometimes he wondered if the stress would kill him before he ever had a chance to retire. He was suffering, he wasn't there enough for his family, and one day it dawned on him that he'd actually asked for this: "I'd climbed to where I'd set a goal, and realized there was more to it that was negative rather than positive." Sometimes it takes all you've got to reach a goal, and then it takes all you've got plus some to maintain it. Stacy saw this happening with Mark: "We kept thinking, well, if we get to this next level, then it will all fall into place. And then the next level came, and it was: 'Yes, there's more money, but it's not balancing out—the hours, the responsibility, the stress, the commuting to L.A.' It still wasn't worth it."

The next level came, and suddenly Mark felt like a parent who was a good material provider but whose moral instruction was hollow. "I talked to my kids," he says, "about maintaining your integrity and ethics, and yet I'm asked to do things at work that don't maintain that. Nothing dishonest, just reprehensible. . . . So I said, 'Okay, I need to readdress this.'" The moral lessons of their immediate environment were, Mark and Stacy felt, even emptier. "Also, there was the ethic of Southern California," Mark explains. "We were just there, and a new thing is this Botox, where people were getting injected [with a botulism strain] so that when they laugh they don't show their wrinkles. That—and not just that, but those kind of things—is just not a head-set that I ever embraced."

Southern California is often recommended—or slighted—as a laid-back place to live. Stacy and Mark would disagree. They've seen the tentacles of the freeway system expand into their backyards, rows of orange trees become rows of houses. The empty fields that they'd known growing up had been transformed into urban grids that quickly became gridlocked. Mark had lived in other areas of the country, but Stacy says her worst fear was that she was going to live and die in Orange County. She started thinking of her father, of what California had meant to him. "My dad got out of Kansas," she explains, "and ended up coming to California, doing his thing. He did it for adventure, and I admired that. Getting out and doing something new and living a different lifestyle than you'd lived as a child."

Both Stacy's and Mark's tone and manner change as they finish describing their lives in Orange County and warm to the subject of what their lives are like now. They had been feeding off of each other's statements in a crescendo of conviction over what led them to change. As they continue, their account calms markedly. Stacy is a dynamic con-

versationalist, Mark ever-so-slightly sardonic at the edges. Stacy is practiced at picking up her sentences exactly at the point she left when her
"high energy" children interrupt; Mark seems to have perfected a kind
of quick thoughtfulness which reminds one that, despite his early hopes
to pursue a career in law enforcement, his college major was philosophy
before he changed to business.

By the summer of 1996, the couple had stacked up plenty of reasons
to leave the life they knew but still confined their thinking to a transfer
or a new job. It took a little cajoling on Stacy's part, but Mark finally
took a long-overdue vacation, and the family drove up to Wallowa
County, Oregon, where Stacy had vacationed as a child. As they drove
into a valley about the size of Orange County, with a population of only
seven thousand, a thought occurred to them: What about living here? As
they explored the valley, their secret desires bubbled to the surface in the
form of jokes. "We were walking through town," Stacy relates, "and
Mark said, 'Yeah, I could get a job flipping burgers and we could live
in . . . ' and he pointed to this dilapidated shack that was ready to crash,
and he said, 'Yeah, we could live there, it would be just great.' And that
was the end of that, but we came home and it was just more of the same
stress."

In the few quiet moments they shared, they had brief discussions of
buying a vacation home in Wallowa, but there really wasn't an airport
nearby, and they were still maintaining a condo and renting a home.
Once that fantasy was ruled out, they made up their minds within two
months. As Stacy tells it: "There were no long discussions, there were no
debates, it was just 'Yeah, okay, let's move there.' There was not a lot of
planning or preparation or 'Well, maybe we should go back and see it
and really decide if we really like it.' It was just 'Let's do it.' We were
both so ready to do it, and that's what we did." Mark chimes in at this
point with: "We probably split a bottle of wine one Friday night, because
I know I resigned on Monday."

In less than a month, they were packed and on their way. That didn't
give their family and friends much time to react, which might have been
a good thing. "They thought we'd taken something when we were up
here, and that we hadn't recovered," Mark chuckles. Stacy remembers
some people dismissing the move as a midlife crisis—Mark was thirty-
five. He allows that it was a crisis, even if he wasn't quite at midlife: "It

was an identity crisis, in that I had tracked out a career plan, that I had met or exceeded my goal, but I wasn't happy. . . . And I hadn't really done anything courageous in a long time."

Mark has lived in forty states, but he says he's never seen a landscape as beautiful as that of Wallowa County. It might take your breath away, he says, but it will also calm your nerves: "A good friend of mine said this, your heart rate slows down. No extra heartbeats. And that's what I would describe it as. I just have no extra heartbeats."

Very little stood in the way of their relocation. Mark's unused vacation time covered their moving expenses. Friends of Stacy's grandmother had a spare house on a ranch that the couple rented until they found a house of their own. They'd always, among their peers, lived in the smallest houses and had the oldest cars. "We'd simply been frugal enough to allow ourselves a bit of a nest egg," Stacy says. "So it was *reasonable* to think that we could go up there. People who lived up there said, 'You will not be able to find employment, you will not be able to make money.' And yet, that was a risk we were willing to take."

Stacy, with her freelance connections, could take a certain amount of work with her. Mark, however, found himself looking at a single column inch of help-wanted ads in the Wallowa County *Chieftain* for positions like electrician, short-order cook, and potato picker. "Potato picker was crucial," Mark interjects, "because I considered it for a short period of time."

Fortuitously, an ad popped up for "sales, service, and consulting" at a tiny local computer company. Well, thought Mark, he'd *used* computers before. "Although," he points out, "I was the person who told the IT manager, 'You need to get our systems up or I'm going to have your job!' I had no understanding of how computers truly operated." Since it was either that or potato picker, however, it was worth a shot.

"All the eggs were in this one basket," Stacy says of that job application. "Not true," objects Mark. "See, my first four years of college, I worked at a grocery store, so I knew how to bag groceries." "Yes," agrees Stacy vigorously, "Safeway was the other thing. He could always go to Safeway. Draw on his experience at Alpha Beta."

Mark admits that he walked into his job interview with the mind-set that "I'm in this little town, and I'm from the big city, and I've got all my ducks in a row. I'd be dealing with this person who's kind of half clued in, and I could walk myself through it. Which wasn't the case at all. I was dealing with someone who was educated, had been a teacher, and started his own computer business eighteen years ago. I mean, he's brilliant."

Mark was surprised that there were two other applicants with more computer experience than he had out there in the sticks. But during the second interview, he managed to convince his future boss that his business experience would be more valuable, and that he could learn computers. He was offered the job and got a hotly negotiated starting salary of $18,000 a year. "In California," Mark remarks, "I was *taxed* more than that." As Mark was getting ready to leave, his new boss closed the deal with "and I know a place where you can get a good deal on a used desk." This to a man whose former company had given him use of a car and paid for his family's vacations in Puerto Vallarta.

But that company car was usually stuck in traffic, even though he left home, as Stacy says, at "four forty-two in the morning." No longer— there's an hour of quality family time every morning before school. These days, his wife and kids stop by on their way to preschool right down the street from Mark's job. Mark comes home every day for lunch and gets home promptly at five. For their first two years, he made the commute, if you could call it that, in a 1974 F-150 Ford pickup, which Stacy relishes describing as "a big old brown thing, with dents, cracked windshield, brown and orange macramé seat covers, gun rack, AM radio. . . . And our kids absolutely loved that car, because it had no shocks, so it bounced around a lot."

Stacy's client list has actually thrived in the rural environment. At first, people at the local chamber of commerce told her that there probably was a need for her marketing and advertising skills, "but people here have a real do-it-yourself attitude, and they're not used to hiring consultants. We don't have that here." So she went to Eastern Oregon University to propose a class tailored to this attitude: "Do It Yourself Marketing for Your Small Business." She taught at night so as not to interfere with what she calls her son's "schedule." The high attendance at her class convinced her there was interest in consulting, and she got a few clients from her students. Cold calls and networking brought her a few more.

Today, she has five steady clients who pay her monthly, and several more who pay by the job. Her business, she says, has brought her "to a nice income level and a nice number of hours. It's flexible, my kids go to day care two days a week, and I make pretty decent money." Mark turns to her to object: "Good money. Give yourself credit." Stacy shrugs: "Okay, so I make good money."

Mark and Stacy brought some valuable skills to their corner of Oregon, but their integration into the community has definitely been a two-way street, and far from the reception they were told they would get as transplanted Californians: "The first thing we did was get rid of our California license plates," Stacy says. Mark adds: "I was told if I didn't do that they'd put a bullet through my window, so . . ."

It didn't turn out that way. "What we found is, assuming you're a nice person, that they enjoy having people from the outside, because it's interesting," Stacy says. They have a family of fifth-generation ranchers as neighbors, and because Stacy and Mark have shown an interest in their lives, they have, in turn, shown an interest in the newcomers. Mark says he's pitched in when it was time to brand cattle and has been invited hunting, which is "a far cry from what I used to do before."

There are a few more far cries in their lives: Mark sits on three local boards, Stacy is chairman of a summer camp board. Mark's a trustee at their church. He hadn't been to church in fifteen years before they moved to Wallowa. They go camping, horseback riding, cycling, and attend outdoor concerts and main street parades where the Birkenstock-wearing crowd mixes with those in cowboy boots. Mark actually sees his children. The only thing Mark and Stacy gave up was the status of Mark's high-powered, high-paying job, which hadn't been working for any of them. They are more than happy with what they got in return: community and room in which to live. With finality, Mark states the obvious: "It *never* crosses my mind to go back."

Stacy, Mark, and many Americans like them have pared the American dream down to its core. The "dream itself" is what they've found in northeast Oregon, divorced from money, status, and consumer goods. "We're never going to be rich," Mark says, "but I guess we decided that wasn't the number one criterion for us. And so we're meeting the *not* rich criteria." Which involves what? Stacy answers: "Now I feel like we have a life. A great life."

FAMILY
NURTURING THE DREAM

What has made this nation great? Not its heroes, but its households.
—Sarah J. Hale

*T*HE American archetype is a solitary figure—a rugged individual, in Herbert Hoover's famous phrase, or a lonesome cowboy or a self-made man or woman. As the people in these pages told their stories, though, I was struck by how often they spoke not of themselves, but of their families. Struck, but not surprised, because I know just how they feel.

My mother and father were my earliest heroes and to this day they remain my most important ones. They did everything they could to impress upon me, my brother, and my sister that we were a *family,* not just a collection of people who happened to live together under the same roof. We knew from my parents' sterling example that in every endeavor, in each challenge we faced, we stood together or would fall together. Our triumphs were shared and our hardships were not endured alone. I was tremendously fortunate to have known such love and I cannot overestimate the influence of that early environment on my life.

I suspect a lot of you reading this know what I mean. To be born into a family that is consciously united and to parents who actively shape your values is a lucky thing, but it seems blessedly commonplace. So much of how I see the world can be directly traced back to some lesson taught by my parents, either by word or by deed: the value my father placed on being, above all, "a good hand"; my mother's ability to always, in her words, "turn a card" or, as she put it to me not long before she died, "About yesterday, no tears. About tomorrow, no fears"; their shared skill at nurturing an idea, a dream, and, above all, their children. I like to think that some of the best things they gave live on in my siblings and myself, nourished by the love that we have found in our own families, with our own wives and husbands and children.

So turns the wheel, the unbroken circle. Good families beget good families; love begets love. And, corny and unfashionable as it may seem in some quarters to say so, with the love of family, all is possible. Family gives us the support of unconditional love. Our mothers and fathers also offer a leg up from the life that they've known. This is the dream of all parents: that their children will have it better than they did. We don't spend much time thinking about it, but this dream was once uniquely American. It's since spread throughout the world, but it started here. The Europeans who came to the New World found a place where they could transcend the strictures of class. The distance from Old World institutions—and, in time, independence from them—made it so.

Progress may require the march of generations but progress is indeed possible. Consider the Kennedy family, who moved from Irish famine to wealth and the American presidency in the span of three generations. Ironic, then, that we sometimes term them "American royalty"—a family whose journey owes all to America's absence of royalty. Many more, if less dramatic, examples dwell closer to home; your family may be one of them.

Interestingly, the notion that you don't choose favorites among your kids also has its roots in the American experience. Girls, it is unfortunately true, faced the same prejudices in America as they had in Europe, at least until very recently. But primogeniture, the Old World custom that heaped favor and inheritance upon the eldest son, did not make it across the Atlantic intact. The impact of primogeniture's relative absence on American life was such that it drew comment from de Tocqueville, who saw this development as part and parcel of the democratic ideal. The microcosmic state of the family, no less than the United States, would be governed by the principle that "all men are created equal." Of course, parents and older siblings have always been there to point out that some family members are, indeed, more equal than others. But in America, the simple fact of birth order no longer dictated whether you were going to continue in and inherit the family trade, or become a soldier, or join the clergy.

De Tocqueville was also among those who saw a difference in how families came together in America. He observed that, in the New World, "Democracy loosens social ties, but tightens natural ones; it brings kindred more closely together, while it throws citizens more apart." Democracy severed the feudal bonds that in Europe ran from the lowliest peasant up to the king and through the church. Not government, not business, but family became the gravitational center of American life.

New institutions have sprouted up, since our nation's infancy, to supplant the structures torn down by democracy. Mass communication has brought us closer together and, paradoxically, contributed to our isolation. Our government has grown enormously on all levels, our federal government, especially, since World War II. Nevertheless, we live in what may be the least paternalistic society in the world. Despite Roosevelt's New Deal and Johnson's Great Society, the underlying message seems to be: "You're on your own." It's a message that cleaves us closer to *our* own.

The role of home and hearth in shaping the American experience reverberates today in the prominence we've given to so-called family values in our political dialogue. We've seen this phrase, which started out as shorthand for a set of conservative ideals, find resonance with folks across the political spectrum to the point where, in our most recent presidential election, "family values" consistently ranked high among the priorities of voters of all stripes. To some, the phrase is a battle cry for a return to religion in our private and public lives. To others, it means keeping handguns away from our children, or legislation, such as the Family Leave Act, that allows us to be with our loved ones when they need us. If our nation is adrift in rough seas, we seem to see family as the rudder that will help us plot a surer course. The family is what we've returned to in our dissatisfaction with the institutions that have grown to replace de Tocqueville's Old World social ties.

Family is integral to the American dream . . . but do we really dream of family? We do. The desire to build a family might run parallel or even counter to career goals, but it still burns brightly in the American heart.

It finds expression in a definition of "family" that has expanded from the original to include extended, expanded, mixed, single-parent, and same-sex household situations. Given such variety, it's easy to see why we have not always managed to agree about the changing shape of the American family.

With family such a big part of all our dreams, I realize that just about all of the people you've met and will meet here could be said to hold an American dream of family. For some, though, family was absolutely central to their experience of the American dream. For Melissa Nelson, the pull of family was so strong that she plunged into utter financial uncertainty rather than miss another milestone in her son's life. Building a family meant all to Bill and Karen McDonald, who traveled far across terrain both emotional and physical to add children to their lives. Generations of a single family have sustained the Star Detective & Security Agency, just as the agency sustains the family today. And the story of Alfredo Palacios, an orphan, reminds us that sometimes family is where you find it.

All have found the power of being part of something that is greater than themselves; and, in typically democratic fashion, all have gone about it differently. In this respect, as in so many others, our American families reflect and inform the spirit of our American nation.

Melissa Gradischnig Nelson

America entered the twenty-first century with an economy that was not only booming but for a time challenged conventional economic wisdom as well. Prior to our flirtation with 3 percent unemployment, most economists held that any figure so close to full employment would be sure to drive up inflation. But while more Americans are working now than ever before, many work for minimum wage in an age when that's ceased to be a living wage. When it can take as many as three menial jobs to get by and when benefits like health insurance are not included, a job is not necessarily an opportunity.

Most of the folks in this book, indeed, most Americans, have experienced low-paying, menial labor at one time or another in their lives. I've even met plenty of people over the years who were happy in what we sometimes call "dead-end" jobs. Usually they're folks for whom something else is more important—family, perhaps, or free time, or even simple peace of mind. Melissa Gradischnig Nelson decided long ago that the balance between work and family isn't really a balance. And tipping her personal scales heavily in favor of family eventually made her a successful entrepreneur and business owner.

Melissa grew up in Des Moines, Iowa, in a well-known and well-regarded family. Her mother was active in the Democratic Party and once even ran for Polk County supervisor. Her father plays trumpet in local bands and has worked closely with community theaters. Melissa's maiden name, Gradischnig, means something in her city.

But when Melissa graduated from high school in 1983, she thought her dreams could only be found in a larger city. She left Des Moines and established herself in Milwaukee. Though she loved the faster pace of the larger city, she discovered that this alone wouldn't settle the question of what she wanted to do with her life. "I always thought I wanted to be a writer," Melissa reflects, "but kind of just never went anywhere with that, I guess. Then I kind of got into a standstill in my life where I really did not know what I wanted."

Melissa met a man in Milwaukee and together they had a son, Nick. But when the couple split, Melissa found her thoughts turning to home. After seven years away, she returned to Des Moines with her eighteen-month-old son, determined to find a way to support him while devoting as much of each day to him as possible. Tight finances, however, soon led to a stint on public assistance. It was an experience Melissa hated.

First there was the shame that compelled her to shop on the other side of town, so no one she knew would see her using food stamps. Then there was the incredible frustration of never having enough. "You'd get so much money a month and you'd get *beaucoup* food stamps," she remembers. "Well, here I had this eighteen-month-old who didn't eat very much, but there was never enough money to last the month. You run out of money, but then you have all these food stamps left over." Melissa did something that she isn't very proud of, but it's something that goes on all the time: "My sister actually used to trade me. Which is, I know, totally illegal, just so that I would have money to buy diapers."

Melissa hated being in this position and harbors strong opinions on the subject still. "I'm always so tempted to go up to the government," she says with conviction, "and tell them they need to change the way food stamps are used. In my opinion, they should not be used for junk food.

But they could buy diapers. Or they could buy toiletries, because those are necessities." After six months of this scraping by, Melissa got two jobs: at a gas station and a Chinese restaurant. Both paid minimum wage.

Being able to shop without shame had its price. Each day held only a few precious hours for Melissa to spend with Nick before she would fall into a deep sleep that would barely prepare her for the next day. "I'm sure even the time I spent with him probably wasn't even quality time," she acknowledges, "because I was just so tired and so burned out." While Melissa was working as many as seventy-five hours a week, her sister was essentially raising her son. The arrangement beat day care, but it was far from ideal. "I feel like I missed a whole year there with him," Melissa says, her voice tinged with regret. "I would go to pick him up then for an evening or a weekend, and here my sister and her roommate would tell me all these wonderful things he'd done all week, that I'd missed out on." When Nick spoke his first words, Melissa was not there to hear.

It got to the point where people started thinking that Melissa's sister's roommate was Nick's mother. After working two jobs for a year and barely making ends meet, Melissa decided, "I'll go without so I can see my son." She knew it would take her from the financial frying pan into the fire, but she simply walked out of her two jobs, vowing never again to let work keep her from family.

"I'm a very determined person," Melissa points out. Determined or not, she was left with only one viable option once she had quit her jobs. A friend of hers had just had a baby and was heading back to work. In need of a cleaning service, she offered the job to Melissa. It paid only thirty-five dollars a week and involved cleaning someone else's floors, but she would be able to bring her son to work. She said yes. Then one of the friend's coworkers became interested, and Melissa had two customers. From there, "it just kind of blossomed." From that first added job to their present roster of about 160 clients, the business that is now called Nelson's Home Cleaning Service has "always been word of mouth," Melissa says.

Des Moines, she acknowledges, is a very small city. And even with the growth it has experienced in recent years, "everybody knows everybody." It's the kind of place where folks will ask their friends where to buy something before they reach for a phone book.

For Melissa, the fruit of this grapevine has been a $200,000-a-year business that has never advertised and has never depended on a loan. In the beginning, at least, Melissa didn't even think of herself as running a business—she was just cleaning houses. But before a year was up, she saw money coming in. It was still a small amount but was nearing the point that could be termed "enough." She realized the time had come to obtain a business license, state and federal ID numbers, and insurance. But she still didn't feel like an entrepreneur. Melissa remembers her one-time answer to "What do you do for a living?" as "Well, I clean houses." Whereas "Now I say, 'I own my own business.' "

This business became a true family affair when Melissa's mother, Sharon, came on board. Sharon, who had spent twenty years running her own marketing firm, was ready for partial retirement. "She decided she wanted to start traveling around the world," Melissa says, "so I was a perfect opportunity for her to do that. She could work a little bit here and there and be flexible and take off when she wanted to." For several years it was just the two of them. When Melissa's mother went off to see the world—sometimes for as long as six months at a time—they always found a friend to fill in.

Melissa found herself turning the standard entrepreneurial path on its head—she actually cut back her hours as her business grew. A husband and another baby provided the incentive. When her second son started kindergarten, she began working from nine until three, so she could drop him off and pick him up. For the most part, she was able to stick to the new schedule. Not working worked out just fine.

As more clients came knocking, Melissa found the new employees she needed among friends and friends of friends attracted to the easy, flexible hours. By her sixth year, she had four employees, all dedicated equally to doing a good job and living a good life. "That's the backbone of my business," Melissa says. "I want everybody to be with their families."

Most of Melissa's employees work no more than thirty hours a week. She insists that they take time off for family events, school plays, even something as small as a school outing. "People just need their priorities," she says. "That's my thing. And that's why I encourage people who work for me: 'Gosh, your daughter's going on a field trip. Go with her. I'll work for you so you can go.' That's important to kids."

Melissa takes care of her employees in other ways too. When Nelson's

Home Cleaning Service gets paid for a contract, she always splits the revenue into thirds: one-third to overhead and taxes, one-third for herself, and one-third to the employees who do the job. Under this arrangement, Melissa's cleaners can earn as much as three times what cleaners usually make. "I *absolutely* do not let anybody, even when you're in training, go under ten dollars an hour," she says with force. "I mean, that's the bottommost you'll ever hit. Most of my people right now, especially the ones that have been with me the longest, are making fifteen to twenty dollars an hour." One of her employees left a corporate job with a stagnant salary where she'd worked forty hours a week for thirteen years. With Melissa, she's making more money working twenty-five to thirty hours a week. Sure, if you do the math, the hours and wage aren't going to allow any of them a lavish lifestyle, only the time to lavish affection on their families.

In 1997, after Melissa had been in business for six years, the *Des Moines Register* ran a feature on her success. It was her first piece of publicity, and the response was tremendous: "My business literally doubled within a week. Maybe even more . . . my phone rang for three days straight, I know that." People even wrote letters, telling Melissa "how proud they were of me." Business picked up, but Melissa's life has remained essentially unchanged. She seems to have taken the expansion as an opportunity to extend her success to more like-minded people. Nelson's Home Cleaning Service now has four employees with college degrees, among them a former teacher who's earning money to go back to school. All of them have come to her through friends and family— Melissa says she's never had to place a help wanted ad, and her personal connection to her workforce means she can always trust them to do a top-notch job.

"I don't have a problem growing," Melissa says, "as long as I can manage it all." She felt a bit overwhelmed, she admits, in the half year or so after the article ran, "doing," she says, "what I didn't want to do . . . taking time away from my family to do paperwork and bids in the evening." So she gave the paperwork duties to a woman who had been cleaning for her. Melissa also caved in and got a PC, which her husband, a computer consultant, taught her how to use.

Nelson's Home Cleaning Service now services 152 homes and eight offices. Offices weren't part of the original plan, but if they call and

Melissa has someone who's willing to work evenings, she'll take the contract. But she always asks the question at the root of her business: "If so-and-so's going to do your office, can her daughter come with her?" So far, she says, it's never been a problem. But for right now, there's no pressing need to expand this business. In fact, Melissa has been encouraging competition: "I actually have a friend who is kind of where I was nine years ago, and I was just talking to her this morning. I'm trying to encourage her to do this—she already cleans houses—to try to make it grow. And I keep telling her, if I can do it, anybody can do it." Des Moines, she continues, is big enough to support at least one more cleaning enterprise like hers.

Besides, Melissa seems to have a rare grasp on the meaning of the word *enough*. She may work only eighteen hours a week in her home office and at clients' homes, but as she puts it, "My kids do *not* go without. I mean, they're not spoiled rotten, but they don't go without. We live in a nice home, in a nice neighborhood. We have the vehicles we need. We take vacations. I mean, I'm not rich, but I'm kind of a miser. I'm a good saver." She still clips coupons.

And what about those million-dollar homes on her client list—has their opulence ever tempted her to strive for the same? No, she says, because she knows the trade-off: "Some of them are the ones that *do* have to work eighty hours a week to make their house payment," she says. "And I just think the family unit is too important." As for her glimpse into how the other half lives, Melissa says that "lots of us have even gotten decorating ideas, and it's just *fun* to see some of these homes that we probably would never have the opportunity to go into."

Melissa's youngest son was in his first year of kindergarten when she was interviewed; her eldest son was twelve and harboring dreams of becoming an artist. Melissa had recently taken him to the Chicago Art Institute, a place she can see him attending as a student someday. Her youngest just opened his first bank account, and while he was depositing some of his change, the teller asked him what he was going to do with the money. He told her it was for college. This is how she weighs the benefits of running her business as she does. "I get out of it the smiles of my kids," she says, and then puts into words the sentiment that runs through her story: "Everything in life is not necessarily about money, even though we all need it to survive."

Alfredo Palacios

Family is more than biology, and it provides more than food, shelter, and warmth. We've already seen how a few carefully chosen words or deeds from a loving parent can make dreams possible. Chris Gardner's mother told him he could make a million dollars. The image of Delores Kesler's father telling her she could do anything is with her for life. We will see in the next chapter how Anthony Rapp's mother made difficult sacrifices that made his early dreams possible. But we know that family does more than inspire.

Family is our first and most consistent support network, and these are the frames on which we hang our dreams. They give us our next steps, turn around our failures, and offer more opportunities than we could invent on our own. We have more of a meritocracy than we did back when I was starting out, but countless jobs and college admissions are still gained because someone is connected. Quite often that someone is related to the fortunate one who is just getting a foot in the door.

That doesn't mean that those without connections in the family, or those without families, are locked out permanently. Our next story is of a young man who grew up without parents in a foreign country but found generous strangers who carved footholds in the often hard edifice of our society. Alfredo Palacios didn't always step with certainty, but with each unexpected offer of help, he became more committed to making his way. With so many people behind him, he feels that dropping the ball at this point would be to let them down. For this very special young man found something we can call family in his small community of South Bend, Indiana.

Alfredo was born in Puebla, in central Mexico. Before Alfredo could form lasting memories of him, his father took his leave of their family. For three years, Alfredo's mother toiled to support him and his sister, and the long days took their toll. One day she stopped working. Shortly thereafter, when Alfredo was six, she passed away from an illness Alfredo still can't name.

She died at home, surrounded by family, and Alfredo and his sister were taken in by an uncle. They lived outside Los Mochis, a city on the mainland near the coast of the Gulf of California. Alfredo remembers selling ice cream with his uncle to workers in the tomato fields, and he remembers the dramatic landscape near the sea. He also remembers that, try as he might, he could not contribute enough to his relatives to ease their burden.

Alfredo had two older sisters who had already left home by the time his mother died. One of them lived with her husband in Santa Ana, California. When he was nine, this brother-in-law came to accompany Alfredo and his younger sister to a new life in a new country. "There was money there," Alfredo remembers the adults in his life telling him, "lots of money. And you could have many things, compared to what I had in Mexico."

A border stood between Alfredo and his closest living relative, but even after the attempts in the late 1980s to tighten illegal crossings, this family's journey sounds routine. "We had to walk through some hills in Tijuana," Alfredo recalls. "I had heard many tales about people coming over here the same way, but at the time, I didn't really get scared. I was just having an adventure or something."

Two years passed with Alfredo living in Santa Ana, where a tight community of immigrants had established themselves amidst the conspicuous wealth of Orange County. By the time Alfredo moved again, he was familiar with being uprooted. And again, he was still too young to fully understand why the adults in his life had chosen to leave their lives behind, only that "there were problems." His sister's husband had relatives in South Bend, Indiana, a city of a hundred thousand between Chicago and Detroit, and that's where they settled.

But before long, the marriage between Alfredo's sister and her husband frayed. They separated and started to look back to California. Then, Alfredo says, "We decided to try something else." That something turned out to be harder than either could have imagined. They moved into the housing projects in South Bend, and Alfredo's sister scrambled for work to support not just her brother but also her two young children.

Alfredo came of age during a dramatic demographic shift that's hard to overstate. Between 1993 and 1999, according to census estimates, the U.S. Hispanic population increased by a third, something you'll hear a lot more about as the 2000 census figures roll in. It's been happening in nearly every corner of the country, but hadn't touched Alfredo's small community when he first arrived. At the time, he entered the public housing community warily. "I thought I could never fit in," he says, "but I did. [People] were good. I had never really talked to black people or anything until then. It was a good experience knowing them."

Alfredo was attending school, and says that while his English wasn't "too good," he had enough from living in California to keep his head above water academically. Meanwhile, though, his sister was finding it increasingly hard to keep the family afloat financially.

As he patrolled the housing projects, as he walked the projects on his own time as part of a community policing project, Corporal Derek Dieter of the South Bend Police Department noticed Alfredo kicking around a soccer ball. "From being in the police all these years," says the twenty-three-year veteran, "you can tell in the first couple of minutes . . . who is sincere and has a vision of what they want to do . . . someone who has something in mind, somebody who's honest, somebody who's caring." Derek had been working with the Community-Oriented Police Enforcement (COPE) program in the projects, a program he says started with a few policemen tossing a football with kids who had nothing else to do.

Alfredo had been holding a wild dream he told few people about and that didn't seem to stand a chance in his environment. He wanted to play soccer for the professional team in Milan, Italy. In his estimation, they were the world's best. In Mexico, any field, any patch of asphalt, any dirt road, is a potential training ground. Any round object stands a chance of being used in a children's pickup game. But in America, especially in Indiana, soccer is a game played in the suburbs.

When Derek saw that Alfredo had a vision, he also saw the potential to get other youth interested in the game. As he explains it, COPE officers were determined to expand the horizons of disadvantaged youth through sports. They picked sports that weren't readily available, either because of a lack of green space or a lack of equipment—sports like golf, soccer, and floor hockey. Here was someone who was an excellent soccer player, someone who needed a chance, and someone who could give a chance to someone else.

Alfredo, in his typically modest and unassuming way, says that Corporal Dieter took him into his team, where he played until he entered high school. Derek, however, calls Alfredo "the king of soccer." The policeman didn't know the rules of the game, had never played and never coached. The team was essentially organized around Alfredo, who took on a role of instructor while Derek picked up tips from high school and college coaches. In 1994, they started a team in a local association, and won the league championship with a collection of kids aged ten to fourteen, most having never experienced team play before. Alfredo and a few others went on the road around the Midwest and to Denver for a national three-on-three tournament. Alfredo racked up more than thirty trophies for his leadership as captain and his team's skilled play.

The premise behind COPE was to get youth interested in athletics, and from there interested in high school athletics, and from there interested in staying in school. By the time Alfredo got to high school, the soccer coach already knew about him. Alfredo made junior varsity his freshman year, and got a few chances to play with the varsity team. He made the grades required to stay on the team in spite of his limited English, even scoring a number of As and Bs: "I loved soccer, so if I wanted to play soccer I had to keep up the good grades. . . . I was serious my freshman year, I was really serious." Most kids would at this point have been on a straight road to college, but Alfredo had a few more obstacles to overcome.

After years in the projects, Alfredo's sister wanted out. But supporting her six-year-old, her four-year-old, and Alfredo was holding her back. Toward the end of his freshman year, Alfredo went to work as a dishwasher in a fancy restaurant. During the summer, he husked corn, thinking that he would save money to avoid having to work the next year. But when he and his sister looked at the cost of housing, he sacrificed his savings to help move the family out of the projects. He says he didn't feel he could shirk the responsibility: "I always wanted to work . . . so I could take money home to my sister. I just kind of felt . . . that I had to forget about soccer or school."

By the time Alfredo was a sophomore, soccer had become a luxury: "Work was right after school, so I couldn't come to practice at all. At the time, [it felt like] work took everything away, because I always wanted to play soccer for a really good college. I wanted to keep going in soccer. That was my dream. But . . . I just had to do something to keep my family going." Work ate up more of his life as his sophomore year limped along. He started working days, as his employer didn't know that he was in school, and finished out the year attending virtually no classes.

Alfredo's and his sister's combined efforts got them out of the projects, and Alfredo says he was ready for a break. In his mind, he thought they "didn't have too many problems economically." But his sister saw things differently and didn't want to be the only breadwinner. Alfredo saw that there were teens who lived "normal" lives—they socialized, played sports, and got good grades. His sister saw that they were still struggling. Tensions mounted and arguments broke out. Finally, Alfredo and his sister realized he had to leave.

After years of keeping his problems to himself, Alfredo finally opened up to a friend he met when he first came to South Bend. This boy's parents, Brenda and Carlos Huitzil, immediately decided that they could easily make a difference in Alfredo's life. They opened up their home, transferred him to a new school, and made him focus on grades rather than work. Suddenly, washing dishes for minimum wage wasn't his only option. "I didn't think I was going to get anywhere," he says, remembering his frustration. "I don't want to put anyone down—but I thought I was going to be like everyone else, working every day of their lives, trying to get somewhere. . . . I didn't want to be that way."

Still, Alfredo entered South Bend's Washington High School as a junior with lowered expectations. If he worked hard, he thought, he might make it into a vocational school. The dream of professional soccer was all but gone, but he still played with the school team. Then, in addition to the support he was getting in his new home, he found a mentor at school. Bilingual education specialist Leonora Battani works one-on-one with Hispanic students, not just on their language skills, but also on issues outside of school that interfere with their studies. "I saw a student with a lot of potential," Leonora says of her first meeting with Alfredo. "A student who wanted to do the right thing for himself. He made up his mind that he wanted to finish high school, and whatever it took, he was going to do it."

Alfredo's missed semester and still-limited skills in written English meant that he would have to work double time to finish high school by the end of his senior year. He was placed on a tough schedule, and got some tough talk from Leonora, who told him she wouldn't allow him to miss school like he had before. "He kind of did whatever I told him to," she says, laughing, "for his own benefit. He understood that."

Leonora says that her student's junior year was incredibly trying for him, but by the time he was a senior, he relied on her very little for help with English and barely missed getting straight As that year. This gave them time to talk about other things, like what he would do next. As he remembers, he was uncertain and fearful of the future, but Leonora encouraged him by investigating colleges. "I couldn't just let her do the work," Alfredo says, so he started to visit some campuses himself.

The extra effort Alfredo had put in over his last two years of high school didn't counterbalance the low GPA of his first two years to the point where he could get into most four-year colleges. Leonora knew, however, that all her student needed was a chance. She pulled strings in her program to get a meeting with the president of Bethel College in South Bend, and introduced him to Alfredo. "I truly believed in Alfredo," she says now, explaining her efforts on his behalf. "I truly believed that he could do this. And I think that that came through to the president, that even though his grades were not the best, he could do it if he wanted to do it." At about the same time, Alfredo's former soccer coach had a conversation with Bethel's soccer coach about a young man who could take their team to the next level of play.

Alfredo and Leonora left the meeting without getting a final answer. There were problems with his GPA, and Alfredo's immigration status stood in the way of most student aid funds. Then one morning, Alfredo says, he got a call from the president. Could he meet with him and some other people at the local Rotary Club? "He never mentioned anything about a scholarship," Alfredo remembers. "He just introduced me to some other people." After graduation, Alfredo got an acceptance letter and notification that his tuition was being sponsored. Now all that stood in the way were the bureaucratic mazes of two governments.

Alfredo had to return to Mexico, the first time he had seen his home country in nine years, in order to obtain a student visa. All he had was the address of a friend's family in central Mexico and a piece of paper saying that he had been accepted to college in the United States. He had no birth certificate and found that he was expected to get his compulsory military service waived. He found himself face-to-face with his past: "The poor people and the little kids asking for money in the streets. I saw so many kids . . . I was just really sad at the time." And hanging over his head was the fact that if he didn't navigate this last hurdle, he could be stuck in a now-unfamiliar country.

Once again, Alfredo was rescued by strangers, some of whom he will never meet. In three weeks, after a series of strings had been pulled on both sides of the border, he had a passport and a visa and the right to enter the United States legally. Alfredo doesn't discuss these three weeks in detail, but simply laughs and says, "There's a lot of corruption in Mexico."

Alfredo was a college freshman when we spoke. He described the natural beauty of the campus, the brick buildings, trees, and fountains, and remarked on how different his life and surroundings are these days. "Every time I go to school," he says, "I want something more out of life. It's just not like before. I want to go further every time I go to school." Alfredo was studying business administration but isn't sure that's exactly what he wants to do. For now, he says that he's after knowledge for the sake of knowledge, taking classes in sociology, psychology, and physiology. Things he never expected he would enjoy.

"Maybe I'm not as great a soccer player as I wanted to be," Alfredo says of his original dream, adding that he hopes to play for Bethel next year, "but I've had better rewards than that. . . . My sister has gotten better, and everything has gotten better for her. Everything's good. Everything around me feels good." Alfredo still lives with the Huitzils, still sees Corporal Dieter and Leonora regularly, and spends a lot of time thinking about how their contributions and the contributions of others came, in a way, out of the blue. "Maybe," he confides, "I didn't deserve it."

A lot of people in South Bend would disagree. There's something about this kid that goes beyond his politeness and willingness to work hard. Neither his mentor on the police force nor his mentor at Washington High could fully explain, but they offered a few suggestions. Both mentors comment on how he never took pity on himself. As Leonora puts it, "He's not a whiner. He's never said, 'Look at me, poor me, I've had a horrible life, I don't have parents.' . . . No. Alfredo's just Alfredo. He comes across like, 'I'm here and I want to do this.' And he appreciates everybody's help, so everybody's willing to help." On top of this, both Dieter and Leonora separately said that he makes a huge difference in the lives of others. Derek Dieter: "Alfredo was put into a bad situation at birth and he learned to cope with it and deal with it and make himself and everybody else into a better person." Leonora: "Everybody benefits from knowing Alfredo. It isn't just the other way around."

Alfredo, Leonora, and Derek all had something on their minds that went beyond their success story. They all know how many others in similar situations weren't as lucky. Alfredo knows several Hispanic students, including his girlfriend, who got better grades in high school than he did but still find their way to college blocked by financial or bureaucratic problems. And then there are those who never made it through high school. The 1997 final report by the U.S. Department of Education Hispanic Dropout Project claimed a 1994 dropout rate of 30 percent among Latinos nationwide, and President Clinton called the problem a "national crisis." The report was titled "No More Excuses."

Derek and Leonora see the faces of this crisis on a daily basis and feel the frustration that comes from watching a kid slide downhill and being unable to stop it. "It's sad to see what's going to happen with those kids," says Derek. "I can pick out seven-, eight-year-old kids who aren't going to have a shot at a life, let alone going to college or whatever, just [because of] the bad family environment. . . . Other than adopting kids and moving them into your own house, there's only so much you can do." Leonora says that knowing she can help is "the best feeling in the world." But she doesn't miss a beat before adding that such influence is rare: "The only unlucky part is that we can't do it more often. That it doesn't happen, not even every year. . . . There's a lot of Alfredos out there. A lot. But sometimes we don't see them or we just can't handle all of them."

When you have little to give, however, there is still something that doesn't cost much in terms of time or resources that can turn someone's life around. Growing up with the help of an extended family, Alfredo learned that the best "push" a family can give comes in the form of trust: "I think trust is one of the best things a family can give you. They can give you money and everything, but if they don't give you trust, at one point you are going to just not care about what they give you. If I wanted to do something bad, I couldn't, because I would let them down." The trust of others, even of strangers, Alfredo found to be more powerful than the inspiration or practical lessons his mentors passed along: "Most of all, I don't want to let them down, because they helped me out to do this. Now that I'm here, I can't let anyone down." I don't think he will.

The Star Detective & Security Agency

Americans value family, Americans value business. So I had a feeling from the outset that a family business would find its way into this book.

But I didn't imagine I would find such a family, and such a business, as the Star Detective & Security Agency in Chicago. Almeda Dunn, Star's president and CEO, has an expansive and enthusiastic embrace of the American dream that reaches back to the dreams of her grandfather and forward to those of her daughters. She stands between a rich history and a promising future, with family at the center of each.

The Star Detective & Security Agency sits in the middle of what Almeda calls the "hood" on East Seventy-fifth Street, a strip once famous for jazz and a center of black cultural life, but now notorious for crime and decay. Star shares the block with a beauty shop, a TV repair shop, and a church. That's about it. The rest is boarded up, and most of the activity on the street comes from drug dealers. At one time, there was a police station nearby, but not even the building that housed it still stands. In the middle of all this, uniformed men and women pass day and night under the American flag that flies from a building that once housed a manufacturing space but now serves as the headquarters for Star. Inside, visitors find very different images than those they might have encountered outside: pictures dating back to the 1920s, pictures of Captain Luegemus Bratton, a stern man with a ramrod-straight posture. In many of the photographs, Captain Bratton stands before an American flag. The pictures hang as a reminder of who founded the company, how it was founded, and why its founder believed it was successful. Velora V. Watson, sales and marketing director for Star and Almeda's daughter, says that her great grandfather "was a big advocate of saying what a wonderful opportunity he had and the dream that he has been able to accomplish by living in America." One of Bratton's favorite sayings, she adds, was: "America: love it or leave it."

Bratton's father was a former slave who used his freedom to walk from North Carolina to Louisiana, where Bratton was born in 1895. When Bratton felt he was old enough—he was no more than twelve— he was struck by a similar wanderlust and hopped a freight train. He had no idea where the train was going, only that it would take him away from the farms that in many seasons produced little more than dirt. Getting off in Kansas City, he worked unofficially in the train station, cleaning the waiting rooms for pennies given to him by friendly rail workers.

Another train took him to Chicago, where he got a job in a foundry and met his wife, whom he married in 1916. He might have settled into this hard but stable career had he not been injured in a foundry accident around late 1921 or early 1922. Almeda says he then vowed never again to work for someone else. Too proud to accept welfare, he struck out on his own.

Bratton lived in the golden age of door-to-door salesmen, and in Chicago, many of them were recent European immigrants who were, like him, trying to grab a piece of the entrepreneurial American dream. Bratton started his agency by accompanying salesmen on their rounds in rougher neighborhoods. Later he served as a collection agent. As his clients established storefronts, Bratton's role evolved from bodyguard to "doorshaker," meaning that from sundown to sunup, he would shake the doors of his clients to make sure they were locked and secure.

Almeda still draws guidance and inspiration from these humble beginnings. And inspiration is required to run a business that employs over four hundred and provides security for government agencies such as the Chicago Transit Authority, Provident Hospital, the City of Chicago Library, and the Department of Children and Family Services—not to mention businesses that range in size from a fast-food franchise to the telecommunications giant Ameritech. You'll also find Star's ushers at the Chicago Fire's soccer matches and the Chicago Bears' football games. They recently kept a crowd of love-struck teens in line at an 'N Sync concert. Star's security officers no longer shake doors; they check IDs and watch surveillance videos. Many of them are trained to deal with emergency medical situations, and a majority of the new hires have completed training in disaster and terrorism response, crowd control, unarmed self-defense, fire prevention and control, and firearm safety. In more ways than one, the business, as Almeda says, "reflects America as it has come along."

Much has changed but much has stayed the same. Almeda still adheres to rules set by her grandfather early on—do no business with drinking establishments, give churches a reduced rate, hire from the community. She remembers her grandfather, who passed away in 1977, as the kind of man who could stop any kind of mischief with his expression alone: "He never had to scold me if I did something that he didn't like. It was just that *look* that he gave me." That look is evident in a 1940s photograph of Bratton reviewing his guards before they take to their rounds. Six African-American men—one of them his son, one a nephew that he raised as a son—stand in a formation, wearing uniforms, badges, ties, and pistols. It's clear from the scene that these men have learned discipline, pride, and honor from their boss, a man who never served a day in the military or police force and only went to school "between crops," but was given the title "Captain" by his clients. Bratton, incidentally, appears to be the shortest of the seven men in the photograph. He's also the last one any sensible person would consider tangling with.

When Almeda was growing up, Take Your Daughter to Work Day often meant sitting in the back of her mother's car on a stakeout. All four of Bratton's children put in some time with Star, but Vivian V. Wilson, Almeda's mother and now Star's chairman of the board, served as a typist, accountant, investigator, and office manager. In other words, she did everything. But it's the undercover work that Almeda remembers most clearly. For a child, it was fun and games, like the time she went with her mother to a beach party. Only years later did she find out that the pictures her mother took were for an insurance fraud case, and the man her mother danced with was claiming to be too injured to work. But as much as Almeda was steeped in the family business, she was also taught to serve her country; at nineteen, she left home to join the navy.

After her honorable discharge, Almeda took a job with the post office in California and started a family with her husband. In 1971, she got a call from her mother, who was then running the office. Star was expanding, jobs were available, and Vivian Wilson was getting ready to pass the torch. "Being raised the way I was," Almeda says, "around the business, my mother coming in and doing undercover work, and me doing some things with her as I was growing up, I didn't even question it." Almeda took her family home to Chicago, ready to learn the ropes.

She found there was quite a bit more to learn than she expected, and she will always be grateful that her grandfather was still around for six years to complete the grooming and see Almeda pass the state certification exams to become a private detective and security contractor. After she passed, as far as the state of Illinois was concerned she could legally run the business. But as far as Bratton was concerned, she had a long way to go. He encouraged her to join the Chicago Police Department and attend business classes. For twenty years, Almeda took a dangerous night shift with the Chicago PD and worked for Star during the day. And, of course, she and her husband raised two daughters. As if that weren't enough, after a few business classes, she says, her eyes opened to what continuing her education would bring to Star. She went on to earn bachelor's and master's degrees in criminal and social justice. It took her a mere six years.

All this training and extra effort went above and beyond what was required of Almeda, but she had strong reasons for wanting to go further. Times had changed since Bratton started the business. The industry had changed, and crime had changed. Almeda also knew that current and future clients might be skeptical of a woman in charge of a security company, even if she was the granddaughter of Captain Luegemus Bratton. True, her mother had been running the office for years but that was while the captain was still around. Almeda knew that her extra effort could help offset some of that. But finally, and most important, Almeda felt and still feels a great weight on her shoulders: "It's my responsibility . . . to make sure my mother is taken care of, my two daughters are taken care of, and that my four hundred ten employees and their families and babies are all being taken care of. I would hate to be the one that something happened to, who dropped the ball, and see that my grandfather's dream was no longer a reality."

While Bratton was rigid and uncompromising about his sense of honor and morality, he also knew that his business had to change with the times. As one of the first black business owners in Chicago, he understood the struggles that the next generations would face as women business owners in a male-dominated industry. "He knew that he was leaving this business to women," Almeda says. "He knew that he was leaving the business to my mother and to myself, and he knew that I had two daughters. . . . He was very aware that this would be a woman-owned business." Almeda won't let the prejudices that stand in her way distract her, but she knows all too well that they are in effect: "I know from my experience that I can't go to downtown corporate Chicago and even be considered for an interview. . . . These big Fortune Five Hundred companies will not open the door for me, and I have tried. I have really tried." The exception, she says, is Ameritech, which gave Star a contract to provide security for one building back in the 1960s. That foot in the door has led to contracts for twenty-seven Ameritech buildings today.

Star's next generation—represented by Almeda's daughters, Velora V. Watson, sales and marketing director, and Dominique A. Dunn, chief operating officer—has grown up knowing that their struggles will be only slightly fewer. But at their side remains Captain Bratton, a figure they proudly evoke and link to their own success. Velora, responsible for bringing in new accounts, makes education her mission on sales calls: "When I go out, the first thing that I think about is what my grandfather would say if he were here. So I educate my clients on our history, the importance of providing jobs for those in the inner-city community, and the importance of women in leadership. . . . I want not only our community, but the whole world to know that we can do it."

Like Almeda, Velora and Dominique grew up in the office and out on assignment. Like Almeda, they joined their mother on stakeouts, not fully aware as they sat in the backseat of her car, snacking and playing games, that mom was working. Velora graduated from Spellman, the traditionally African-American women's college, in Atlanta in 1986, and pursued a career in advertising for three years before returning home to Star, injecting valuable expertise into the business. Dominique, like her mother, got a degree in criminal and social justice but already had experience in the field: "When I turned eighteen, I did my training; they had me in uniform, working every shift." The one she hated most was the graveyard shift, midnight to 8 A.M.: "I used to think I was so mistreated at the time. . . . But I was always told by my mother and my grandmother both that you would never know what the officers are going through or what they have to deal with if you don't experience it. Now I appreciate it, but then I did not." She worked in the ranks during summer vacations from college and for a few years afterward, until she was ready to work in administration.

The next generation has already embraced the family's heritage, legacy, and traditions, but both they and their mother know that there's a slight difference. Almeda explains: "When we were children, you didn't ask why. My children ask why, but me, in my age group, we didn't ask why. Even when we were adults." As Velora and Dominique learn the business, they have questioned and will continue to question a few of the traditional ways of doing things, something their mother says she has encouraged: "I understand the frustration of not knowing why you are doing something." Their questions have never been due to a lack of respect for tradition, but rather part of a process of combining the old with the new. And as it turns out, Dominique says, the old ways often win: "I may try to do something on my own, but when I look back on what was laid out for me, it's like, if I'd just done it that way in the beginning, it would have saved a lot of trouble. . . . It's live and learn."

It's something that all families do. Sometimes, Almeda says with a laugh, they just "buck" one another. The difference here is that it's played out on a stage where what works and what doesn't can be proven. And in the end, they all have the same goal: to keep the business in the family and growing. "There *will* be another generation," says Almeda, thinking ahead to her children's children. Selling the business to a larger corporation is simply not an option, but expansion is. Almeda plans to move Star from its current 2,075-square-foot office into a newly constructed headquarters in the same neighborhood, where it will stretch out in over 11,000 square feet of office and training space.

Moving with them will be the same collection of photographs and mementos from Bratton's era; the traditions of the door shaker will continue even as Star takes on new problems and solutions. One of those traditions is embodied in a copy of the Constitution that Bratton had framed and hung, which serves as a reminder of both the opportunity and the difficulties this country gave him. "My grandfather said that these are the things that this country is made up of," Almeda remembers. "He was very aware that at the time it was made up, they didn't consider blacks as who they were talking about, but my grandfather did." The Constitution hangs not only as a symbol. Star's security officers are also taught that this document gives the citizens they encounter, and may have to detain, inalienable rights. In this family business, the Bill of Rights is also a guide to customer service.

Bratton knew that the term "American dream" wasn't invented for him, but he built a dream anyway. He knew that powerful forces were intent on keeping him out of their version of the ideal American society, but he still embraced the ideals behind America. That's a difficult mental balancing act, but one that Almeda has mastered. America, right or wrong, is where she lives, and where she either finds or fights for opportunity: "A lot of times people don't realize that African-American families have been a part of this American dream, just like any other. . . . You might talk about immigrant families that came here voluntarily. Well, no matter how you got here, you are in America. At some times the opportunity wasn't as easy for some people, and it was hard, but the point is that there was and is opportunity in this country."

Star's new headquarters could be called a symbol of this opportunity.

But if anyone needs clarification as to what that symbol means, the family behind the building will offer it in the form of three flags that will fly above the entrance. The Stars and Stripes will fly next to the red, black, and green tricolor banner of black pride. Next to that will fly the city's flag. Each flag represents a community—America, black America, and Chicago. Each of these communities has benefited Captain Bratton's descendants, and each community in turn has benefited through them. The flags say clearly who Star is and speak just as clearly not only to the struggles they have endured, but to the pride they feel in being a part of the continuing American story.

Bill and Karen McDonald

Has anyone managed to reach adulthood without hearing the words "Wait until you have kids of your own"? I don't think any comment annoys kids more, but that's not why parents say it—the annoyance is just a fringe benefit. No, parents say these words because having children really does change you. It changes the nature of your dreams. Ask a parent: no matter where they're from or what they've accomplished, most will tell you that raising a child is the toughest thing they've ever done. It's impossible to go through it without being forced to learn something about yourself.

In the process of building their family, Bill and Karen McDonald learned enough about themselves to merit a pair of Ph.D.'s. Their first child, Julie, was the happy conclusion to a long struggle with fertility problems. Their second child, Anna, arrived only after they traveled to a place Bill had once sworn he'd never return to and wasn't anxious to remember.

Karen and Bill seem perfect for each other. She's a prosecutor; he's a retired police captain. Both are from New York, and when they met, both were thinking about getting out. Working in public service and law, they both had great careers they truly believed in. But both also felt the higher calling of family.

Karen is still amazed that a "little Italian Catholic girl" could have her career. The first in her family to graduate from college, she went from the Manhattan district attorney's office to the Department of Justice in

Washington, D.C., to the U.S. attorney's office in Phoenix. The hours are long and the work is emotionally taxing, but Karen wouldn't have it any other way. According to her husband, "There's no question in my mind that she could name her job and name her place with any law firm here that does criminal defense work . . . but that's against her grain." One case she prosecuted in New York really drove this home. The opposing counsel had made a name for himself defending mob bosses. He showed up every day in a limo. After Karen won the case, he told her "without coming out and saying it," that she could become a wealthy woman working for him. Was she tempted? "No," she answers, "not in the least. Not in the least."

Bill loved being on the police force and was next in line to be police chief of a Westchester County town when he suddenly retired after twenty years. "I loved the job," he says, "but I think after I had about four years on the force, I was looking forward to my twentieth year so I could retire." He was close to his twentieth year of service when he met Karen.

They both believe in their work and in working hard (Bill now supplements his pension as an insurance investigator). But they both know where to set limits. As Bill explains, "Life is short. We own a beautiful home, we've got a really neat boat. We have to make time for us. And for our family." And that seems to be enough. To hear Bill tell it, less would also be enough: "I've offered to move us into a double-wide and just live on my police pension. We're in the right town for that."

Once Bill and Karen were settled in Phoenix and "assimilated" to the western lifestyle (Bill, like a true transplanted easterner, went as far as buying a cowboy hat and boots, and listening to country music), they were ready to start a family. That's when Karen learned she had serious fertility problems.

She felt cheated; they had made so many plans and sacrifices for the sake of having a family. She endured months of fertility treatments that brought on "hormonal chaos," only to find another surprise around the corner: "In the middle of it," as Karen tells it, "I stop menstruating. They test, and it's like, 'Oh, you know you are sort of in the beginning of menopause.' And I'm thirty-six years old!" Now the prospect of having a child seemed very distant indeed.

She stuck with the treatments, though, and her fertility doctor eventually "pulled a rabbit out of the hat," as Karen puts it. "I got a call from the doctor one day; it was just another blood test of dozens and dozens of blood tests I've had for one thing or another. But he's got his whole staff around the phone and they all yell, 'You're pregnant.' " She didn't believe him: "The thought I had was, 'Oh no. I have to get a new fertility doctor, because this guy is really messed up.' "

Karen's pregnancy wasn't easy either. "The whole time I'm pregnant I have to take a needle and jab it into my stomach. This flipped me out beyond belief. . . . I'm still working. I'm in the grand jury one day indicting a case and the very next day go to the hospital and induce labor." Julie finally arrived, and, Karen says, "She was a very colicky baby. High-stress infancy with her. We just learned to incorporate a certain amount of craziness into our everyday lives."

But once this craziness was incorporated, Karen went looking for more: "Poor Bill, he's got two grown children from his first marriage. In fact, he's got a grandchild who's older than Julie. . . . But I'm saying 'I'm not done yet.' "

The fertility doctors said there was no chance she could have another child. The option of adoption, which she had avoided, became her only one. "When I was having fertility problems," she says, "no one could say the "A" word to me. . . . But Julie wasn't fifteen minutes old when it hit me like a ton of bricks. I was really wrong. I would have a second biological child if I could, but it doesn't make a difference. It's the relationship you have with the kids after they're there in the world."

Chasing a dream can take you down some unexpected roads. Or back down some old roads, as Bill and Karen were about to discover. Bill is a Vietnam veteran. He served one year in the mid-1960s as a crew chief and gunner on one of the thousands of Huey helicopters that became a symbol of the war. Stationed in the Mekong Delta, Bill was shot down twice. But when Karen raised the possibility of adoption, the first thing Bill thought was "Vietnam."

"Vietnam is a period in his life that we never really discussed in great detail," Karen says. "He doesn't like to talk about it. But he comes to tell me that when he was stationed in the south there was an orphanage nearby that he used to visit." Bill was twenty years old then, and was out taking a walk with a friend when he passed an orphanage run by Catholic nuns. The nuns pulled the children inside. "They were very protective," he says, "as they should be." Bill and his friend came back a few days later with "purloined" supplies. They gained the nuns' trust and took time off from the insanity around them by playing with the children.

Bill pulled out photos he and his friend had taken and showed them to Karen. They were covered with scratches and had faded with age, but the children's faces, boys on one side and girls on the other, convinced them both that their next child would be from Vietnam.

She and Bill attacked a mountain of forms that made all her legal paperwork look like a molehill. An agency found them a candidate for adoption and sent them a picture of "this adorable little child." Karen remembers the girl's face well—it was framed on her desk next to a picture of Julie for three weeks. Then, a month before their scheduled departure, the roof fell in. "We got the horrible phone call," Karen remembers. "The mother had shown up at the foster care home and took the child back. She changed her mind." Good for the baby, perhaps. But for Bill and Karen, already attached, the news was devastating.

Prospect number two came into and out of their lives in a matter of days—all because of a missing piece of paper that the U.S. government required and the Vietnamese government wouldn't provide. Still, they stuck to their travel schedule, and a picture of prospect number three—a baby girl named Truc Ly—arrived by fax just days before their departure. At this point, Karen says, the picture wasn't the thing: "Quite frankly, [now] it doesn't matter what comes out of the fax machine, a kid with three eyes. . . ." Soon after they got the fax, they were off to Vietnam.

Bill's heart started pounding as soon as he got off the plane in Ho Chi Minh City (formerly Saigon) and made his way to the immigration area. "I was beside myself waiting for my turn to be confronted by the soldier there behind the counter. It took me a week of just being reassured by my surroundings that everything was okay. I expected to be ridiculed, I expected to be harassed, I expected a lot of things. And it just never happened. The people were as friendly as I remember they had been when I was a young soldier there."

One thing that was particularly unnerving was the absence of aircraft. Bill remembered the Vietnamese skies humming with planes and helicopters, but now they were calm. Karen watched Bill relive memories thirty-five years old as he slept: "He wasn't sleeping well. He was fighting a lot of battles in his sleep." This is something Bill doesn't remember: "I didn't wake up in a cold sweat, I don't remember a problem sleeping. When I got back from Vietnam the first time, I probably spent a year doing that."

A strange coincidence made Bill's readjustment easier. Their guide, appointed by the adoption agency, was a former South Vietnamese soldier by the name of Dominic. He told Bill that he and his family were some of the last to leave the American Embassy on April 30, 1975. It turned out that Dominic and Bill had been stationed at the same small compound in the Mekong Delta at the same time. "There's no question that I probably flew him into battle more than once," Bill says. "Now to find him as someone who is working with us to adopt a baby was almost surreal."

One other particularly surreal experience sticks in Bill's mind. With Dominic as guide, Bill, Karen, and the other families in their group went out by bus to the Mekong Delta for a day trip. At the end of the trail, they boarded sampans, flat-bottomed skiffs that are the only means of transportation on the small canals around the Mekong River. "We're being paddled through these canals with jungle growth just hovering above us, barely seeing the sky in patches, the woman and the man paddling our boat, wearing the conical hats. And it was unbelievably quiet.

"What was really going on for me for that whole ride, I called it an out-of-body experience. I'd never been in a sampan before. I had never been under the jungle growth slipping through the canals in a boat. I was in a helicopter sitting behind a machine gun looking for these people. . . . As we're paddling along, I keep looking up. At one point, as we're approaching the Mekong, there was the throbbing of an engine that sounded just like a helicopter coming from one of the boats. I think that was the closest I had come to wetting my pants while we were there."

The trip lasted a couple of weeks but it contained a lifetime of intensely emotional experiences. None, however, matched the moment Bill and Karen met their daughter-to-be's birth mother. The adoption agency had recommended a meeting, but Bill and Karen approached it warily. They finally decided it would be a good thing for their adoptive daughter. It turned out to be something they will never forget.

After a week of preparing themselves for the encounter, it began to seem as if it wasn't going to happen. Their guide had advised against it—too emotionally confusing, he thought—and Bill and Karen assumed that might be the end of it. But suddenly they got a knock on the hotel door telling them to be downstairs in five minutes. The mother was waiting.

Through a translator, they listened to the heart-wrenching story of Truc Ly's birth mother. She had fallen in love and became pregnant. That's when the father disappeared. Her housing was tied to her job on a rice plantation, and so without work, she was out of a home. Trying to raise her daughter while living on a beach, she made the most difficult decision a parent can make—she decided that her child would have a better life, at any cost.

Bill, Karen, and the birth mother relied on a translator. "We didn't know how much was passing between us," Karen says. "But we did get that she was trying to explain how it was impossible for her to keep this child. There was an embarrassment and shame to what she was trying to communicate. She was crying, I was crying.

"And then I realized . . . I think I've always had this little thing in the back of my mind, a little prejudicial thought. The politically correct thing to say about adoption is the birth mom loved you and did the bravest thing. But I always thought if it were me, maternal instincts would win out. I'd find a way to keep the kid and have it all. And then I saw this woman."

Karen had an epiphany that day that "just hit me in the head like a two-by-four." Talking to the woman who had given birth to the girl she'd be taking home, Karen realized "what an incredibly brave thing she was doing. It was an incredibly loving thing to do for her child. There was no lack of love for that little girl in her act of giving her up. I knew that in an instant. I felt really rotten about harboring this little thought that somehow she's to be faulted for this."

The meeting was rushed by the translator, who seemed uncomfortable with the process. Karen gave the birth mother a photo album she had prepared, with pictures of themselves, their house, their dog, and their parents. "She clutched it for her life," Karen says. Then the translator stood up and said the meeting was over. "But I just couldn't leave it like that. I turned around and went back to her. I took her hands and said, 'Look, I don't understand what you said, you don't understand what I'm saying, but I'm telling you, 'Look into my eyes, I'm going to take care of your daughter. I'm going to take care of your daughter. Don't worry.' And off we went." The adoption was completed, and Truc Ly became Anna McDonald.

Having children changes you. Anna's birth mother will go through life holding a tiny piece of the American dream represented in photos of her daughter's new home; Bill and Karen now live with a new perspective on the meaning of family. Karen explains: "I realized that biology has little or nothing to do with it. It's the act of doing for someone. That's the thing that makes love develop. . . . And yet, I think about it and there's a sort of connection that we have to this other country and this person, the biological mom on the other side of the world. Not to be too flowery here, but it makes the world a much smaller place, and makes the world feel like a community." As for Bill: "I like to think of this relationship, this family that I have, as almost akin to being reincarnated."

Bill and Karen are holding a letter from Anna's birth mother, written in Vietnamese, that explains to Anna why she was adopted. They know that it won't answer all of Anna's questions. They know that in foreign adoption there aren't any easy answers. Karen has wondered if they are "exploiting the country yet again." They both wonder about how Anna will approach her heritage. They both know that even changing her name has implications. But at the same time, they have the perspective of their first daughter, Julie, who chose the name Anna from a children's book on foreign adoption. Seen through a child's eyes, these complicated issues vanish. Bill and Karen called Julie every day when they were in Vietnam. All she wanted to know was "Do you have my baby sister yet?"

Making a Name
Dreams of the Spotlight

Fame is a bee,
It has a song —
It has a sting —
Ah, too, it has a wing.
                    —Emily Dickinson

*A*MERICANS are not the only people on earth to entertain dreams of fame, but they have the best chance of achieving it. Such are the fruits of a country and an age where the media grapevine has grown as thick as kudzu.

The nature of fame has changed mightily in our lifetimes. Today's roving public eye has augmented the Emersonian notion of fame as the reward for building a better mousetrap with a gallery of pretty faces and folks known for a single trick or deed, and I humbly submit that the change has not been for the better. Once upon a time, the only names spread far and wide were those who belonged to people who had, to borrow a page from Poor Richard, written things worth reading or committed deeds worth the writing. Now we know not only the names but the faces as well of far too many people whose central talent seems to be their knack for attracting the camera's gaze. These are the people we see peering out at us from the pages of glossy magazines, from billboards, and yes, most of all, from the television screen. Their numbers are swelled by the ever-growing ranks of others who stumble into the spotlight for their Warhol-allotted fifteen minutes before passing once again into obscurity.

All of which makes plain the need to distinguish from the outset between fame and celebrity. To my way of thinking, at least, the famous are those who truly belong in life's pantheon. Americans like Jonas Salk and Franklin Delano Roosevelt, Martin Luther King Jr. and Clara Barton. Muhammad Ali and Martha Graham. William Faulkner and Woody Guthrie. People whose names and deeds exist independent of their image.

And the celebrities? Well, they're everywhere—the latest teen heart-throb, last week's game show winner, the bit player in a scandal. Former librarian of congress Daniel J. Boorstin had it just right when he wrote that "the celebrity is a person who is known for his well-knownness." Boorstin, justly famous in his own right for the breadth and depth of his knowledge, had the drop on celebrity from an early point in our country's media explosion. In 1962, at about the time I was getting my start at CBS in the fledgling occupation of TV newsman, he published a seminal book on the subject, titled *The Image*. Boorstin's book contained such spot-on observations as: "A sign of the celebrity is often that his name is worth more than his services"; and "The very agency which first makes the celebrity in the long run inevitably destroys him." In other words, he who lives by the public's appetite for novelty will die by it as well.

There is, of course, a middle ground between fame and celebrity, occupied by accomplished people whose name and image have been spread farther and wider than would have been the case before the mass media machine really kicked in about fifty years ago. Before I knew of television, I dreamed of being a newspaper or radio reporter. I like to think that I would have been a good one, known to those in my paper's circulation pool or those within the reach of my station's antenna, but such people are generally known only by their colleagues and the most dedicated followers of the news. Without the instant-recognition qualities of "the face" to latch on to, very few reporters become well-known apart from their stories. And this would be just fine with the over-whelming majority of broadcast journalists I've met and worked with over the years—especially the best ones, for whom doing the news on television is about immediacy and reach, not fame.

This last, I think, is absolutely essential. Yes, there are scores of actors, musicians, artists, even reporters and businessman today whose wide-spread celebrity is mostly due to the growth of the American mass media. But the truly good ones are those who would keep on doing what they're doing even if the audience were small or if no one were watching at all. The American philosopher George Santayana put it well when he wrote that "the highest form of vanity is love of fame." Fame is NASA-grade rocket fuel for the ego, and the danger is that you will cease to pay service to the skills and determination and people that brought the spotlight upon you in the first place, in favor of the spotlight itself. When it's turned off, you may find that after you blink and your eyes readjust, those talents and those people who made it possible have fled.

I was drawn to the people in this chapter because they all have a healthy view of fame as the by-product of a job well done. Their stories bring to mind my earliest brush with people I considered famous, growing up in Houston when it was still a growing Sun Belt city with a small-town Texas feel. In the winter months, I would often pass by the vacant-lot rehearsal space of the Flying Valentis, a nationally known family of circus trapeze artists. The Valentis would spend long days practicing their triple somersaults, and occasionally you'd actually see one or another of them take a long fall into the safety net below. When I'd see them return from a summer of touring with limps and bruises and assorted limbs in casts, it dawned on me that life in the limelight was no cakewalk.

Each of the folks here has a strong work ethic—just as strong as that of the entrepreneurs we've met. If one can make a generalization, their dreams are born of idealism rather than the practical concerns that so often provide the drive for dreams of fortune.

According to Eric Maisel, an author, psychotherapist, and expert on creativity, Americans such as these have "bought into the American dream without consciously buying into it." Early in their lives, those who aspire to creative pursuits—and I'd include sports here—quite often reject, sometimes subconsciously, the notion of a "career." They may not be in complete rebellion against American middle-class values, but they do retain a few of those youthful misgivings about what they "should" do as responsible adults. What they do believe in, Eric insists, is freedom: "Insofar as there is a stilted and conventional side to the American dream, that's too small for them. But the founding principles of America embodied in the Constitution and the Bill of Rights, the deepest sense of the American dream, they buy into entirely."

Eric's comment, distilled from years of experience in counseling artists, is consistent with what I heard from the people you'll meet in the pages that follow. When asked to define the American dream, aspiring filmmaker Adam Ballard answered immediately and simply that "it's a good idea." Actor Anthony Rapp followed suit: "I think that the foundation of the country, the language of the Constitution, is pretty remarkable in what it aspires to create. I do think that the policies in the country often fall short of that—the policies of ignorance or nonpolicy." Anthony's words also serve as a reminder that idealism can survive the heady taste of success. And for many, fame can provide a useful platform from which to promote deeply felt causes.

Life lived in the public eye carries its own unique lessons, and they must be squared with life's more universal demands. Countless athletes and artists have learned the hard way that the same tunnel vision that can sustain and drive a budding career can become a liability, especially when faced with setbacks. The ones who survive are those who manage to adjust and to "keep it real," as in, "rooted to the realities of life." Chicago Cubs pitching coach Oscar Acosta, whom you'll meet here, found ways to turn the adversity he met on the road to success in a career pursued just outside the spotlight. Anthony Rapp, who resisted the very word "career" for most of his life, did not find full comfort in his acting success until he had ironed out some long-standing wrinkles in his relationship with his brother. And best-selling writer Jacquelyn Mitchard, who may be my favorite story here, didn't write her first novel until she was forty—and only after she had consciously rejected the idea that growing up means giving up on "childish" dreams. Amen.

Young Adam Ballard, still at the beginning of what looks to be a promising career in filmmaking, will no doubt learn his own lessons from the obstacles life puts in his way. His story reminds us of the pure source of some of the best aspirations. Think of the hopes contained in a Little League team, a first chemistry set, or in a school play. I still remember vividly the radio reports my journalistic heroes filed from faraway and exotic-sounding locales and how they beckoned my boyish mind to adventure. These are the dreams of youth, and maybe America responds to them so strongly because we are still a young country. We're also a country that deeply believes in equal opportunity, however imperfectly we may at times practice it. The belief that anyone can fulfill these dreams can go a long way to carrying them to fruition.

The mass media's role in creating the American cult of celebrity has given it a lot to answer for. But it's also helped create room for people of genuine talent and drive to make a living, sometimes for those least likely to succeed in conventional ways. Could one silver lining on the dark cloud of America's obsession with fame be that we follow and feed the spinning wheels of the fame machine because, deep down, we want *everyone* to succeed? Maybe, but then we ought to mark well how we define success.

Jacquelyn Mitchard

The stack of clippings on my desk is about an inch thick. I'm looking through articles from the *New York Times,* the *Los Angeles Times,* and what seems like every small, big, and small-town newspaper in between. I have a few pages torn out from *Newsweek* and *People* and a pile of television news transcripts from an alphabet soup of networks. All detailing the fascinating life of novelist Jacquelyn Mitchard.

In 1996, Jacquelyn provided a true story too good for reporters to pass up, and few of them did. Her classic rags-to-riches tale had everything, and if that weren't enough, she proved to be a master of the sound bite, a fount of home truths, and a consistently down-to-earth person. Since she began living in the public eye, her personal life has remained irresistible to the media.

The clippings tell the story of how Jacquelyn's first novel, which she wrote at age forty, was born of personal tragedy and desperate financial circumstances. They reveal how much she was paid by the publisher and for the movie rights, what her agent said to her when she sold the book, and how she erased Oprah's first two phone messages, thinking they were practical jokes. I find out where she bought a vacation home. There are details about her six children and her second husband—how they met, how old he is, and what he does for a living. One article goes through her daily routine; countless others tell me that her plots come to her in dreams. A photograph accompanying one article somehow conveys her high energy and enthusiasm—maybe it comes through her sideways glance and youthful appearance. Or perhaps it's the smile, that of someone who has had a weight lifted from her life.

Insofar as you can know someone through reading about them, I feel as if I know Jacquelyn Mitchard. A big reason for this is Jacquelyn herself. Her interview voice, if distinct from the one she employs in private, is that of someone unfazed by the attention, but who obviously enjoys the ride. She comes across as refreshingly candid, at ease, quick to answer without overreaching. Her weekly syndicated newspaper column dips into her home life to illustrate what Jacquelyn believes are experiences shared by families everywhere. Her writing career, she says, is a public performance, comparable to acting or teaching. To do this job well, she realized a long time ago, requires some sacrifice of privacy. So while she calls herself an average working mother, she is fully aware that her balancing act involves not only managing work and family, but also managing her fame.

For those who missed it, Jacquelyn's American dream developed like this: she was a mother of four, married to an accomplished journalist, working part-time at the University of Wisconsin in Madison, and pursuing a satisfying, if not always lucrative, freelance writing career. One night, a novel came to her in a dream, but being surrounded by practical matters, she compartmentalized it for later. Then, after thirteen years of marriage, she lost her husband to cancer. Within a year, she was facing dire financial problems in addition to her profound grief.

Friends and family offered love and support, but a great many also delivered a message that Jacquelyn decided to reject: give up on writing. Get a normal job. Let those dreams go. "They were all from people who loved me and were well meaning," she says, but adds that the message was, for her, incredibly stifling: "Kid games have to stop now. It's time to grow up. And for a great many people, the words 'grow up' mean 'give up.'" It was a message she ultimately decided to reject: "It's enough to have to lose your mate and your children's father without having to lose your stake in ever being happy or effective again, too."

Perhaps she could have been effective, if not happy, in a more predictable career. But that decision would have confined her role as parent to that of material provider, and little more. She knew that the message she wanted to give her children was nothing like the message she was hearing, and she knew that they would take their cues from her actions. The worst scenario actually writing the novel could have provided, she says, was a slightly more desperate financial situation. To Jacquelyn, that possibility weighed lightly when compared to what she had a chance to gain: "It put a lot of teeth into the arguments that I make as a parent, that no matter what happens to you, no matter what grief befalls you—and a significant amount of grief befell these kids really early in their lives—it doesn't really give you permission to downsize your dreams and to live in fear. So I felt that by doing this, by being able to do this, I was able to say to them, look. Even me. Even your beleaguered mom was able to cobble together a second act."

The novel she dreamed of became *The Deep End of the Ocean,* the story of a normal American family ravaged by the grief of their son's abduction. Her agent took two chapters, the first piece of creative writing Jacquelyn had done since college, and got her a two-book deal worth $500,000. Michelle Pfeiffer bought the movie rights before publication. The novel sold well on its own but was sent into the stratosphere when Oprah Winfrey chose it as the inaugural reading assignment for her newly formed book club. Millions of copies were printed as reviewers praised it and feature writers told and retold the story behind the story. The thunderbolt of fame strikes more often in America than it used to, but rarely does it hit the same target as frequently and as strongly as it hit Jacquelyn.

What changed? This is a question Jacquelyn hears often. It's a question we reporters seem to never tire of asking the famous. We know that readers, viewers, listeners . . . want to know what's on the other side. It's a matter of simple curiosity, sure, which at its worst even verges on voyeurism. For Jacquelyn, having to contend with just that sort of public curiosity has been the biggest change.

She has had to come to terms with fame, and with the added attention given not just her but those around her. Coping with this often glaring spotlight has been an ongoing process, one made slightly more complicated by Jacquelyn's forthright nature ("I have the personality of a golden retriever") and her frequent interviews. "The only thing that I've been sort of surprised by," she says, "is the willingness to sort of probe the privacy of people who didn't write the book, and some of the questions have surprised me, about my husband, about my husband now and our lives. But I think I've done a pretty good job." Jacquelyn leaves her children out of the photo ops, even against their wishes: she tells of their annoyance, for instance, at her not allowing them to appear in a

People photo spread and admits that she's been "even more strenuous about protecting their privacy than they would have liked."

One simple step to protect her family's privacy was to buy a house in a "more rustic" area outside of Madison. It's a busy house, with five children of widely varied ages and a small staff of assistants. A lot goes on there that Jacquelyn insists isn't for public consumption, and the family has invented a signal to let one another know what stays home: "ITH" or "In the House." These ITHs aren't embarrassing or scandalous items, but the fact that they belong to the family makes them more precious: "We don't have anything in particular to hide. We're not really a very dashing group of midwesterners. But it's an increasingly loud and revealing world, isn't it?"

Early in Jacquelyn's career as a novelist, a production company that wanted to make a TV movie out of her life approached her. At first, she was receptive—"I'm always willing to let folks give me money"—but as she saw the possibility that the project would threaten her family's privacy, she called it off. "I thought, no, I'm not going to do this. This is sort of taking fiction beyond the beyonds. I would rather tell stories. . . . Like Emily Dickinson said, 'Tell the truth, but tell it slant.' "

Having set effective boundaries and barriers against the American publicity machine, you might expect Jacquelyn to follow the lead of those many celebrities who, when asked, tell us that "nothing" has changed. But the author of the nationally syndicated column "The Rest of Us" knows that her life isn't exactly like the rest: "Everything changed," she says, "except the things that were essential then and are essential now." The events that changed her life she describes as casually as a change of careers. It was a dramatic change, she agrees, but hastens to add that "work is a slice of your life. It's not the entire pizza."

Entertainment, in the form of novels, TV series, movies, and music, has become one of our most important exports. Jacquelyn's first novel alone has been translated into about a dozen languages. But beyond creating the individual pieces that fold our culture into the world culture, American artists have helped to redefine what it means to be an artist. Jacquelyn's approach to her work is a clear example. First of all, it's work. "It isn't just a way for the inside of my head to talk to the outside," she reminds us, "it's the way that I support my family."

These days, we seem to want more than stories from our writers. We like to see their faces and hear about their personal lives. And as our artists come down from their garrets, we can discover that they aren't really terribly different from those of us in the workaday world. According to Jacquelyn, writing fiction "doesn't set me apart, because I'm not considering this some sort of art that can only be practiced where the air is very thin and refined." Again, she points out, "It's my job."

This increasingly common view of the writing life definitely has an effect on what is produced. Some say the result is novels written solely for the talk show circuit, Hollywood, or Oprah's book club. On the other hand, the potential commercial benefits can have a democratizing effect on an art such as writing. Artists, Jacquelyn believes, don't have to exist in a separate class: "I've been a writer for twenty-five years, and I've always tried to maintain that it's perfectly possible to live an ordinary life, strive for the middle class, strive for middle-class values, and still be as fully tortured and committed a writer as you might need to be to produce good prose." Jacquelyn believes that to make a living through a creative endeavor, even a good living, "shows that dreams don't always have to be fragile and ephemeral. They can really put tofu on the table. They can put you on your farm. They can be a way to enjoy real life."

The art that Jacquelyn produces sometimes has an uncanny way of feeding into her real life. The story she told while on the circuit for her second novel, *The Most Wanted,* was of how she met her husband. A character in *The Most Wanted* falls in love with a man who comes to work on her house. Jacquelyn mentioned to friends that this guy she had written was too perfect to be real, but one day his likeness walked into her house to lay tile on her bathroom floor. They are now married, he has adopted four of her children (the fifth is grown), and he and Jacquelyn have added a daughter to the family.

It's her family, more than anything, that keeps Jacquelyn from becoming a casualty of her own fame, or as she puts it, "someone who believes their own press releases." Being a parent, she believes, is wonderful because of the way it lets you know how little you know. She counts herself as "awestruck by the amount of influence I have in their lives and equally awestruck by how they take me down another peg."

The issues of fame aside, Jacquelyn's American dream is of living a sane life with a supportive family. She just happens to have an unusual job. Those who follow her column know that her family is somewhat unusual, too, in how it came together—through birth, adoption, and remarriage. More akin, her son-in-law says, to a family fern than a family tree. But that isn't what's important: "The American dream doesn't depend on one sort of family, and I'm not going to make a plug here for nontraditional families, but it certainly doesn't depend on the way one given family looks." Bill and Karen McDonald, whom we met at the end of the last chapter, would agree. Much more important, Jacquelyn maintains, is "the way they feel about what they're doing, and the way they feel about the importance of what they're doing." Whether nuclear, extended, biological, or bound solely by love, "the ideal structure for a family," inside or outside of the spotlight, Jacquelyn concludes, "is one that remains so."

Anthony and Adam Rapp

When interviewed for this book, Jacquelyn Mitchard spoke of why she chose to end her first novel, a story about a family's loss and recovery, with a scene between brothers. Their mother remains in the background—they can hear her, but the moment belongs very much to them and them alone. "The bonds of siblings are keener and more lasting than the bonds that bind parents to children," she explained, "because they operate below the level of the parents' radar." They are, she said, "a lifelong bond, where the bond with your parents never can be lifelong." The best end for her story, she felt, lay in a moment that encompassed the future.

Anthony and Adam Rapp are two brothers who have extended their lifelong fraternal bond into their respective lives in the arts. Anthony is a thirty-one-year-old actor with over twenty years of experience—on and off Broadway, on the big screen and the small screen. Adam, three years older than Anthony, is author of fifteen plays and four novels. Their dreams, which have always been as distinct and individual as are they, bring us to another intersection of the dreams of fame and family, a busy and confusing corner of American life.

Anthony and Adam agree that they weren't very close growing up. While their relationship rarely degenerated into open hostility, they shared little common ground while moving in radically different worlds at early ages. They took turns telling their divergent stories in Adam's new apartment in lower Manhattan. As forthcoming as they both are, the extent of their mutual respect and friendship comes through in more than just their words.

Over twenty years ago, one of the Rapp brothers began his ascent while the other flirted with decline. They and an older sister were living with their single, working mother in Joliet, Illinois, an edge city with a rough edge. By now, a good part of Joliet has been swallowed into the greater Chicago area and is dotted with tract housing. But back then, they say, it was one of those semirural, semi-industrial spaces that attracted all of the problems of a large city without any of the benefits. "In our apartment complex, where we lived for twelve years," Adam says, "there were probably ten or twelve huge buildings, there was a pond, and then there was a cornfield. It was really sort of a strange mix." Anthony describes it as having been a place with few options for escape.

The family struggled on a single paycheck, won by their mother as a third-shift nurse. By the time he was eleven, Adam says, he was in trouble. His shoplifting, petty vandalism, and association with "the wrong kids" were alarming to his mother. His infractions landed him in a school for boys that, according to Adam, was somewhere "between reform school and a halfway house." He says it turned out to be "one of the scariest things I've ever experienced in my life."

Adam was jolted from the safety of his small and humble home into daily contact with a much rougher crowd of kids from Chicago. If you are curious about what the fear he experienced tastes like, you can read Adam's second novel, *The Buffalo Tree,* set in a nightmarish juvenile detention center where the authorities are just as sadistic as the worst offenders. Adam's twelve-year-old character narrates the story in a language that conveys the turmoil of a boy trying to live through something that could break a grown man.

While he says he wasn't old enough to fully understand why his older brother wasn't living at home, Anthony does recall that even the sight of this school was fearful: "It's sort of a shameful memory for me, but I remember once going to visit him. I remember not wanting to go inside and trying to get the courage . . . so I could visit Adam." Adam spent a thankfully short two months at the school. In quieter moments between violence and threats of violence, he actually made a few friends and made the basketball team. In the end, he says, the school definitely toughened him up.

But he'll also admit that it didn't straighten him out. Back home, a zoning quirk landed him in a wealthy junior high school, where, he says, "I had this chip on my shoulder about being a poor kid, and I got in five fistfights my first week back." The course he was on could have led him straight back to juvie, but his grades and athletics eventually got him a scholarship to a military school, a strong step toward getting both straightened out and toughened up. At the same time, it would be a step that would take Adam farther from his family, especially his brother, Anthony.

Anthony had experienced his first taste of acting at the summer camp where his mother worked as a nurse. His stage debut came in the role of the Cowardly Lion, in a camp production of *The Wizard of Oz*. "I fell in love with it," he says, and he allowed a dream to take hold of his six-year-old imagination. He remembers the story his mom told of how he broke into the world of somewhat more serious theater: "I got an ad in the paper for an audition for a local theater production of a musical of *A Christmas Carol*. I called and scheduled myself an audition. I was like eight."

As Anthony performed in community theaters, his mother was processing praise and advice from a growing group of fans. Anthony belonged on bigger stages, they said. He should be in Chicago, not Joliet. In 1981, at age nine, he made his professional debut in a road tour of *Evita*. In 1982, at age ten, he won a part that would change his family's life.

Adam had by then started to fit in as a self-described "jock," with less potential for causing trouble but still far removed from the life his younger brother was beginning. "I'll never forget this. It was my eighth-grade year, and I had a basketball game, and my mom came into the locker room at the end of the game, which is really weird, that a mom would come into a locker room. . . . And she said, Anthony's got this Broadway thing, we're moving to New York. And I thought . . . 'Cool.' "

Anthony had won a part in a Broadway production of *The Little Prince,* and their mother took it as a sign that her child's stardom was right around the corner. "And then three days later," Adam says, "we were on a plane."

Anthony understudied for the part of the Little Prince while preparing to play Fox. He soon replaced his study, which made his future look even brighter. Then, following a two-week preview run, the play suddenly folded. The family was stuck with little money and meager hope. They lived on Staten Island in a cramped apartment without a refrigerator and with box springs for beds. Anthony remembers clearly talking with his mother about how he might earn the family some money by singing on the Staten Island Ferry.

Adam, meanwhile, was doing little but bouncing his basketball and bouncing off the walls. When relief came to the family with Anthony touring in a production of *The King and I* with Yul Brynner, Adam realized that things had changed. Something in the family was upside down. "It was like we were two different classes. Here he was, earning his own money . . . and I was living at home in this little apartment, and he would come home and he would have toys and things, and I was wearing my uncle's hand-me-downs in the next bed. It was strange . . . a very different way to be brothers."

Anthony was still of an age to be fairly unaware of what was happening outside of his acting career. Looking back now, he says, "I'm sorry it made life more difficult for Ann and Adam, but I hope it's balanced out to some degree. I know Mom got a lot of pleasure from it, but I know she regretted some of the choices she made in terms of how she handled some of those things with Ann and Adam." Anthony also believes his mother was pursuing a dream of her own: "She always loved the arts, and to see one of her children excel at it . . . I think she got to be a part of something she really loved."

Over the next five years, the family moved with each success and slump as Anthony appeared in Broadway plays and made his screen debut in *Adventures in Babysitting*. Even as their financial situation stabilized, and even though attending a military boarding school insulated him from much of the turmoil of the constant moves, Adam developed "a weird feeling . . . of feeling almost emasculated in a way." As he explains it, "Here I was, the older brother, and I always thought it was supposed to be the other way around. Yet he was the one making money for the family at times. He was paying our rent." When Adam was in danger of not being able to pay for military school, it was Anthony's money, almost two thousand dollars, that kept him in.

One thing Adam knew with certainty was that he didn't want any part of the arts. His dreams were influenced by the athletics that he says saved him from delinquency, and by his mother's career as a nurse. "I admired my mom, we used to talk about how she wanted to be a doctor. . . . She was an amazing nurse, and I always thought she was, like, this healer. If I sprained an ankle, I would be healed in like two days. It was amazing." He saw himself as a heroic doctor but also harbored dreams of playing in the NBA or covering center field for the Chicago Cubs.

At Clark College in Dubuque, Iowa, Adam took premed courses and captained the basketball team. He had no idea that he could or would ever want to be a reader until he walked into an elective poetry class during his sophomore year: "I immediately fell in love with it. In the class. At that moment. And I changed my major the next day." No one was more surprised than Adam himself, who was hit with another discovery when he walked into his first writing class: "My whole life changed. I knew that's what I wanted to do."

One of the first things he did was share his new passion with his younger brother, who had been writing short pieces since he was a teenager. Adam admits he had some catching up to do if writing was now really his dream. He'd never seriously read fiction before and didn't even know where to start. Anthony sent him recommendations, which Adam devoured. Their correspondence became collaborative as they passed stories back and forth. Writing became the common ground these brothers had lacked all their lives, and they both slowly and surely moved to occupy this new territory.

On some level, Adam says, he might have suspected that his younger brother was gay before he accidentally opened a door in Anthony's apartment and saw something suggestive. If anything, Adam says, his brother seemed "asexual," both because he was a "nerdy guy with glasses," and because, after all, he was his baby brother. But even if he had some inkling, Adam's experience on that visit to New York during his senior year in college jarred him. "I sat in a chair, and literally stared at the wall for four hours. I don't think it was out of terror." Adam at this point pauses to search for the right word and finds it. "I just think it was . . . I was just sort of in awe. In awe of what was just presented to me."

He says he didn't feel judgmental, sickened, or confrontational. In fact, he didn't feel like talking about it at all. Anthony says he offered to broach the subject, but Adam casually dropped it, giving no clue as to what he was thinking. What he did instead was write.

Even before making that trip, Adam had started work on a story about a man who comes to New York, discovers his brother is gay, and "how it made him feel totally lost." As they had in the past, Adam shared his story, and Anthony contributed to it. Anthony: "He would show it to me, and I would read it, and I would write a scene. That's kind of how we talked about it." Adam recalls that Anthony contributed dialogue in critical places, and adds: "He just had a better sense of style, and I think that definitely helped me shape and find the story. . . . We definitely worked some stuff out, but even sitting here now, I didn't realize we were working something out. It wasn't conscious." The short story turned into a novella, and became Adam's senior thesis.

The actual conversation happened later by phone, when Adam was back in school. Adam says he's a little "surprised at myself that it was very easily accepted. Between my friends and coaches and teachers and military school, for God's sake. . . . Coming from that world, the world of midwestern jocks, I was surprised." He remembers a time in military school when one of the cadets was found to be gay. The young man was hauled out in front of the entire corps of cadets assembled in formation, placed in a van, and driven away.

After thinking about it for a moment, Adam credits his mother for teaching him tolerance, even though she had a more difficult time accepting Anthony's coming out than Adam did. All good nurses, especially those who work in jails, like their mother did, must have or must learn to have a measure of tolerance in order to do their jobs. Anthony, at any rate, knew that his brother fully accepted him after they had been roommates for a while. "When I knew it was really, really okay," he remembers, "was when I'd been seeing this guy a lot, and he was staying over a lot, and Adam asked me, 'Why doesn't he move in?' They'd become really good friends. That was that."

As a footnote to this critical moment in these brothers' lives, it should be mentioned that Anthony describes himself as "queer" rather than "gay." People, he says, need labels, but to him, the "gay" label invalidates the female partners he has been with in the past. "So it's sort of an effort to be inclusive of my own life experience, and not separate and say 'that was not real, this is real.' " He also likes the subversive quality of the term: " 'Queer' to me says, whatever you want to make of me, fine. And I like the notion too that it's claiming a word that's been derogatory in the past and making it something positive."

Regardless of how one may feel about his choices, Anthony has done something very in line with the American dream. He has defined, refined, and established his own identity. He has chosen a term and a way of thinking, rather than allowing another person or group to do it for him. In the middle of New York, Anthony has appropriated the same spirit that populated the frontiers and brought immigrants to our shores. He has chosen to remake himself.

Adam moved to the city after graduation, where he joined the small army of English and writing majors who squeeze a living out of the lower rungs of the publishing industry. For Adam it was an education in the writing life: what authors go through, how much (or how little) they are paid, and their relationships with the publishing houses. He also learned what it's like to live in tight quarters—he and his brother shared a one-bedroom apartment—and survive on Ramen noodles. It's a testament to his tenacity that he wasn't discouraged from pursuing writing as a career.

His first novel, *Missing the Piano,* about a young man sent to military school while his mother and sister travel with *Les Miserables,* was written during sleepless nights and during the workday when his boss wasn't looking. But Adam unexpectedly, especially to himself, became interested in "what people could do three-dimensionally" with writing after watching Anthony in the Broadway production of *Six Degrees of Separation.* Venturing into playwriting was a bigger step for Adam than learning how to write dialogue. Even today, he says, "It kind of doesn't make any sense to me, to tell you the truth. How it happened. I hated the theater, I hated what it did to our family." At the same time, it turned out that writing plays was a way to exorcise leftover feelings about his past: "A lot of my plays are really dark. . . . Things are actually being destroyed onstage. So part of me thinks that I was initially destroying the theater, reacting to that time in my life."

Playwriting also gave Adam a chance to collaborate with Anthony on *Ursula's Permanent,* a play that, when mentioned, inspires a pair of side-long glances and chuckles. The inside joke, they say, is that the authors now think it's, well, not their best work. Adam's writing career is now a balance between writing novels (which are typically sold to the young adult market, even though his protagonists are dealing with very dark themes that adults could deeply understand) and writing plays. His novels are written in a more consistent, workmanlike fashion than his plays, which he takes on only when he feels he *has* to write one. One of his most recent, and most highly praised—*Nocturne*—will run at the New York Theater Workshop in 2001, and may be the play that establishes Adam as a world-renowned playwright. The fact that the same company put Anthony in *Rent* is a parallel not lost on either brother.

Success in the arts requires the right combination of talent and luck, and so it's remarkable that two brothers could have both been so fortunate in both departments. As they detailed their careers, Adam explained that he had just moved into the apartment where he sat a week before. It's the first place in New York where he feels at home. He hasn't had to keep a "day job" for a year and a half, but he knows that he's still one missed check away from signing up at a temp agency. "It's bizarre," he says. "But that's the way it is, and I don't care."

Anthony, as his fans know, set his career on more solid ground with a certain musical called *Rent*. The production started modestly in a workshop and went on to become the best-loved production of 1996, with Anthony in the role of the filmmaker who "narrates" the story. This was when Anthony got a taste of what it can mean to be famous. "*Rent* was insane," says his brother. "If we were hanging out at any given time on the street, people would come up to him. . . . I mean, not to be rude, but getting home became a problem."

Anthony moved on from the *Rent* cast in 1998, but he's still recognized and says he's felt like he's on the cusp of some sort of "rock 'n' roll life." Some adjustments had to be made, but Anthony has found a way to appreciate the attention without letting it go to his head or keep him indoors. "I think it probably also has to do with who you are. Who you are with yourself and how comfortable you are with your own fame." Still, Adam's reaction to his brother's celebrity is: "I don't know how you do it."

Adam certainly doesn't mind having his name attached to a play or on the cover of a book, but for his last two novels, he declined to have an author photo on the dust jacket. He prefers to stay in the shadows. Then again, he admits he liked the attention he got on his author tour. How much fame is too much? Adam still isn't sure. "I'm not saying I want to be reclusive," he says, "but I think I'd like to be more . . . I don't know. I'm still resolving that. Because I do like it, when people admire and respect you and come up to you and say things."

In the end, for both the Rapp brothers, they simply want careers. This was a term that Anthony avoided for a while, not liking the word's association with suits and ties, but he now says he's proud of his career. Adam is looking forward to the day when his career can support a family. After years of highs and lows, a stable and sane creative life has great appeal, even if it brings fame.

Both are grateful that they reached a point of relative stability before their mother passed away. Back in Joliet, she was struck with cancer just as Anthony was getting started with *Rent* and Adam was finishing his second novel. As sick as she was, she made it to Anthony's opening night, and got to see a copy of Adam's novel *The Buffalo Tree*. It was the first copy off the press, sent overnight to ensure she would see it. Anthony recalls how she "held on and held on and held on."

Before their mother let go, there were long conversations. She came to accept Anthony's homosexuality and expressed regret over how difficult her choices had been on Adam and Ann. But when she let go, she was also confident that her children would survive.

Back in New York, Anthony and Adam have discovered family, not just between themselves but in what Anthony calls "the extended family" of artists and friends. Although they now live separately, for five years the brothers shared a four-bedroom apartment with a series of "revolving" roommates, many with similar struggles and dreams. And *Rent,* of course, is the story of an artists' community on Manhattan's Lower East Side. Adam calls the actors and directors who bring his plays to life siblings and says that working on a play is like having a family for two months. "I think that's probably why I do it," he says. "[I'm] sort of re-creating the right kind of family."

In each corner of America, from the urban bohemians scraping for rent, to the clean-cut suburbanites working for their mortgage, Americans are determined to create families. I found that to be the case again and again in the exhortations of the folks in this book. Even those who live in the worlds of fame and fortune, where you would expect to find nothing but glitz and flash, I found dreams coming back to family. But as we have seen, American families don't just happen. They are lovingly fashioned and molded. They are, I began to believe even more deeply as I worked on this book, the most important work we can do to achieve any American dream.

Oscar Carlos Acosta

As pitching coach for the Chicago Cubs, Oscar Acosta is on close terms with a dream that has tantalized generations of American boys. He also knows how profoundly painful it can be to lose that dream. "There was a young man who came to our tryout camp the other day," he says when asked about some of the aspiring players he has seen. "At twenty-eight, he was trying to pursue his dream to be a professional ballplayer. He was out on the mound and he threw his warm-up pitches, and right away I knew that he did not have what it takes." Oscar is a busy man with a promising pitching staff to develop. But he also knew what the moment meant to that aspirant.

"Instead of bursting his dream at that time, we let him have his ten minutes in the sun, pitching at Wrigley Field. Then I pulled him aside, and I could tell that he knew what I was going to say to him." Oscar tells this story with sympathy. When he was twenty-three, someone had that talk with him.

Oscar was "discovered" pitching in the small New Mexico community of Elida in the late 1960s. Situated between the Texas border and "the middle of nowhere," Elida's 250 residents forged hardscrabble lives on the flat, dry grasslands, primarily as ranchers and ranch hands. Oscar's parents had emigrated from Mexico. Both had limited educations, but Oscar's mother was determined to see her four children graduate from high school, even though she knew that "opportunity" was something that typically passed their town by.

"I knew I was headed for a life on the ranch, that's all I knew was going to happen," Oscar recalls, adding that gaining his high school diploma did not make him think differently. Oscar had, like most kids in his community, learned to ride a horse at the age of four. By age six, when he learned how to feed calves from a bottle, he was working. As soon as he had the strength to lift a sack of feed, he was going out on the rounds with the other ranch hands: "Everybody starts pretty young there. I just thought that was kind of the way of life. That's what it was about." The life he knew held few rewards. Oscar says his father, even after working as a ranch hand his entire life, made little more than seventy-five dollars a week.

"Baseball was kind of the furthest thing from my mind," Oscar says. Even when he and other kids managed to carve out time for a game, even when they could find eighteen players in a community where the high school graduating class numbered ten, they often couldn't gather together enough equipment. They didn't always have the support and attention of their parents, who mostly were working until sundown.

In Elida, "Basketball was our main thing," Oscar explains, "simply because it brought the community together at night." The community would also come together for an occasional rodeo, a sport that taught Oscar a few valuable lessons. Oscar rode bareback broncos and bulls, endeavors that guarantee you will have to learn to get back up after being knocked down.

If it weren't for a few committed parents who patched together a Little League, Oscar would have never experienced more than the infrequent pickup game on a dusty field. To find an opponent, Oscar's team had to travel at least thirty miles on Saturdays, taking with them the few players who got a temporary reprieve from the ranches' busy spring. Oscar didn't realize it, but hefting bags of feed, riding broncos, and shooting baskets had made him into an athlete. But sports for him were just fun and games. His future life, he was certain, would look a lot like his father's.

Forty miles away from Elida lived a man who loved baseball and spent his weekends traveling from one Little League game to the next. Oscar had no idea who he was, but he came to know who Oscar was, and learned that he had a powerful pitching arm. He also knew a baseball coach at Dallas Baptist University, and passed along the tip that he should come to Elida if he was interested in a promising young pitcher.

Oscar was completely unaware that people were talking about him until a letter arrived from Dallas offering him an athletic scholarship. It just dropped out of the blue, leaving Oscar at first confused, and then elated: "When I found out there was something I could do, I was ecstatic. I had an opportunity to do something and try to be something. There was more determination when that became a realization." No one had ever gone from Elida to the major leagues before. Oscar suddenly could see it happening and suddenly had something to fight for.

If Oscar was confused at first, his parents were completely baffled. His mother was the first to come to terms with the new possibilities: "My mother understood it was education," Oscar says, adding that of four children, he was the only one who had the opportunity to go to college. His parents had only seen him play once in his life: "Daddy was never a big sports fan. He thought it was a waste of time. He thought I needed to find a job and become a man." But in the end, there wasn't much discussion about it. "It was just something I wanted to do, and I left and went out and did it."

There are probably more fictional accounts of Americans being discovered and propelled into the spotlight than there are actual "discoveries," but the idea has incredible power. To go from having no dreams and no escape from our dreary lives to having the world at our feet. To defy the odds. As it dawned on Oscar that he could be "somebody," a dream took him in its grip and wouldn't let go. It changed him into someone he still has trouble recognizing.

"Going to Dallas, it was like going to Hollywood. I had made a giant step in my life. I knew that something was going to happen for me." His arm grew stronger, as did his determination and confidence. Except for the fact that he met his wife in Dallas, the world outside of baseball meant little. He didn't go to church, he barely paid attention to his schoolwork: "I knew that the only thing I had was a good arm, and that I could play. . . . I wanted to play and sign. That's all I wanted to do. Dummy me, academics were the furthest thing from my mind. It was just standing in the way of my progress." After only a year, he transferred to Lubbock Christian College, just two hours from his hometown. In the summer leagues, he was tested by former professionals and top college players. In his mind, he passed the tests. He felt he could compete against anyone at the collegiate level and was ready for the next challenge.

In 1977, Oscar was drafted into the minor league system of the Philadelphia Phillies, then a powerhouse of the National League. Oscar met Ryne Sandberg, drafted in the same year and now in baseball's Hall of Fame. He rubbed elbows with George Bell and Bobby Dernier. But instead of being humbled, he saw himself in the same league. The dream was still unachieved, but to Oscar it was already a fait accompli: "I knew then that it was going to happen if I had to force it." The dream became so vivid that it completely blinded Oscar to everything else. "I became so consumed I lost sight of life. I lost sight of a lot of things—my perspectives and priorities," he says candidly. He even lost sight of his family, which now included two daughters. He was going to drive himself into the majors, and nothing could stop him. "I thought I was in control." Today, he acknowledges, one of the things he couldn't control was a nagging pain in his pitching arm.

Professional athletes hold a special place on the American dreamscape. They are often our first childhood heroes, the earliest examples of success that children can understand. But as a career, athletics is terribly unforgiving. If you don't "have what it takes," no amount of training or practice will put you into the game. If you are injured seriously, you're out, and that's usually that. In this country, we'd like to believe that you can do anything you set your mind to. Pro sports show us clearly, depressingly, that this is not always the case. For every winning touchdown, grand slam, or buzzer-beating shot, there are thousands of dreams dashed, deferred, or destroyed.

"I never would give in to the pain in my arm," Oscar remembers. "I never did say anything, I just kept throwing and throwing. Then they finally realized that my velocity had gone way down. I kept telling them it was nothing. I was afraid they were going to take my uniform away from me. When they did take it away from me, it was like my whole world had been shattered." The diagnosis was a torn rotator cuff. These days, it might have been treated, but back then his career could only have been saved if he'd sought medical attention earlier. But he never went to the doctor, fearing he'd lose his place in line. Oscar, now in his early forties, has gained the perspective he needed so desperately back then. He speaks frankly in his tough west Texas accent about a twenty-three-year-old who, after growing up with nothing, lost his shot at fame simply because he acted with determination. And isn't that how the ambitious are expected to act?

Oscar thought that he had lost everything, but there was still more to lose. Oscar found himself at Lubbock Christian College as a coach. It was the only way he could support his two children. The realization that his dream was dead in the water, and that he was back at his old college, just hours from his hometown, started taking an emotional toll. "I think that my fire and my dream had just died out. I'd given up. I just kind of fell flat on myself and my life. . . . I thought that I was destined to do the same thing that my father had done, and that was to go back and be a cowpuncher the rest of my life." Within five years, Oscar gave up on coaching, his family, and his future.

Oscar was twenty-eight when he left coaching and resigned himself to what sounds like slow suicide: "I think I had to learn to lose everything in my life, which I did. I hit rock bottom. . . . I lost my family. I became somebody who didn't know who he was. . . . At that point, my wife just couldn't take it anymore, and because I didn't have the quote-unquote uniform, or something to recognize myself with, I thought that life was over."

Those who make it to the top tier of any endeavor, be it film, or writing, or baseball seem in some measure to share the ability to exert laser-sharp focus on a long-term goal. The problem is, it can turn into tunnel vision. Especially when you push away the people who have the best chance of helping you.

During the two years after his wife left him, Oscar traveled on what he calls "a downward spiral as fast as I could go." He was dead broke. He didn't see his children, and he fell behind on his child-support payments. In February of 1988, he says, he got a call from his mother. His kids wanted to know where their father was. A week later, he got a call from Doug Gassaway, a man he calls his guardian angel. Doug was "always there, it seemed, at the right place and the right time."

Doug was the scout who had signed Oscar to the Phillies back in 1977. This time, he was calling to see if Oscar was interested in getting back into professional ball. A coaching position was open in the Texas Rangers' minor league system. Those two phone calls, from his mother and from Doug Gassaway, helped give Oscar the courage to give his American dream a second act.

"It kind of all came back together, but by the same token, I understood and realized that I couldn't be in the driver's seat of my life. Somebody else had to take over. A higher power had to do it. . . . If I was in control again, I would shipwreck, and I would end up right back where I started—a ranch hand the rest of my life."

For Oscar, reclaiming the identity he lost with his uniform meant relying on others. To his belief, they were agents of a higher power. He would have to accept help from his former mentor, his friends, and most important, his family. After two years of divorce, he humbly reconciled with his wife and children. His identity would, he swore, never again be tied exclusively to baseball. He would be a coach second, a husband and father first.

For eleven years, Oscar rebuilt what he had lost. He discovered that he liked coaching in the minors and was good at it. He coached for the Rangers and the New York Yankees' minor league teams before accepting a minor league managing assignment with the Cubs. He learned to take these blessings as they came . . . and while he fought for his team, he no longer felt as if he was fighting for his life. As he says he explained to his daughter: "If the good Lord wants me to be a minor league instructor . . . that's what I'm going to do. No way am I going to get in the way again and try to take over, because it doesn't work. If I'm going to be in the minor leagues, that's what I'm going to do."

Oscar didn't know at the time that an episode in his early life was about to replay on a new level. Oscar was visiting Elida for Thanksgiving in 1999. Unknown to him, his name was moving to the top of a list in Chicago. The Cubs called to ask if he would be interested in interviewing for the position of pitching coach. The telephone interview, a few days later, turned out to actually be a job offer. Oscar was finally in the major leagues. Looking out the window of his mom's home in Elida, he saw symmetry in his life's course: "And I was at home in my hometown. I thought, 'This is where you started, and you've made full circle. You've acquired a dream because you never gave up.' "

The toughness Oscar has acquired over the years comes to play in his new job. The professional ball club, he says, is a pressure cooker: "It actually does take a special group of people to be able to perform at this level. I didn't realize that until now. The expectations. The demands for perfection, for the W—the Win. That's what it's all about." Learning to accept what comes stands Oscar in good stead when his pitchers are on the mound and it's out of his hands. "Sometimes," he says, "you feel like you can still participate"—exert an influence on events—"and you just can't."

The dream has come true for his family as well, whom Oscar credits for sticking with him through several relocations and changes in fortune.

He and his wife now have a son in addition to their two daughters, and have settled in Portales, New Mexico, about twenty-five miles from Elida, where his children go to school. Oscar joins them during breaks in the schedule and the off-season. It's as if Oscar no longer has to run from the town he once felt trapped by. "Elida is a safe haven for my children. . . . It's a very good community. The values of family are embedded, entrenched in people." Oscar says he recently made it to one of his son's Little League games, which is often impossible during the professional season. His son played on the same field where Oscar learned how to pitch. "This was a big deal," Oscar says. "It was like watching myself. Like my life had started all over."

If there's one thing Oscar would like to impart to his children as they pursue their goals, it's the lesson he had such trouble learning. It's a message that a surprising number of people interviewed for this book say about the American dream: "You have to rely on other people to help you get it. You have to rely on other people. You can't do it alone. You have to have a very good family base, and you have to have that support."

Adam McFadden Ballard

Compton, California, is a quick freeway ride from the Dorothy Chandler Pavilion, Mann's Chinese Theatre, and the American Film Institute. But to most children growing up in this notorious city just south of Los Angeles, Hollywood may as well be on Mars. "You grow up there," says Adam Ballard, who did, and "you're looking around and nothing is good. You look around, all you see is negativity. You feel that's all there is out there." Adam adds that he knew people there who'd actually never been out of this small inner suburb.

Compton was once idyllic enough to serve as the short-term, postwar home of George and Barbara Bush. That was long before the rap group N.W.A. titled their debut album *Straight Outta Compton,* painting a picture of a city where murder was routine and rage was forever. That album became known as Compton's main contribution to American culture. Adam wants to change that. Drastically.

Adam has known he wanted to be a filmmaker from the age of nine, when he would create scenes with his toys and pretend to shoot them with his play camera. Today, this twenty-one-year-old is a film student at the Art Center College of Design in Pasadena and was called "the next big thing" by *Videomaker* magazine after he directed a public service announcement for the Boys and Girls Clubs of America. So what sort of films does this product of Compton dream of making? "Good family films. Films that everybody can watch." When Adam shared this dream with his cinematography instructor, the professor was silent for a moment. Then, according to Adam, he replied, "Wow. No one's ever said that to me before."

How did this wholesome vision grow against a backdrop of violence and hopelessness? Flashback to Compton, April 29, 1992: Adam and his father are completing a house-painting job. Over the radio, the verdicts are read. Adam's father wastes no time in collecting his son and heading for the relative safety of home. He knows what is about to break.

The riot is already in full swing as they pull onto Compton Boulevard and head for their apartment. A tractor-trailer slams into a gated business, and looters swarm in. Buildings are already burning. There's not a policeman in sight.

In the week following America's largest civil disturbance since the Civil War, Adam notices in the alleyways boxes that used to contain TVs, VCRs, camcorders, and bulk meats from fast-food restaurants. The twelve-year-old boy understands the anger but is saddened by the sight of the burned and gutted buildings. Today, he sums up his mixed feelings with a terse statement: "Personally, I think they should have trashed more of those liquor stores."

Adam and his family—a loving and protective mother and father, a younger brother and sister—had moved to the L.A. area from Virginia just a year before the Rodney King verdict and the riots that ensued. They had a solid family network, and Adam's dad found jobs as a security guard. Their first apartment was, in Adam's words, a "roach motel," but their next apartment, a two-bedroom on Compton Boulevard near the Compton/Gardena border, was clean, well kept, and affordable.

"The area where I lived wasn't altogether too bad. We had our share of bad times, but it wasn't altogether bad as people imagine Compton would be," Adam recalls. There are good areas and bad areas within any "bad" neighborhood. The level of violence and tension can change block by block. On this particular block, Adam says, there was no shortage of prostitutes and drug addicts, but in Adam's memory, they were part of the fabric of the neighborhood: "It's actually pretty cool, because all these guys who hung out there, they were all crackheads or whatever, but they would always look out for us. Everybody had each other's back over there. . . . When my mother came home late, and was putting the car in the garage, they would watch out for her while she was back there. That was pretty cool."

Adam's mother was pretty cool herself. On holidays, especially Thanksgiving, she bought extra turkeys and prepared plates for the women who did business on the boulevard and the men who called the streets home. Then she would distribute the plates herself.

Adam knows that his parents' protectiveness, more than anything else, made his life in Compton sane. He remembers the day he brought over three newfound friends: "My father wouldn't let me hang out with them. He didn't like them." Though upset at the time, Adam is now glad that his father took a hard line—"One of the guys ended up getting shot, another one of the guys is just a waste. I just saw him not too long ago. He's on drugs, he doesn't do anything. Another one of the guys ended up in jail."

In the face of a city that teetered on the edge of lawlessness, Adam's parents took their protectiveness one step further. Rather than send their children across gang-infested territory to a deteriorating school where metal detectors pass for an investment in children's futures, Adam's mother schooled him at home.

Adam never had to spend a day in a Compton public school. His mother, who had some college credits but no degree, passed the state test and got support from the South Bay Faith Academy in nearby Redondo Beach. The Academy provided materials and offered specialized classes that Adam's mother felt she couldn't teach, such as Spanish, science, and history. Learning with other students two days a week, Adam says, took care of some of the social isolation that could have arisen from his home schooling. At the same time, he learned about how isolating Compton can be: "I was the only black student there, and I felt I couldn't relate to some of the students. They were all from Redondo Beach. They didn't know anything about where I was from."

Adam's mother kept him on a strict schedule, with lessons coming one after another across the kitchen table. Their "classroom" put a heavy emphasis on the practical. Adam remembers an early math lesson in which he learned to balance the family's checkbook, pay the bills, and complete a budget. That kind of experience, he feels, made addition, subtraction, and averaging important, useful, helpful, and even fun.

Being home-schooled obviously meant that Adam was almost always home. If he did get out in the afternoon, he was under strict instructions to be back before dark. "I hated it back then," he admits, "running home, trying to get in before the streetlights came on. But now I'm glad [my parents] were like that." So Adam did what most kids do when they are stuck inside. He turned to television. "I was a living *TV Guide*. I knew every show, every movie that was going to come on TV."

We Americans have a complicated relationship with "the tube." We (and I'll definitely include myself here) constantly grumble about what a bad influence TV can be, but we still watch (and I'll continue to do what I can to make my corner of it something in which I can take pride). We passionately discuss television violence—on television—every time an American child commits an act of violence, but even the owners of the loudest voices will sometimes, when they can't take the high energy of their own tykes, pop a tape into the box and plop their impressionable child in front of it.

Television is easy. Easy to watch, and easy to criticize. But young Adam found a third way between "on" and "off." He watched and then incorporated what he saw into his dreams. The more he watched, the more he wanted to imitate what he saw. Not the actors, but the camera angles, the direction, the writing. He saw right through TV's fantasy world and focused on how the fantasies are made. With his family's help, it took only a few steps before these television fantasies became Adam's dreams . . . and his dreams became concrete goals.

Adam recently spoke to an outreach counselor at Art Center College of Design about his efforts to recruit inner-city youth: "I was telling him how some of the kids, they don't know that stuff is actually available to them, that they can become successful artists, that they can make money at it. Black people especially, they think that if you're not a doctor or a lawyer, you're not making money. But there are careers out there, where you can actually design buildings, paint, draw, become an illustrator, and be real successful, make money, and provide." Adam never experienced that doubt firsthand. When he told his parents that he wanted to be a filmmaker, they moved quickly to keep his dream alive.

Adam's grandmother took Adam, then fourteen, to a public access station in Pasadena that offered training on their equipment. They discovered that applicants had to be sixteen to get in, but the administration was willing to bend the rules for someone as committed and knowledgeable as Adam. His experience there, the first time he had ever laid his hands on a camera or an editing deck, confirmed his desire. He "fell in love with it." That first day, Adam knew: "I would make movies for the big screen."

He could learn and practice on the public access channel's equipment, but he still couldn't check it out on his own. The expensive hardware he needed to pursue his goals seemed forever out of reach, but a little creativity and support can buoy even the priciest dreams. Adam's father, who was working as a security guard in a wealthy apartment complex, discovered that when rich people move, they often prefer to make new purchases later rather than pack now. The building's castoffs included an old twin-lens reflex camera that Adam uses for still photography to this day. When his grandmother, who worked at a record company, took Adam to a video shoot at a major studio, he grabbed a box of scripts in the trash to learn how they are formatted and presented. Somewhere a few rejected screenwriters can take heart in the fact that their trashed scripts served as inspiration for at least an audience of one.

"That was just a start," Adam continues. The next break came again through his grandmother, who looked up an old colleague back in Virginia. Harry Young, who had been vice president of original production at the Family Channel, was running Youth Entertainment Studios (YES), a nonprofit that gives inner-city youth a chance to use their summer vacations to launch careers in film, video, and entertainment. Students form teams and are expected to have a finished project by the end of the two-month program. For advice and counsel, YES brings in working writers, executives, and celebrities to mentor youth on their projects and teach them about the vast range of jobs behind the scenes: "Real nuts and bolts," as Adam calls them, "that you can't get anywhere else."

For Adam, it was a real chance to start turning his dreams into reality. "I loved it. All the students loved it. We put all our heart and soul in our projects." His first summer at YES, 1995, he directed a short music video about a "bad seed" who turns his life around, with his cousin and fellow student performing as rapper. Next year, he directed, produced, and cowrote a short film about abuse in teenage relationships. The experience gained on these projects was valuable in itself, but Adam gained something even more tangible, something every aspiring filmmaker needs. He started building a reel, a sampling of work that would later get him into film school.

Being in the L.A. area and having a flexible school schedule allowed Adam to ply the visiting lecturers for jobs. Fresh back from his first YES program, he interned at Nickelodeon under two executive producers and helped the directors of photography and lighting. For a few months during that time, he also served as assistant to the director of creative affairs at Yab Yum Records, an independent and eclectic label.

Adam had tucked all this experience into his belt before he got his high school diploma from South Bay Faith Academy in 1997. He was immediately called back to YES to direct the public service announcement for Boys and Girls Clubs of America, and he entered community college in the fall. Although he probably had more hands-on experience in filmmaking than just about any applicant his age, the film centers at UCLA and USC seemed remote. Home schooling had given him both practical and general skills, but he hadn't prepared for the SAT. And even the in-state tuition at UCLA seemed like a fortune.

But there were still plenty of opportunities. Adam interned at CBS Children's Programs—"That was cool, because I had my own little office and everything"—took an animation course at the UCLA extension program, and produced and shot studio and performance videos for musicians such as Herbie Hancock and Jonathan Butler. It was hard to wait for film school, but in the end, Adam was glad he did.

Adam was positive that Art Center was the right school, and the early expertise he showed in his reel got him accepted, but coming up with the tuition was another story. He found it in an informal financial aid package: "During my first term, I wrote letters to my family and friends asking for their support, and I got checks in the mail. From family I hadn't talked to in years." He asked just about everyone he knew for contributions, thinking all along that most of them would just trash his letter and laugh. But he found that he already had a fan base. "It's just crazy," he says of the support he received. "I still just sit back and think about it sometimes."

Adam is now working on short projects and music videos, and learning about special effects and equipment he never dreamed of having access to before. For now, he's working small while dreaming big. Rap videos are good practice, and his old neighborhood often serves as a location. He's working on a short animated film about children's nightmares that will go on his graduation reel. But at the same time, he's thinking about the feature films he hopes one day to direct.

This aspiring filmmaker was under the strong influence of Stephen Spielberg's movies when his dreams were coalescing. He still loves Spielberg's early adventure and fantasy movies but says his list of influences is expanding. He's learned a lot from watching the visual and storytelling skills of Martin Scorsese and Brian DePalma, but their content isn't something he wants to emulate. He's been charged by the films of Spike Lee and the recent crop of black family films like *Soul Food, Love Jones,* and *The Best Man*—"films showing us in a positive light"—which also, he adds, can be enjoyed by anyone. "The characters in those films, anybody could have played them. It could have been about a white family."

It all comes back to family for Adam, the same place it all started. He's latched on to something that Hollywood often forgets as they pinpoint and target demographic groups—families like to watch movies together. They shouldn't have to split up in the lobbies and walk to different ends of the multiplexes. "A lot of this stuff coming out of Hollywood now, it's garbage," Adam growls before pausing and adding diplomatically, "It's just not the kind of stuff I'd like to direct."

Adam would like to honor his family with more than just a thank-you in an Oscar speech. "My whole goal is to bring my family in on this. My sister's into writing, my little brother, I could see him as a producer type." If fame comes, he wants to make sure everyone who helped him along the way benefits: "If I blow up, they all blow up."

This explosion, Adam knows, is still a ways off. But in keeping a distant goal ever present in the moment, he has already come far. Those who dream of fame are, more than just about any others, taking a long shot. Their dreams may seem to them, as Jacquelyn Mitchard pointed out, ephemeral, distant, impractical, and even immature. The only way, if we look to a young man like Adam, who still has a long way to go to bridge the gap between a beginning like Compton and a dream like Hollywood, lies in recognizing one's gifts: "If you have something within you, then I feel that nothing can stop you. . . . It's God-given. I think if you have a gift inside of you, it's there forever, and that's your best chance to get out of whatever situation you're in."

EDUCATION
LEARNING TO DREAM

Unless a people are educated and enlightened it is idle to expect the continuance of civil liberty or the capacity for self-government.
—Texas Declaration of Independence

A teacher affects eternity. He can never tell where his influence stops.

—Henry Brooks Adams

*M*y own American dream began with my first day of college. Sam Houston State Teachers College, as it was then known, in Huntsville, Texas, may not have been Ivy League or even ivy covered, but it was undeniably an institution of higher learning. It was there I found my first mentor, in journalism professor Hugh Cunningham, and it was there I began the journey of discovery on which I am fortunate to still find myself.

I don't know how Professor Cunningham, still young and surely smart and dedicated enough to have had his own very successful career in journalism, ended up teaching in Huntsville, but for me, finding him there was a tremendous break. I know it's a lot to lay at the feet of one person, but I can honestly say that I can't see myself having gotten where I am today without having crossed his path at the crucial time I did. People like Hugh Cunningham show you that the phrase "good teacher" is redundant and "bad teacher" is a contradiction in terms.

Education in any form is a lifelong thing, and its effects are often far from obvious or immediate. It is rightly considered a foundation or point of embarkation for any dream. But for me, as for so many Americans, its pursuit was also in and of itself the realization of a dream. My father, like his father before him, had dropped out of the tenth grade to work in the oil fields. My mother, who held visions of going further than was considered normal or even becoming for young women in her day, was also forced to quit school to help out her family financially. By graduating from high school, I had gone further than my parents had ever been able to. And when I set foot on Sam Houston State's little campus, I became the first in my family to attend college.

For a large and growing number of young men and women, pursuing a college education has become a matter of course. We forget that it has not always been like this in America. Before World War II, especially, college was the province of the few, and even finishing high school was a luxury many couldn't afford. I remember a man who visited our house when I was young, and how my mom told me afterward in near-reverent tones that he was "a college man." My folks weren't able to do it themselves, not in the hardscrabble times they knew before and during the Great Depression, but they made it clear that the value they put on education was high indeed.

They were not alone in this, for education has always been central to the American experience, uniquely so. Our democracy and our New World freedom to move beyond the circumstances of our birth have bestowed it this privilege of place, one that was recalled most recently in the past presidential campaign. "Reading is the new civil right because if you can't read, you can't access the American dream," said President George W. Bush in one of his standard stump speeches. "If we want prosperity to mean anything, if we want to make sure that every American can master the new job manuals and seize the full promise of this new and changing economy, surf the World Wide Web, prepare for the twenty-first century, then we have to shake up the status quo in our schools," proclaimed former vice president Al Gore in his campaign oratory.

The founding generation, good Enlightenment men all, knew well that their grand experiment rested on education. If the new government was truly to be of, for, and by the people, We the People could not be ignorant. As our education went, so would the ship of state. Intellectuals of the American Revolution, men like Thomas Jefferson, Benjamin Franklin, and his friend and fellow Philadelphian Benjamin Rush, wrote and spoke with passionate eloquence of the new nation's need to school its young in not only the arts and sciences but in civic virtue as well.

Theirs was a noble ideal, but it would be some time before the free, compulsory schooling that the Puritans had implanted in New England spread nationwide. It would not be until the middle of the nineteenth century, amid the broadening democracy of the Jacksonian era, that school would become a commonplace of American life. From that time, formal education has steadily, if imperfectly, grown to include all Americans.

Our own age has seen enormous strides. None more important, in my estimation, than the integration of our schools. It would be hard to overstate the importance of the Supreme Court decision in 1954 of *Brown v. Board of Ed. of Topeka, Kansas*. It was education's Emancipation Proclamation, a powerful force for drawing African Americans into the main of American life. And with it, our nation moved closer to the promise of its organizing principle that all our dreams matter.

Mark well, integrating our educational system did not come easily, either before or after it became a constitutional imperative. Some of my earliest and most harrowing experiences as a reporter came on the front lines of that battle in the South, and *battle* is indeed the word for what it was. The debates over our schools are seldom placid affairs. They are fights over the future, for the values that our society will reflect and inculcate, and they are waged on the precious personal grounds of our own children's lives.

Of course, education does not only give us the tools to run our democracy; it also equips us to better our lot in life. In this role, too, education is central to the American dream. And it must be available to all if equality of opportunity is to be more than a well-intentioned phrase.

Going back as far as I can remember, I was fortunate enough to be surrounded by adults who challenged me and expanded my horizons. My mother and father and grandmother, who taught me to read and write—first and foremost. But also the social worker—Mrs. Rose, I think her name was, though I'm sorry to say I'm not sure—who took me to the local library for the first time, and a succession of teachers and coaches who have touched my life in ways big and small.

I knew that I would be able to find other folks for whom education brought the American dream closer to reality. I also wanted to get the stories of some of the people who have dedicated themselves to educating others. In Rubylinda Zickafoose, a child of migrant workers who fought for an equal education and now teaches elementary school in Florida, I found both. Rubylinda and others like her remind us that, for some, education isn't just a means to an end but the dream itself.

Curtis Aikens, a television chef in Georgia, chafed against the shackles illiteracy imposed on his talent and native intelligence. When his business failed, Curtis found the courage to ask for help. By learning to read at the age of twenty-six, he is living proof that it is never too late to learn. Now he uses his celebrity to spread the word that illiteracy can be overcome.

Former software tester Trish Dziko turned her Microsoft stock options into a foundation that works on the leading edge of what may be the greatest educational challenge of the twenty-first century: closing the so-called digital divide. Her efforts to introduce inner-city kids to high-tech corporate culture and vice versa reinforce the lesson that not all learning takes place in a classroom. Though not a teacher by training, Trish sets an inspirational example by taking it upon herself to wield education against a problem about which she cares deeply.

While our attention drifts first to our hallowed four-year colleges when the topic turns to higher education, Karen Altland knows that for those who can't afford the time or expense, vocational training is a form of education very much in step with the American dream. It's the path she herself took from factory worker to a career in health care to vocational instructor. After spending twenty years of her life in a dead-end job before a school changed her life, she knows how dreams and education walk in step.

These are people for whom education is an explicit part of the American dream, or for whom it represents the dream in full. Like the mother and father who blessed me at an early age with their esteem for learning, they are hardly alone. And like family, education in its boundless variety is a touchstone for just about everyone's life. Books could be filled with the stories of those who have found it so. For all of us who turn to it to improve our lives and the public, collective life of our country, education connects us with the spirit that animated the earliest American dreams.

Rubylinda Zickafoose

I remember my teachers, even the first ones. Some were a direct part of my life for only a short nine months, but their influence on me was such that their names and images have stuck: Mrs. Spencer, who collaborated with me on a one-page school newspaper in the fourth grade; Mrs. Simmons, the principal at my elementary school, who seemed to be able to actually smell mischief; and Miss Bresky, who fearlessly strode through the rough halls of Hamilton Junior High School. These people gave me at an early age a deep and abiding respect for teachers.

I wince whenever I hear the old saw "Those who can't do teach." It simply isn't true. To me, teaching is patently a labor of love. My feeling seems to be borne out in a study by Public Agenda, a nonprofit, nonpartisan research and education group. The report "A Sense of Calling" claims that 96 percent of the teachers they surveyed teach because that's "the work they love to do." And if they had to do it all over again? Eighty percent said they would. Seventy-five percent said they planned to teach for the rest of their lives. In very few, if any, professions would you find this depth of commitment.

Teachers aren't just putting down stepping-stones for the sake of others, they're living out dreams of their own. The low pay and tenuous social status our society offers teachers pains me, as does the thought of their trying to teach fifty students at a time in crumbling classrooms. It takes a very special person to continue with this career, to even hold on to this particular dream.

I believe I could draw at random from a list of public school teachers and come up with a good story. But I wanted to find someone who really had to fight to become a teacher, and I was lucky to hear about Rubylinda Zickafoose. If Rubylinda had struggled as hard as she did to become an actress, I feel sure she'd be a household name by now. If she had poured her energy into building a business, she'd be a millionaire. But when Rubylinda was eight, she decided that she would become a teacher, and her stubbornness made it happen. Today she teaches at Palmetto Elementary School in Florida. Her passion for teaching hasn't wavered, nor has her passion for learning. She's currently a Ph.D. candidate at the University of South Florida.

Rubylinda's grandmother counted 102 grandchildren before she passed away six years ago. Rubylinda, born Rubylinda Hernandez, is one of two who have received their bachelor's degrees. She's the only one who's earned a master's degree. Rubylinda's grandparents were migrant farmworkers who emigrated from Mexico, and her parents were migrant farmworkers who were both born in Texas. She, too, worked in the fields, from the age of eight. It's a hard life, and even harder to break out of, a fact to which the rarity of college degrees in her family attests. Rubylinda notes that children can be raised blind to life outside their circumstances; even when parents try to break the cycle, because if "you can't read, and you can't write, and all you know how to do is sign your name, this is not the land of opportunity." The chances to move up may be there, but "you can't see the opportunities" or "you know they're not within your reach."

Rubylinda did learn to read and write, but it wasn't until she had reached college that she felt she had truly broken out of her family circumstances. It's not surprising, then, that she believes that the true value of education is liberation. "When you are educated," she says, "and I don't just mean a formal education . . . it opens doors, it opens vision, it opens your mind and it opens your heart. It's just amazing how much you see . . . and it can be overwhelming at times."

Rubylinda was lucky to have parents who insisted that each and every one of their children graduate from high school. Rubylinda remembers when one of her older brothers decided he would drop out of school to work in the fields full-time. All this sixteen-year-old really wanted were the set hours and the simplicity. He thought he could buy a perfectly enjoyable life of "games and weekends" one bushel at a time. "My dad said, 'Okay. Fine.' " Rubylinda's father took her brother out of school and put him to work—"I mean hard," Rubylinda says for emphasis. "My dad did the extra effort to tell him, 'This is your quota for the day, and you will not stop until you get this quota done, and if this is the lifestyle you want to lead, expect this every day of your life. It's not gonna get easier. It's not gonna get any better. The sun's not going to get any less hot.' " In two weeks, Rubylinda concludes, her brother was begging to go back to school.

During the school year, Rubylinda's family kept a home base in rural Immokalee, Florida. When they could, her parents labored in fields near town, but sometimes their work took them as much as four hours away. Every May, the picking season got started in earnest, and the family would pack a few belongings into a pickup truck with a camper shell on the back and travel to Virginia, North and South Carolina, Tennessee, or Texas—wherever the crops were ripe. Rubylinda and her four siblings slept in rest areas, sometimes under the truck, sometimes on the grass— but never in so much as even a roadside motel—until they arrived at their destination.

Rubylinda remembers the little things that meant everything to a young girl. "This one time in particular, I wanted to take a shower so bad. I just wanted to take a shower!" The drive dragged on and on, and they finally pulled up to a beautiful two-story Victorian farmhouse at two in the morning. "I'm unpacking and I'm gonna go take a shower. I'm going to *hit* the shower and I remember my mom saying 'You can't.' " The shower was downstairs, and downstairs was full of workers: "That was the first time it hit me. There were three or four families staying in this two-story house, and we were all sharing one bathroom and one shower." In the morning, of course, there was a long line. "I remember just throwing my hands up and just crying, because all I wanted to do was take a shower!" she remembers with a laugh.

This particular house was palatial compared to the usual barracks they stayed in while on the road. Most didn't have running water. Rubylinda typically "showered" in a basin with water from the forty-gallon cans provided by the bosses. It was a complicated operation, and often Rubylinda was just too tired to go through with it. Her description of those days that wore her out from age eight deserves to be quoted at length here. It's something to think about the next time you slice up a tomato.

You start out in the morning . . . the earlier the better because that way you're able to kind of escape the heat of the day, if the quota's met. Usually the big boss and the owner of the acreage are the ones who determine how much we're going to pick for the day. . . . The faster you pick, the more you get, so you're always in competition with the other people, but at the same time . . . the more money you need the harder you're gonna work. Sometimes, especially the men, you see them flying, running to dump their bucket in the truck so they can come back and start picking again. It's piecework where you get so much money for every bucket.

Dad would usually take one of those coolers full of water, and sometimes it would look soooo far away. And you'd think, "Okay, if I can just make it to the water, I'll make it for the rest of the day." I remember the sun being so hot. So very hot. And when you pick tomatoes, you're bent over. And the wind? You can't feel it because you're between rows. Of course you feel the sun, and sometimes the sun reflects off the plastic, so you're usually *very* hot. Your face is really, really red and burned and sweaty. It's incredibly hard work. People really earn their money. I remember my dad saying, "We don't have much, but everything we have we earned with the sweat from our bodies."

In addition to tomatoes, Rubylinda's family picked potatoes, onions, cucumbers, bell peppers, eggplants, and strawberries. It was the only life her parents knew. Rubylinda's father had a third grade education, and her mother less than that, as Rubylinda discovered one day when she was eight years old.

Rubylinda remembers the day she decided that she had to be a teacher as if it were a vivid dream. She came home from school with a friend, her report card proudly clutched in her hand. She found her mother sitting on the porch and pushed the report card into her hands. "I'm smiling because I think I did really well," she recalls, and her mother opened the card and examined it closely, "but it was upside down." Rubylinda stammers that she remembers her friend "saying to my mom, 'Are you stupid? Can't you read?' And my mom's face fell in her hands and she cried for such a long time."

Eight-year-old Rubylinda tried to comfort her devastated mother, who, after years of hiding her illiteracy, had been found out by a child. "I remember promising her that I was going to grow up and I was going to be a teacher, so I could teach her how to read."

It was a promise that Rubylinda's mother did not forget. In that moment, she caught a glimpse of a better life for her young daughter, and it solidified her commitment to see her children through school. From that day on, anytime Rubylinda slipped or lost interest in her studies, her mother was there to remind her that she needed to teach.

Rubylinda would need those reminders along the way. As it was, her public schooling was geared toward a vocation, not college. The differences between her and her classmates was made painfully evident in sixth grade, when she was pulled out of her regular classes and put in a special program for the children of migrant workers. "You're labeled with this migrant sticker," she says, "and you have to go to these migrant classes, which I *absolutely* hated." Rubylinda felt that the school was simply saying that she wasn't smart enough to cut it in regular classes.

After she came home one day crying, Rubylinda's father went to the school and insisted that she be taken out of the migrant classes. Although she may have been pulled out before the end of the year when she was needed in the fields, her father argued, she was able to attend school every day for the majority of the year. Rubylinda sat through a meeting between her father and her principal and watched him fight the system with a strong voice. He succeeded, and on the way home, he told her it was her turn to fight: "My dad gave me these piercing eyes and told me, 'You will show this man that you can do this, because I just put my word on the line for you.' "

It took some difficult catching up on Rubylinda's part, but she proved herself to her principal and made the transition to high school full of confidence. There was no question in her mind that of the different tracks the high school offered—vocational, general education, college prep—she would be on the one that would take her to college. And in her first meeting with her guidance counselor, her dreams were again dashed in an instant: "I'm very, very smug in my confident manner, saying 'Okay, I want to go to the college prep program. I want to go to college, I want to be a teacher.' And he says to me, and I still see it, and hear it to this day. He says to me"—Rubylinda quotes him in a whisper—" 'But you're a migrant.' "

Rubylinda could not believe that she would have to fight this battle again. "You're taught all through school," she says, "be whatever you want to be, dream the American dream, do what you want to do, be the best you can. You're told this over and over, and here I tell this man what I want to do, and he comes back at me with 'But you're a migrant.' That didn't fit in. That didn't fit." Her counselor put her into a cosmetology program.

Rubylinda admits that cosmetology had a certain appeal to her at the time—"What teenage girl doesn't love doing hair and playing with makeup?"—but she also knew that cosmetology wasn't the reason why she wanted to stay in school. To some extent, she heard the messages she had received about what was possible for her and what was off-limits. They weren't just coming from her high school. Many of Rubylinda's female classmates were becoming young wives and mothers. And she began to see herself in that role.

Rubylinda was fifteen when a man in her town, almost ten years older than she, proposed marriage. Her parents hit the roof. They even considered sending her to California, far away from what they saw as a terrible mistake. Then they tried to change her mind. Rubylinda explains, "He came to ask [my father] for my hand in marriage. It's a custom to usually wait a week, and then they come back for a reply. . . . So during that week, my mom and dad gave me the same treatment they gave my brother." Rubylinda's parents showed her in painstaking detail what her life would be like. They got her up at four-thirty. They had her do all the cooking, pack all the lunches, and clean all the laundry before she could go to school. It didn't work for Rubylinda. "I was the stubborn type," she says. "I took it on as a challenge: 'I'll show you.' "

Also in the back of her mind was the idea that her husband would support her decision to go to college and have a career. She even thought that he would pay for her education. At least that's what she told her mother when she reminded Rubylinda of the promise she had made seven years before. When her suitor returned, all Rubylinda's father felt he could do was make him promise that he would not pull her out of high school.

Today, Rubylinda describes her now ex-husband as a "very, very, very dominant" man, someone whose idea of tradition was to keep a wife away from work outside the home. He didn't see why she needed a high school diploma but he kept his promise to Rubylinda's father. The weight of keeping it, however, fell foursquare on Rubylinda's shoulders. Her parents had tried to show her: she had to get up at four to cook his breakfast and pack her husband's lunch before he went to work in the fields. She then went to school until one-thirty, to her job at a grocery store until evening, and then home to cook, clean, and study. The routine carried her through her junior and senior years in high school.

After graduation, she learned about a job as a teaching assistant at a local elementary school, and something stirred again within her. But before she could take advantage of her first real opportunity, she had to beg, plead, and cry to her husband to let her have a career, or at least try. She got the job and "absolutely fell in love with it." She remembers feeling that "this is it! I remember now why I wanted to be a teacher!" Her new work rekindled the promise she had made so many years earlier.

For five years Rubylinda took classes without her husband's knowledge while she held a part-time job at the community college's media center. "I kept saying 'I'm just working, I'm just working.' " As she got closer to her goal of earning a degree, however, she realized she would have to take some classes at night. The time had finally come for her to tell her husband that she still wanted to be a teacher. She says it took all the inner strength she had to convince herself that she could live up to her dream.

After graduating from community college with honors, Rubylinda applied for a job and a scholarship at the University of South Florida. She realized now that her hope that her husband would pay for her education was totally naive, so she had to figure out a way to attend without taking either money or herself out of the home. She says today that it was pure luck that she didn't have her first son until after she finished at the community college.

One day, while Rubylinda was sitting in the university's media center, something happened. "I remember feeling the world opening up. I remember feeling my mind being challenged, and going 'Yes! I did it! I did it!' I remember sitting through humanities classes and looking at the art and saying, 'Wow. I can go there someday.' I remember sitting through geography and really thinking about how there's a whole other world. . . . I remember feeling the opening of my mind, and the opening of my soul, and the wanting more and dreaming more and hoping more." I recall having a similar feeling in the course of my education, as my college journalism professor turned me from a young man with an interest in the news into a reporter. It is the music made by a mind that finds itself, and there may be no more beautiful sound.

And it changes you. It changed Rubylinda. For one, she had completely lost the ability to stay in a relationship with a domineering husband. They were divorced shortly after she started teaching, after it dawned on her that she could support herself and her son on her own.

Rubylinda started teaching at Palmetto Elementary School right after she finished her bachelor's degree in early elementary education at the University of South Florida. Did she find that teaching was everything she had dreamed? Well, she's been honored by Manatee County, the Milken Family Foundation, and the Sallie Mae Foundation as an educator with rare talent. She went through the grueling national certification process in 1999 and succeeded beyond her own expectations.

Exceeding expectations should be old hat by now for Rubylinda. And she shows little sign of slowing down. She was just about to earn her master's in reading, and readying herself to take on a Ph.D. in brain research and reading. The hunger hasn't subsided. While her second, "wonderful" husband, their children, and her parents sometimes wonder if she will ever be able to pull herself away from learning more, Rubylinda believes that she will never get enough: "There's always a book under my arm."

In her classroom, Rubylinda finds constant reminders of where she began. There may be a migrant child stuck in a corner because he or she can't speak English, or a student whose anger and pain is deeper than what a six-year-old can endure. "Slowly," she says, "I try to peel away those little pieces of anger one at a time. . . . I pull them out of that corner, and I say 'You will. This is the expectation, and you will rise to the expectation because I will help you rise." Rubylinda knows, better than most, that "all you have to do is want it bad enough." That's something that Rubylinda's mother is discovering as she learns to read. Rubylinda says she's suffered some setbacks and frustrations, but she's been brilliant in her math courses at the community college. She hasn't had it easy.

Education alone might not make you a fortune or bring you fame, but Rubylinda sees that it gives you something very personal and permanent. "I've seen life without education," she says, "and I see what I have now and how blessed I am to have the ability to know, and to reason, and to learn. It's something that goes with me wherever I go, and no one can ever take that away from me." In this light, education isn't just part of the American dream, it's a tool for living the dream every day. Once gained, nothing can take it away.

Curtis J. Aikens Sr.

As Ruby's mother is discovering, learning to read late in life is a long and difficult process. It takes a very committed student and teacher to write a happy ending. For Curtis Aiken, there's no question that the struggle has been worth it.

Curtis puts a face to one of those literacy statistics we hear but sometimes cannot believe: he went through high school and five semesters of college without learning how to read or write, one of millions of Americans who fall through the cracks and keep falling. Curtis believes today that he would have disappeared completely if he hadn't, at age twenty-six, finally asked for help. Now, at age forty-one, he's molded himself into a celebrity chef, with three cookbooks to his name and his own show on the Food Network. Of his literacy tutors, he says, "They didn't change my life, they *saved* my life."

Conyers, Georgia, was a small rural town when Curtis was growing up, but he says his parents always encouraged their children to think beyond the way their lives were then. They were "worldly," Curtis says, in the way they reminded him that "the world didn't end at the boundaries of Georgia." They also wouldn't let their children think that they were poor or disadvantaged in any way: "We knew we weren't rich, but looking back," Curtis says, "we didn't have anything. But we never wanted for anything." Curtis wore clean clothes to church, and will always remember his family's Sunday dinners. That's one of the reasons he decided to become a chef.

As Curtis started his formal education, America was passing through the turbulent era of school desegregation. Although he and his classmates would face tremendous obstacles as black children in formerly all-white schools, Curtis knows that his greatest obstacles were those he erected himself.

In the third grade, Curtis made a decision that would determine the course of his life. As he sat through a parent-teacher conference, he heard his teacher praise him: " 'I just love having your boy in my class,' " Curtis remembers her saying. " 'He's a great kid, he's sweet,' and then I heard a 'but.' And I thought, 'Oh no. What's this. "But he's dumb? He's stupid?" ' " Well, no. She didn't say anything close to that, but she did say that he had some reading trouble, and she thought it would be best for him to repeat the third grade.

"I was shocked. I was floored. I'm thinking to myself, 'Well, I'm not gonna let anyone ever call me dumb or stupid again.' So instead of learning to read, I learned to hide the fact that I couldn't read." Bad choice, as Curtis would find out. Faking it took a good deal more effort than if he had simply asked for help. As he grew older, he felt that if anyone found out his secret, the label "stupid, dumb" would be much bigger and harder to shake. So he dug himself deeper and deeper into a hole.

We've all heard of children graduating from high school, and even going on to college, with little or no reading and writing skills, and most often it is the schools that get blamed. Curtis, however, declines to point a finger, except at himself. Most of his teachers, he feels, were ready to give him a hand if he asked. But they were also completely fooled by what Curtis calls "the tricks of the trade." The trade, in this case, was about conning everyone. "I had two things going for me," the younger Curtis realized. "I remembered stuff—I had pretty much total recall—and I had a likeable personality." He learned he could charm his way out of tough questions before the class. He developed the kind of personality that teachers wanted to believe in. If he was called on to read a passage, they believed him when he said he had a sore throat, and went on to the next kid.

And so it was always the next kid who got the attention. Curtis was passed by. "One of the things I remember thinking about was, if you sound smart, people think you're smart. So I had this great facade of being this smart, confident boy." He says he built his vocabulary and charisma by watching TV and listening to recordings of great black entertainers—Flip Wilson, Richard Pryor, Bill Cosby, Redd Foxx, Sidney Poitier. They used big words, they were likeable, and they projected the confidence that Curtis needed to pull off his scam. And, Curtis adds, "When they really wanted to do the Anglo talk they did it."

Most of his grade school teachers were completely taken. In the fifth grade, however, Curtis met up with a teacher who wouldn't be fooled. So he adjusted his game plan—he started acting up. He realized that being a pain in the neck was also a sure way to be passed over. Once again, he advanced, and went on to high school with no one the wiser. Sadly, Curtis was no wiser himself.

The game changed in high school, with Curtis discovering that a course load heavy on electives and light on academics, coupled with athletics and student government, could bring him a diploma. He could do basic math, he could guess at multiple choice. The only real problems came up when he had to turn in an essay question, and the strategy became one of creating confusion. "I had, and kind of still have, the worst handwriting in the world," Curtis explains. He would "write" a paper that no one could read, expecting the reaction "What the hell is this?" And then he'd pull out the charm: " 'Well, which question are you talking about?' So in the course of a conversation, they'd read the question, and we'd talk about it. 'Well, here's what I'm saying.' " He'd then walk away, with the teacher thinking that he had at least been paying attention in class. Good enough for a D or even a C.

It would have been hard indeed to fail Curtis Aikens: star football player, student council member, winner of a statewide cooking competition (he was the only boy in his home economics class). And now, though he doesn't blame his teachers, he does have some lessons for them. "Now when I talk to teachers," he explains, "I say, listen, it's not just the bad kids that you gotta worry about. Sometimes it's those sugar sweet kids who are having problems too, but they're afraid to talk to you about it because they have the reputation of being a nice kid. That was me. I was that nice kid, who really wanted a teacher to grab him and say, 'What's up?' "

On top of being nice, Curtis was headed for a football scholarship. He remembers a photograph of himself signing his letter of intent to Southern University, ringed by his beaming family. He was supposed to be the first in the family to graduate from college, and he represented their hopes and dreams. Curtis should have been beaming along with them. "But my face just looked like this sheer face of horror: 'Oh, no. Here I go again. Four more years of having to fake this.' "

The ploys of high school were evidently not going to play in college unless he exhibited real pro potential and the administration was forced to let him slide. He barely made it through his first year at Southern, and then transferred to the University of Georgia. He knew he was running, that he couldn't stay too long in one place. Finally, halfway through his sophomore year, he dropped out.

"My dad, he was so heartbroken that I had left college. . . . Everybody thought I was supposed to be a success, but no one knew I couldn't read. Not my mom, not my dad, not my brothers and sisters, not my school.

And I remember, I wanted to say, 'Dad, you know what, your kid can't read, man. I can't read! I'm just faking.' "

The American dream seemingly out of reach, Curtis thought he could settle for a California dream instead. The Golden State's promise of rebirth had strong appeal, and with both San Diego and the San Francisco Bay area tugging on him, he flipped a coin to decide. His fate settled, he headed north and got a job in a grocery store.

Life should have been much easier than it was in school. Curtis says he had little trouble telling the difference between smooth and chunky peanut butter, between 2 percent and nonfat milk. It was all in the packaging. But his manager turned out to be one of the few people he wasn't able to win over, and the two fought constantly. After one particularly bad argument, he went home to plot a new course. When he got there, he did something strange.

"I got a pad and paper like I could write something. I don't know why I took it out, but that's what smart people do. They write down their ideas. This is one of the things I'd learned—that smart people write down their ideas. And the first idea that came to my head was to start a produce company. I wrote the number one down. But I never wrote the idea out. I didn't know how in the world to write that."

His idea was to go into a business that he could run on, as he says, "a handshake and a smile," with a minimum of letters. He'd noticed buyers from restaurants coming in for produce. He could do that. He could selectively pick produce from wholesalers and deliver it to restaurants. He knew little about produce, but he knew plenty about talking to people. The grocers at the produce market were happy to share: "These guys taught me everything about buying mushrooms and onions and tomatoes. It was like being in the college of fruits and vegetables."

His first account bought two hundred pounds of mushrooms, which took three trips to deliver in his Honda Civic. He got the restaurant to pay COD, so he could cover the check he had just written to the produce market. It was all "a hustle," he says, but he was in business. "The whole idea was to keep it simple, kind of straight line. I'd get the order, I'd pick it up, I'd deliver it, I'd collect the money. No overhead. As long as I kept that formula, I did great."

Curtis even developed a microlanguage of produce to help him deal with crates. He learned to recognize that two *P*s meant the box contained apples, two *T*s meant lettuce. An apex followed by a vertex, *AV*, stood in for avocados. Curtis couldn't sound out the letters, but he didn't make many mistakes.

At the wholesale end, he couldn't have run his business without trust. He could pretend to read an invoice but ultimately had to believe that it was right. To pay the wholesalers, he usually had to leave a blank check: "There's no way I could have pulled off my scam if I had to write a check to [for example] Crescent Produce. I couldn't spell 'crescent,' " Curtis recalls, adding, "but every single purveyor had become a friend. They wanted to help me, they wanted me to succeed. They trusted me and I had to trust them."

As Curtis says, he could have strung this tiny enterprise along indefinitely as long as it remained tiny. But businesses have a way of running away from their owners, especially when the owner is someone eager to please. He soon found himself with seven employees, serving seventy-five accounts. The larger players in the business started to take notice. They could afford to play a game of lowball. Curtis couldn't, and more quickly than it had grown, his business crumbled.

At the same time, Curtis was feeling the undertow of his illiteracy. Driving across the country, he found himself stuck on the side of the road, unsure if he was headed in the right direction, simply because he couldn't read the word "Arkansas." In the airport, he found himself staring at the arrival and departure monitors until he got the courage to ask someone where his connecting flight was. The world started to look like a very limited place.

Deep in debt, with all his employees let go, Curtis seldom left his apartment except to service his few remaining accounts or work his part-time job: "You don't date anyone when you don't feel good about yourself. You don't really have friends to socialize with. . . . So a bag of chips and a Coke and my television were my friends." One night, a public service announcement from Literacy Volunteers of America came on that spoke directly to Curtis: "It said, 'Don't be ashamed, don't be embarrassed. We can teach you how to read.' " And, Curtis adds, they knew the secret to getting him to make that call when they said: " 'And we won't tell anybody.' "

His first tutor let him down by leaving the program, but then he was hooked up with a husband-and-wife team he only remembers as "Steve and Ginny." Steve was a student, Ginny a nurse. They were the first people Curtis felt he could tell his secret to: "It was like the world was lifted off my shoulders when I said 'You know what? I can't read, and I want to be able to read.' To be able to say that to somebody and not have them laugh or pick at me or think I was dumb or stupid . . . was my biggest fear, and they didn't do it."

Curtis flew through the literacy training program, in part, he was told, because he already had a large vocabulary. But he could also feel the way his life was about to change, and that, more than anything, impelled him forward. He says he now reads about a book a week and has read maybe close to a thousand books since he learned how it's done. He carries a laptop with him on his frequent trips. He enjoys a laugh every time a conversation turns to books because he can participate without faking it. The Twenty-third Psalm was the first piece he read on his own. He had known the fear, and now he could feel the comfort.

On the surface, Curtis's life changed little. He didn't tell anyone that he had just learned how to read—it was still a stigma. After a few years in New York, working for a market that catered to upscale restaurants, he returned to Georgia. Once back in Conyers, he started a produce company with his family and took French lessons. Before he could read, he says, his confidence was just for show. Now it was brimming over, looking for an outlet.

On vacation in Key West, Curtis visited Hemingway's home. Old Papa didn't exactly become a hero to Curtis, but he did get him to thinking: "I was up in his workshop, by myself . . . and, I swear, this feeling hit me. It was either the ghost of Hemingway or God saying, 'Boy, get your butt back to Conyers and start writing.' " This was only four years after Curtis had learned to read. Back in Conyers, he sold himself as a food columnist to the editor of the local paper. He wrote his first column on how to pick the perfect fig.

As his writing developed, Curtis started to see how he could use it as a platform for more than just his ideas about produce. One week, he wrote about some of the racial tensions in Conyers, and the mail response was overwhelming and positive. Steve and Ginny's gift had become a way for Curtis to move people and get them to think. Now Curtis saw that he could give the way his tutors had: "I then wrote a column about illiteracy and got tons of mail. I didn't tell them *I* hadn't been able to read, but I wrote about all the adults in this country who could not read and the fact that if you're reading this column you can help."

Back in the chapter Making a Name, we met people who thought that the best by-product of having a known name was the chance it gave them to speak out for a cause. Curtis says he made celebrity a goal for no other reason: "Ten, fifteen years later, it sounds so naive, but I said to myself, 'Well, you gotta make yourself a celebrity. I'm *gonna* become a celebrity so when I talk about the fact that I couldn't read . . . maybe these other nonreading adults will say, okay, if he can do it, I can do it too.' "

Curtis knew enough about the game to use his connections. He called an old high school friend who was then in theater in Atlanta, and told her everything: how he fooled her and everyone else, how he finally learned to read and write, and why he wanted to get on television. His tearful confession moved her to call and write every station in Atlanta, and one called back.

It was fall, and a network affiliate could see Curtis doing a short piece on pumpkins for their midday show. "Of all the produce items in the world," Curtis laughs, "I knew the least about these damn pumpkins. But I could read. I could actually go to the library and research pumpkins." His short segment, he says, made the producers "go crazy." He even spiced up his segment with a quote from Henry David Thoreau: "I'd rather have a seat to myself on a pumpkin than be crowded on a velvet cushion."

The personality he had developed to hide his illiteracy made him perfect for television. He was outgoing, funny, somewhat self-effacing. His appearances kept getting longer and went out to larger audiences, especially after he published his first cookbook. His audiences were growing, as was his confidence. But it took years before he could muster the courage to confess his own illiteracy on camera. He finally talked a producer into doing a segment on illiteracy, and he felt he was ready to let the world know that he had learned to read in his twenty-sixth year. He did it on *The Home Show* on ABC, as a guest host with Sarah Purcell.

"We were doing a story on how television can help people learn to read. It was about using closed captioning. And I actually misread the

TelePrompTer. On live television. I actually asked Sarah Purcell a word on TV. . . . I wasn't even thinking about the fact that I asked until two or three seconds after I did it. I broke down and started crying on national TV." There was nothing left to hide, and no way to hide it: "The whole thing just blew up."

Curtis thought he had really screwed up, that no one would listen to him, that his television career was over, and that if the show had reached any illiterate adults, they would only be more convinced to hide their problem. But the opposite was true. It's been said, and I agree, that at its very best, nothing can top television. No other medium has its potential for immediacy. Curtis's "screwup" had been one of those moments where television was at its best, where everything was real. The phones lit up, at the station and at literacy centers across the country. "It was a great day for literacy," Curtis concludes, without a hint of embarrassment or regret. Or even self-effacement.

His story finished, the TV chef climbs up on his soapbox. The only reason he wanted to share all of this is because he has a cause: "Illiteracy is a problem that all of America can unite around. It doesn't know race, it doesn't know money, it doesn't know boundaries. This is one thing we can all get together on." That cause fully and completely contains Curtis's version of the American dream: "I don't get bored anymore, because I can read. I don't get lonely anymore, because I can read. I'm never out of friends anymore, because I can read. But I'm still trying to obtain the American dream, because I want to give everybody the ability to read. I know that sounds hokey, but there it is."

Trish Millines Dziko

Curtis Aikens has a Web site, of course. I can't see anyone raising their eyebrows over the fact that a successful TV chef has a Web site. Of course he has a laptop. Such are the times. Curtis's embrace of technology underscores not only how far he has come since he learned to read but also just how pervasively high-tech we've become.

That's all well and good for those who have the skills and access, but it also means that those who don't will be left even further behind. The digital divide is on a different order of magnitude from education gaps

America has experienced in the past. Like traditional literacy, technological literacy opens doors and worlds beyond the immediate application of the skill. But technology, unlike written language, changes dramatically every few years. Those who don't learn and learn young are likely fated to forever play catch-up. The have-nots are faced with a learning curve that becomes steeper every day they remain outside the gates.

As information-loaded wires spread out to touch every industry, every career, every opportunity, the chances at an American dream for those without technology skills diminish. When Technology Access Foundation executive director and cofounder Trish Dziko attended college in the 1970s, education in information technology was a choice, not a necessity. "I could have chosen any career," she says. "But to kids coming up these days, it's like reading and writing. You *have* to know it."

Trish sees the digital divide in stark terms, one of the reasons she left a millionaire-track job to found her nonprofit academy for inner-city youth. For Trish, it's a simple matter of: "Fix it now, or deal with it later. Fix the schools, fix community agencies now, or build more jails later. That's how it is. Teach kids how to innovate and be independent now, or stifle innovation later." In her view, a DSL line to an inner-city school is a lifeline—not just for the students who will use it, but also for the corporations, public service agencies, and citizens of all races and classes who will ultimately benefit.

Four years ago, Trish decided she would no longer wait for the day that information technology was standard in the public schools. She decided she would no longer wait for IT companies to reach out to minorities. Her Microsoft stock options were ripe, and the time was right. Trish turned her small fortune and expertise toward children who needed, desperately, the lessons she got in college. For her, the decision to leave was what they call a no-brainer.

Growing up, Trish was taught by her mother that life "was all about making life better for somebody else." Her mother cleaned houses for a living and took in three of Trish's cousins in addition to raising her daughter. She saved for Trish's education and bought the family a house, yet always seemed to have money and time left over for the church. "It seemed that somebody was always knocking on the door because they needed help with something, or there was always something going on with the church—fish fries, baking. That was the lesson that my mother taught—that you got to help each other. So this is how I grew up. You never really think about it, you just do it."

Growing up in the New Jersey coastal town of Belmar, Trish saw that "all the rich people were white, and all the poor and lower-middle-class people were black, and that's just the way things were." The longstanding American divide of the color line separated the part of town where Trish and her mother lived and that part where her mother worked. There may have been a gap, but Trish's mother saw education as the bridge: "It was always drummed into my head that I was going to go to college. I was going to do something."

Only once, in Trish's recollection, did she consider another path. When she was thirteen, she says, "I pooh-poohed college. I really don't know why." Just like Rubylinda Zickafoose's parents, Trish's mom pretended to take it in stride. And just like Ruby's parents, Trish's mom knew what to do: she put her on the job. "She just let me say my little spiel, and . . . by that summer, she had me cleaning toilets and scrubbing floors with her. That was sort of her message to me that this is not what I want to do." Now that she's older, Trish is happy to say that "it worked."

Trish applied herself academically and athletically, and got a basketball scholarship to nearby Monmouth College (now Monmouth University). She says she was the first woman to get a full scholarship to this institution. But just months before Trish graduated from high school, her mother died of cancer. Trish got through living on her mother's savings and her dreams for her daughter. She says she also got extraordinary support from her basketball coach.

Trish had always been a gifted math student. She preferred to apply mathematics rather than study it in the abstract. Besides, she knew that she would need to start a career the moment she left. By fate—a conflict between basketball practice and the electronic engineering lab classes she wanted to take—she landed in the computer science department.

This was the mid-1970s, long before programmers were writing code for Windows and the Internet. Trish never even saw a PC until 1982, when she was well into her career. It was all about the command line and the mainframe, for end users as well as programmers and testers. And there were no promises of great wealth after graduation—just a good job. But Trish loved it and still does: "You know, it's pretty cool when you figure these things out. I like that, the way you can do things different ways and get the same result. . . . So I just gravitated toward that kind of stuff." Trish was never ashamed to call herself a "geek," but she didn't just sit in front of her screen—the problem-solving aspect that drew her in led her to also immerse herself in all the logic courses the philosophy department had to offer.

After graduating in 1979, Trish started with a military contracting firm, testing software on radar systems. Today she calls it her "affirmative action job." After discovering that a white woman in a similar position, but with no college technology training, had been hired at ten thousand dollars a year more than Trish, she started to look around and ask questions. Turns out, she says, all the minorities at the company were making less than their white counterparts. "That's when I realized okay, affirmative action. They needed to hire me." Nevertheless, her attitude at the time was: "So that's fine. I'll go ahead and do my job." Seven months later, she found something else and moved to Tucson.

This second job wasn't much better, and so she moved on to San Francisco, "without a job, like a fool, in the middle of the recession." For six months, Trish lived out of her car while looking for the next thing. When she found it, she got her first exposure to the personal computer, the Internet and bulletin board systems, and Unix, the operating system of choice for "geeks" like Trish. It was still extremely difficult for a black woman to gain entry into a field dominated by young white males, but she believed she was building skills that could get her past that.

In 1985 she moved to Seattle, "again without a job." It wasn't until she arrived that she first heard the name "Microsoft." They were a small company over the hill, known as the "velvet sweatshop." They produced something called DOS, a system Trish found really limiting when compared to Unix. When Trish moved out of a management role at a small firm that was losing money, she became an independent contractor and bagged Microsoft as a client. She started working for them full-time in 1990, when Windows was still just a glimmer in Bill Gates's eye.

This was obviously the place to be. "We were there," Trish says, "to make something happen that nobody else had made happen before." The culture was like nothing she had experienced before. "When you go to Microsoft, the assumption is not that you know everything," Trish explains, "but that you'll figure it out." For Trish, her new job was a great fit; she says today that she "learned more in those eight and a half years at that one place than I had in my whole career." And, as we all know, it wasn't just Trish's career that was changing. She was at Microsoft as the whole "technology revolution" was really taking hold. "How can you beat that?" she asks.

Well, one way to beat even that would be to pile stock options on top. "When they were first giving out stock options," Trish remembers, "they were giving them out like you wouldn't believe." Trish knew that they would be worth something but says that she and her colleagues had no idea they would wind up being worth so much. "The first time I vested, and I looked [at the stock price], I thought, 'Wow, I have that much?' And that was just a quarter of my options!" Not long afterward, Trish realized she could afford to leave.

For her entire career, Trish had been forced to work within a culture that she believes has difficulty with diversity. "I'm not saying that [people I've worked with] were racist, I'm just saying that, you socialize with people that are more like you, and you hire people who are more like you. That's just sort of human nature." The information technology industry *is* heavily populated by young white men, a trend that was even more marked at its beginnings. Microsoft tried to deal with this homogenous culture by establishing a diversity department, and Trish took the post of senior diversity administrator. Trish established the group Blacks at Microsoft with the intention of lessening the culture shock she felt was inevitable. But she ultimately found that change is hard, especially when the problem can't be attributed to blatant racism, sexism, or ageism. "They don't want to change, because why should they? They're comfortable, and they're doing things they want to do."

Trish's reaction, throughout her career, was to try harder, move ahead, and always go further than halfway. The strategy served her well, career-wise, but she couldn't do it forever: "I got tired of adapting. I got sick of it." She also realized, as she saw more minorities and women enter the field, that their schooling and work experience had ill-prepared them for the culture shock they would face. To change the culture, more minorities and women would have to get involved. The only way to get them involved was to get them young.

Trish was walking in a Seattle park with her partner Jill Hull, a social worker by training who was struggling with the way public schools warehoused kids with "behavior problems" in classes where no learning took place. The previous summer, Trish had taken a group of these junior high students with her to Microsoft and had seen a change take place: "I mean, these kids were rowdy. I got them on the shuttle, and I'm thinking, 'Oh my God. What am I doing?' " She brought them into the testing department, where six high school interns were hard at work. "And you did not hear a peep. They were *so* interested in what was going on. . . . This incredibly complicated stuff really grabs their attention. And they have fun with it." As they remembered this outing, as they talked about what social services were already available, they saw a need, an opportunity, and a chance at more fulfilling lives.

Looking back, Trish reflects that the walk in the park was where the idea for her Technology Access Foundation (TAF) first took root. TAF opened its doors in fall 1996, with backing that came mostly out of Trish's pockets. Today, TAF is getting grants from companies and foundations like Intel, Adobe Systems, UPS, The Kellogg Foundation, and notably, Microsoft and the William Gates II Foundation.

Instead of building the organization from the ground up, Trish and Jill offered to run a consortium for social service agencies already involved in the community. The agencies responded enthusiastically to their core ideas: using technology to get kids interested in school, getting parents into the act, and placing students from inner-city schools in valuable internships around Seattle.

The first order of business, Trish says, was to get the internship program started. This part of the plan wouldn't demand much infrastructure, would give TAF a presence in the business community, and would give students an immediate reward. "It was a success the first year," Trish beams. "You know, we had no idea what we were doing, when I think about it. But we made it all up along the way. . . . Now we have employers calling *us* up. That's pretty cool."

TAF interns have worked at companies like Microsoft, Alaska Airlines, the Seattle *Times,* UPS, Real Networks, and Go.com. Before they go in for the summer, they get extensive training at TAF during the school year, starting with the most basic technical skill: problem solving. Because of schools where, as Trish puts it, "everything is done for them," a lot of the teenagers TAF sees "don't know how to solve problems. . . . We make them think for themselves, we make them responsible for themselves."

Most of TAF's students come from schools with large minority populations, and so the diversity training in TAF's internship program is just as important. To Trish, the results are both amazing and amusing: "We talk to them all year. Right from the beginning I tell them why we started this, I tell them what the environment is like, and they hear it from the volunteers." The students might hear the message but tend to wonder how different it could really be. "The first week of employment—to a kid—we get phone calls." Trish laughs and lowers her voice to a whisper to quote her students: " 'There are no black people here!' Well, what do you think we've been telling you this whole time?"

She also reminds her charges "that's what we're trying to change, and you're the ones who are going to make the change, because there's going to be so many of you out there, by the time you're an adult, you're not even going to notice.' "

The diversity training runs both ways. Trish changed her career in part because she got tired of being the only one who would adapt. Employers who take on TAF students have to send their managers to a day of diversity training. They have to understand that while they can expect a lot from these students, many of them are, in Trish's words, "scared to death being in the middle of corporate America." Even as they get past that fear, there are small and large cultural differences employers need to understand. Trish offers an example: "If you expect the kids to call you by your first name, you might have a hard time, because there's this whole respect thing. They're going to want to call you Mr. or Ms. So-and-so." These little efforts toward understanding can make a world of difference, according to Trish, in getting both student and employer past their differences. That done, they can get down to work.

And these kids really do work. Trish says that one employer just asked a student to come back for a second summer, a girl who once had some problems keeping up her grades in school. "They're trying to get their dibs on this kid now, right? Because they're worried that some other employer is going to take her. It's pretty funny." Summer of 1999 contained a milestone for TAF—their first intern who was offered twenty dollars an hour. Trish is certain that two of her students, both girls, will be offered salaries of fifty thousand or more when they graduate from high school. "I'm already talking to their parents," she says, "about what they're going to do about this."

This could become an ongoing conundrum. Trish wants all her students to go to college, but she can't send them down the hall to scrub toilets if they tell her they don't want to go, as Trish's mother did to her. Not when these kids are being drafted like star athletes.

"I worry about their patience," she admits. But the first student to break the twenty-dollar mark made what Trish thinks is the right choice: "We were all holding our breath that he would go to school. And he's at the University of Washington. We were like 'Pheeew.' " To these kids, making money is a very big deal. A lot of their public school classmates don't have jobs or work at minimum wage. "You know, everybody wants to 'live large.' . . . We try to tell them that money's not the be-all and end-all, that getting the college experience is important, even if they just go to a two-year school."

TAF backs up that message with a promise. If you don't keep your grades up in school, no matter how well you do in your internship, you get one chance, then you're out. "We have a lot of leverage here," Trish says. "This is not a school, we don't have to train you. And that *really* changes things, because you always have the one or two kids who want to test you. And I don't have a problem making an example of them." This doesn't happen very often, especially now that word has gotten around and TAF is suddenly the place to be after classes let out. "I'd say seventy-five percent of the kids came because they heard from other kids who were in the program. So it's become a 'cool' thing. Which is what I really wanted."

Some of Trish's newer students aren't yet of the age where being cool is a concern. TAF's TechStart program uses the computer as a tool to develop problem solving and communication skills for children as young as two. Working through community agencies and schools, TAF tries to provide exposure to equipment that, at least in middle-class homes, is becoming as common as the television. She and her staff believe that you can't get them started too young.

Trish's own children might disagree. "My two-year-old could care less about the computer, and I have a feeling that the rest will follow! I'm going to be the one with the kids that never touch a computer, great!" She's tried to draw her in using a Winnie-the-Pooh CD-ROM but says her daughter "just looks and then two minutes later she's just sort of looking around the room for something else to do." Trish and her partner have three children, and Trish, as much as she loves what she's doing, is feeling their pull. "I'm gonna be out of here before I'm fifty and hang out with my kids. . . . I'll probably always be president of the corporation, but not in terms of day-to-day hands-on policy." She will stay long enough to see TAF move to a new campus, which they hope to build near their current location in southeast Seattle. "But then," she concludes with the confident smile of someone who knows she's made a difference, "I'm out of here."

Karen Altland

Trish Dziko's philosophy of "get 'em while they're young" is clearly the ideal. Everyone should get the same chance from an early age, when their dreams are still strong and pure. And our educators and institutions would, in a perfect world, meet them more than halfway to ensure that their youthful dreams aren't undermined by their youthful errors.

Sometimes, when I hear the story of someone like Karen Altland, I can believe that while we aren't living in a perfect world, we may be closer than we think. Karen knows that we don't always get 'em young, but she also knows that education means dreams don't have to die.

Karen made time for an interview on a Sunday, one of the few Sundays she wasn't plunging deep into her work. Typically, she puts in a sixteen-hour day at the Academy of Medical Arts and Business in Harrisburg, Pennsylvania, where for nine years she's worked as a medical assistant instructor. Long before classes start in the morning, long after they finish in the afternoon, she's meeting privately with students, giving additional classes to students who need to make one up, or giving them extra practice with procedures or tests in the lab. "I'm very dedicated to my job," she points out, as if it needed pointing out. "Very dedicated. But it really doesn't seem like a job when you're enjoying your work like that."

Some great teachers, Rubylinda Zickafoose for example, always knew they wanted to teach. While it's hard to pinpoint a reason for dedication like hers, it probably has something to do with her living out a lifelong dream. Other teachers are great because they've been there. They see their own past in the faces of the students they stand before. Their determination comes from the desire to pave a way for them, just as it was once paved in their own lives. Karen falls into this category—she never suspected she would ever have the chance to do what she does today until she got her first chance at higher education.

"If someone had told me twenty years ago that I would be doing this, I'd have said, 'Yeah, right,' " Karen says, laughing. Twenty years ago, she was certain that dreams were something achieved by other people. Her own dreams of entering the medical field, perhaps as a nurse, had enjoyed only a brief moment in the sun before a hard reality set in. Karen was raised by a factory worker and a roofer, and was always aware that the family was struggling. The training needed to become a nurse seemed far beyond their means.

"The financial bill on my mother's part didn't seem possible" for Karen to take any sort of medical training, she says. "She was working to support three children. It was kind of hard. She worked a lot of hours, and as a matter of fact, I found myself taking care of the younger ones myself at a very young age. So it was a little rough." But the same reasons behind her dreams of a career in medicine made her good at answering her family's call and got her through. "I've always been the type of person who cares for other people, their feelings, and kind of takes charge of things . . . and like I said, from a very young age. I've always enjoyed taking care of other people."

Karen, now in her forties, remembers her neighborhood in York, Pennsylvania, as a tight-knit working-class community, a place she has trouble recognizing when she passes through today. "Now it's not so nice, but then it was. I go down through there now, oh my gosh, things have changed so much." While she doesn't remember her community as a violent place, violence did overtake her brother when he was fifteen. "He got into a fight somewhere in York, and the other guy pulled out a knife," she recalls. "It was just an argument, but this guy pulled out a knife and stabbed him. And there he was, fifteen years old and then gone. His whole life was taken away from him. Pretty useless."

Watching a close family member die senselessly, seeing her mother go through a series of medical and emotional problems following the murder, deepened Karen's desire to care for others as a profession: "It was something that really, really stuck by me; I was so young that it just stuck with me." But even as her desire to enter this field deepened, she saw even more clearly that it was unlikely. She was helping raise her baby sister, and she saw her mom's situation worsen. "It seemed like I matured nine years," she recalls. "It felt like I was twenty." And, to raise this point yet again, as Jacquelyn Mitchard said back in our chapter on fame, for many of us, growing up means giving up.

You can learn a lot from growing up fast. Karen learned that she could rely on herself. She learned that others could safely rely on her. But when she was sixteen, she learned that there's such a thing as growing up too fast. "To be honest," she says, pausing to clear her throat, "I got pregnant. I got married at a very young age. By the time I was twenty-one, I found myself with three children." Although she went back to get her GED, Karen resigned herself completely to the life her mother had known—as a factory worker.

"At that point, to be honest with you," Karen says, "I didn't think my life was going anywhere. I said, 'Oh my gosh, I'm going to do this for the rest of my life.' " The work she had to do, the treatment she received from this particular factory, seemed to ensure that the rest of her life would be trying, frustrating, and monotonous. Karen fed shoes through a machine, one after the other. "You know the seam you have in the back of your shoe? I ran that through the machine and it held them together." The work had to be done quickly, and the materials were heavy. And her compensation was tied to her efficiency. "I worked piece rate. So toward the end of the week, you got a little tired, but you knew . . . that's what your paycheck depended on. There were many days I dragged myself in to work and I couldn't keep my head up—I had the flu or whatever. It's real hard when your livelihood depends on going to work for one day. That is hard."

Hard on her, hard on her kids. Karen remembers one day when her daughter had a fever of 104, but her employer told her that wasn't enough of an excuse to let her part of the assembly line go shorthanded. "So here I am dragging my youngest one to a baby-sitter, which I feel terrible about. [The work] is just real rough. They'd come up to you and say 'If you don't get this out by the end of the day, we'll fire you.' It was real bad. That piece rate stuff kills you."

Karen did her best to keep her job from killing her outright for twenty years, but all the while she felt like her life was at a dead end. Except for the raising of her children, there was little meaning to pushing through each day. She might still be at that job, she realizes, if her place of employment hadn't gone the way of so many other garment factories in the United States. Luckily, this one offered a contribution to job retraining as part of a severance package to their employees. Karen was stunned that she suddenly had the chance to go back to school this late in life, but the first thing that came to mind was that original dream of working in medicine: "It was always in there," she notes. It just took the offer of an education to bring it out.

The nature of the medical field had changed since Karen originally dreamed of working as a nurse. As she researched her options, she found a career that would put her in the field quickly, one that would bring her into contact with patients, giving her a real chance to "take care of other people." Medical assistants have long been part of the support system for doctors, but as managed care revamps our health system, we can expect to see more medical assistants, and we will expect more from them. According to the Bureau of Labor Statistics, medical assistants are in one of the top ten fastest-growing professions as projected for the years 1998–2008. Of all the professions in health care, only home nursing aides are expected to grow as quickly.

Medical assistants are trained generalists. They are expected to wear the hat of a front-office clerk but also draw blood, take histories, perform electrocardiograms, change dressings, and remove sutures. They aren't at the level of physician assistants, who help diagnose and treat, but they are still an increasingly important mainstay at doctors' offices, hospitals, and all manner of facilities in between. Many medical assistants are certified and are required to pass an exam every five years, part of an ongoing standardization of the profession. For many, it's a stop on the way to becoming a physician assistant or a registered nurse. But for Karen, who wanted to work in medicine but couldn't afford the long work toward a medical degree, the position looked perfect.

The only problem, as she saw it at the time, was that she would have to go back to school. "I'll be honest with you," she says, "when I first came to school, I was terrified. It had been a while, and since I had two more children—I had five altogether—and I had gone through divorce, and through the years it was ups and downs the whole time." Her youngest child was a year old, the school was over an hour away, and the program was intensive.

Karen says she'd studied hard in high school, but she'd never experienced anything like this nine-month crash course designed to give the broadest view possible of the medical world. The anatomy courses were in-depth, and the first time she had to draw blood from a fellow student she thought she would faint. To this day she doesn't think she would have made it if it weren't for the home front. "I had a lot of support from my husband, which really made things easier. You gotta have someone to back you up." Her children were astounded—"The older ones were like, 'Mom, I can't believe you're doing this' "—but ultimately proud that she was taking steps to go from an unskilled factory worker to a trained and certified professional.

As she attended classes, Karen noticed how similar her classmates were to her. They were young and old, male and female, white and black, but more than a few were people who had "come from really rough lives and decided to change their lives around." Karen graduated in 1992 from the Academy of Medical Arts and Business with a 4.0 grade point average. She'd done it, and on a grand scale.

But even that difficult time wasn't as tough as the tiny bit of self-doubt that crept in as she finished her studies. "The hardest part—and this was very intimidating—the hardest part for me was 'Okay, I went through school. Now, can I really do this? Can I apply everything?' " Her course work was immediately followed by an internship, a test that even a 4.0 student might face with uncertainty.

"My first day on the job, I was ready to walk off. I was real nervous: I was so nervous I couldn't even get a blood pressure, because all I could hear was my own heartbeat in my ears. . . . It's very hectic in there. You have to be very, very careful as far as documentation—very in-depth. . . . It's a whole different ball game from sitting in school all day. You're actually doing it." On her first day, she says, she saw just about everything she'd been trained to handle. It was a busy family practice, so she did glucose testing, drew blood, removed sutures, did pap smears, and assisted with minor surgery. "It was real hard." At the end of the day, she thought to herself, "I don't want to come back here again."

So what kept her going back? "I wanted this. I thought, 'You made it through school, you can do this.' " In about two weeks, she continues, she felt she knew the routine. She felt she was firmly in a new career.

Karen went back to York to take her first job, with a Planned Parent-hood clinic. She found that kids in her old community were now growing up even faster than she had. She drew blood from young children's arms to test for HIV infection. She saw a deep and dangerous ignorance about pregnancy and venereal disease among boys, girls, men, and women who "just don't know about what unprotected intercourse can do." A "real eye-opener," she calls it. "A lot of them had a very poor home life. They were looking for love in all the wrong places, if you know what I'm saying. A lot of times sex was the only way for companionship . . . and I'm not talking about fifteen, sixteen. I'm talking about eleven- and twelve-year-olds. It's just incredible." The worst part of the job, she remembers, was when she had to inform some of these kids that they had an incurable and possibly fatal disease—that their lives were forever changed.

The experience made an impression. Karen continues to volunteer for Planned Parenthood. She reminds her students—all past high school age, some in middle age—that these days unprotected sex is nothing more than Russian roulette.

After working at Planned Parenthood for almost four years, Karen got a call from her alma mater. They offered her a part-time teaching job, which became a full-time job after a year. Where she had once been intimidated—first by going back to school, then by starting a new job— here she had only unbridled enthusiasm. "I thought, from a lot of my experiences," she points out, "I'd be able to really help some of these kids."

In her classroom she found a bag as mixed as the one she'd dropped into years before. There were the eighteen-year-olds, fresh faced and struggling to keep up with a steep learning curve that barely resembled what they'd gone through in public school. Often they find encouragement only from their teacher: "A lot of the students have had no family support. Ever. Everything has been negative in their lives. These are the ones I find I need to really motivate." Sometimes they come to her with stories from home, stories of parents who told them they're just too stupid to finish the course or work in the medical field. "No," Karen tells them, "you're here. You've taken the first step. If you want this, you can do it, but you've got to want it."

Then there were the returning students, as old as fifty, who'd been through layoffs, divorces, or poverty. "That's why I can relate to a lot of my students," Karen says, "because I've been there, and I know it's rough. Trying to go back while having children, trying to go to school and work part-time. My heart just goes out to them because it's so hard."

Karen never tells her students they're going to have it easy, but she can confidently tell them that there will be a reward: "Three-quarters of my students get employed as soon as they go out," she avows. Everything she teaches them counts for something in the real world, every minute they're in class is just as important as the last. That's why, when a student misses a day, Karen is on the phone as soon as possible. Whether they were absent because they had to put in extra time at work or because they had to take care of a sick child, they always get a chance to make it up. And that's why Karen's days are so long—some of these extra classes have to be squeezed into a slot at 6 A.M. But she claims she's never had to drag herself out of bed to make one of these appointments. "When I get up in the morning, it's not one of these jobs where I don't know if I want to go in today. I can't wait to get there to teach. It's just so rewarding."

A few years after Karen fully committed to teaching, the Academy of Medical Arts and Business expanded their medical assisting course to offer an associate's degree. Karen waded into this program, adding the course work to her teaching responsibilities and volunteer work. She's been hard to stop ever since. Additional certification as a Red Cross instructor now allows her to teach first aid. She continues to take the state medical assistant exam, even though she doesn't need that certification these days: "I kind of like to know what they're asking the students." Her peers have definitely noticed—Karen's landed awards from two trade associations in her field and was twice voted instructor of the year at her school, an award based on her students' evaluations.

These awards are welcome but are little compared to the hugs from returning students who go on to thank her for being so hard on them. Little also when compared to the letters she gets from doctors praising her former students' work. Even less when compared to the feeling she gets after hearing about a student who has gone on to become a registered nurse or physician assistant. She really had no idea, before she started teaching, how rewarding a career could be—that she could touch the lives of over 1,500 students in direct and tangible ways. "When I was in the shoe factory," she says, "I never had a boss come up to me and say, 'Nice job today.'" Now it comes from all quarters, and from her husband and kids, who saw how tough it once was. "It's a whole new world," says Karen.

Higher education is more than the vaunted four-year colleges and universities that were once only for the wealthy and lucky. We might forget that we can find real education, real educators, and real opportunity in vocational and community colleges. Dreams are made possible here too, and to a more diverse crowd. Both are needed, both are valuable parts of our educational system, but Karen has no doubt about where she would rather teach. "A lot of the other colleges, the classrooms are huge—not to say anything bad about colleges because colleges are wonderful—but a lot of the times a lot of the professors don't even know the students' names. You're more or less a number." That may work for some, but Karen knows her students are often coming from lives where no one cared, and she insists that their education should be the opposite.

"I teach my students the way I teach my children," Karen concludes, "from the heart. I want them to know that I care. . . . I want them all to succeed. I read a phrase somewhere, sometime, and it really stuck in my head. 'No one cares how much you know until they know how much you care.' " In American dreams, nothing matters more in the beginning than having a mentor who cares. Once we have someone who can open our eyes, we gain the means to open countless doors.

INNOVATION
PIONEERING DREAMS

I like the dreams of the future better than the history of the past.
—Thomas Jefferson

𝒯HE man who had written the Declaration of Independence wrote the words above in a letter. It's just a small part of one of the richest collections of correspondence in our history, between Jefferson and John Adams, but it speaks volumes about our national spirit.

The letter dates from 1816, a year when the torch of leadership was passed from the founding generation to the long line of heirs to their dream of a democratic republic. As former presidents, Adams and Jefferson had themselves been the first elected successors to George Washington; now they were aging revolutionaries, watching an America that was no longer guided by their hands move from unsteady infancy to uncertain youth. We know from their letters to each other that they did not like everything they saw, and even harbored some deep fears. Together with their fellow Founding Fathers, they shared a proud history and doubts about the future of their experiment. And yet Jefferson cast his lot firmly with what lay ahead.

It was, then and now, the American way. Some of our forebears, years ago, looked across the Atlantic to a New World. And the Louisiana Purchase, Jefferson's signal presidential achievement, put before our young nation the west that forged the pioneer ethos. In our gauzy recollections of an idealized past, we sometimes forget that, in America, nostalgia is something we have developed only recently. When we take a clear look back, we see a people determinedly looking ahead, a nation of relentless trailblazers and horizon gazers. It is in our blood, from the tenth-generation *Mayflower* descendant to yesterday's Pacific Rim immigrant.

A new continent demanded innovation from the start. The first American inventions were adaptations of agricultural equipment, as Europeans adapted to an environment that the Native Americans knew from long experience. Over time, as goes the bittersweet American story, we came to adapt the environment to us.

But our forward-looking ways are more than a reaction to our natural surroundings. They spring just as much, I think, from the unique circumstances of our nation's birth. After all, far from tracing its history back to the mists of time, America was conceived by a conscious act and not all that long ago in a historical sense.

Of course, innovation takes place in small nations, in those with long histories, and even under totalitarian rule. But nowhere, it seems, do so many national attributes encourage it as in America—something that's been borne out in the extraordinary burst of pioneering energy that has led so many to call the twentieth century the American Century.

The world got its first widespread glimpse of this during World War II, in which the American GI came to be renowned for his battlefield, seat-of-the-pants ingenuity. Historians have pointed out that a sense of democratic entitlement no doubt contributed to even the lowest-ranked grunt's sense that his opinion and ideas mattered.

The same sensibility has reigned in peace. It has given rise to such diverse American achievements as jazz, the polio vaccine, and the mass production of the automobile. It has given us moving pictures and the explosion of communications that, among other outcomes, allows people like me to report what is going on in our world to an audience of once-unimaginable size and geographic diversity.

This is not to say that all this change has been unqualifiedly for the better. But if technology has been a modern mixed blessing, it, like our Constitution, is rooted in noble, Enlightenment ideals. Long before the problems of toxic waste and urban sprawl, the revolutionary generation believed that the same rational approach that they brought to their great democratic experiment would let them conquer the problems that so bewildered their age. Probably no one personified this drive more than Benjamin Franklin, the first American to become a scientist of world renown and the secular patron saint of American innovation. I wanted to gather the stories of some of the men and women who walk in his footsteps today.

I found one of his direct heirs in George Hatsopolous. Like Franklin, this Greek immigrant made breakthroughs by experimenting with electricity. And by taking the American inventor Thomas Edison as his personal role model, he has turned his genius into a great business success as well.

At least to this writer's way of thinking, space exploration is the ultimate pioneering act. Reporting on the triumphs of our space program has not only brought me some of my greatest professional thrills but also some of my proudest moments as an American. In astronaut Eileen Collins, I found someone who has pushed the frontiers of both sky and our ideas about the respective roles of men and women.

This chapter begins with Thomas Jefferson, and it ends too with a man whose work lies in the tradition of the Genius of Monticello. Though a formally trained scientist himself, Shawn Carlson has devoted his life to encouraging the endeavors of amateur scientists. Two hundred years ago, learned people such as Jefferson faced a world much more receptive to scientific work that did not have its origins in the academy. By opening the realm of discovery to anyone with a good idea and the drive to pursue it, Shawn is doing his part to keep this American dream true to its democratic roots.

As Jefferson looked to the future, he could not have hoped for more.

George N. Hatsopolous

"Creating is probably life's biggest reward," says George Hatsopolous, "whether you create a family, you create an invention, or you create a technology or theory." George's statement goes right to the heart of what motivates so many of the people in these pages—the entrepreneurs who create companies, the parents who create families, the philanthropists who create opportunities. It isn't so much an American urge but a human one—no matter where we start, no matter how far we go, the desire to build something that will outlive us is strong indeed.

In the popular imagination, at least, Thomas Edison stands as the quintessential inventor, a man who left behind a legacy that drove the twentieth century. What he could not have known is that he also switched on a light in the mind of a young boy growing up in Greece in the 1930s. George was six years old when he took the Wizard of Menlo Park as his role model, not only for his lightbulb and phonograph but for the business he built in General Electric. George took it as his model of success and endurance.

"As a teenager in high school," George continues, "I read more about Thomas Edison and his accomplishments. I remember when the war broke out and the Germans occupied Greece, I was thinking not only what kind of organization I wanted to create, but also *where* to create it. Where would be the most fertile ground to do that. And I had concluded quite distinctly that I wanted to come to the United States."

Getting George's story doesn't take much reportorial digging. He responds to more than one question with the warning, "That's a long story, but if you have the time . . ." We do. I love a good story, and George's are better than most, humbly and engagingly told. George is a man who built a business that had sales of four billion dollars when he retired as CEO in 1999 and became chairman emeritus. His company has been responsible for hundreds of patents and has spun off twenty-four publicly owned companies. There's no doubting his razor-sharp business sense, but his eccentric, inventor's sparkle makes it clear that he is about much more than empire building and bottom lines.

George has always been a dreamer. Not a mad scientist, but a dreamer—though his actions during the Nazi occupation qualify as at least verging on crazy. The Germans had come into people's homes and sealed all radio dials to the German station only. "There was no communication with the outside world," George remembers. "We didn't know who was winning, what was happening." There were frequent inspections to check if seals had been broken. If they had, then the entire household was sent to a concentration camp. "So I got the idea," George says, "maybe I would build some illegal radios and sell them to friends of the family."

He couldn't buy the components, so he scoured the junkyards for capacitors, inductors, resistors, and vacuum tubes. In the laboratory he'd set up in his garage, he assembled receivers and sold them by very quiet word of mouth. Eventually, the resistance found out and asked him to build a few transmitters as well. "And that was another customer," George says calmly.

All this went on unknown not only to his parents—"My father didn't find out until after the war ended, and he nearly killed me"—but also to the Germans stationed in the same house. "They took the living room and the dining room and left us our bedrooms. One army officer would come down to visit me and say, 'What are you doing?' And I said, 'Well, I'm doing various odd things in electronics.' " And that was the end of that conversation.

In George's mind, this encounter didn't even count as a close call. "It's funny," he remembers with a laugh, but he found this "a wonderful time for a fourteen-year-old. A lot of excitement. Sure, there was no food, but that was secondary. Of course, all the burden was on the older people, but for me it was fun . . . terrific fun." George was also quite taken with the way the stratified Greek society was leveled by the war, with everyone in the same boat and on the same forced diet. His parents invited the trash collector and the street cleaner to their parties, something this well-off family would never consider doing before. He and a friend remarked on this, and took guesses at how long it would take after the war for everyone to go back to normal. "Well, it may take a year," speculated his friend. "In reality," George says with some disappointment, "it took two weeks."

George's extended family had its share of scientists, many of whom were professors at the Athens Polytechnic Institute, Greece's premier university. Two of George's uncles, in fact, had served as president of the Polytechnic, so his family was delighted that George had taken the initiative of setting up a laboratory in the garage, even though they didn't know what he was doing in there. They believed that he would be the third family member to sit in the president's chair at the Polytechnic. But George had other plans. He wanted to live and work in the "country of innovations and inventions."

After the war, he did indeed attend Athens Polytechnic, but he kept his long-range plans to himself. He intended to graduate from their five-year program in mechanical and electrical engineering and then pursue his Ph.D. in electrical engineering in the States. But three years into his studies, he found out about a scholarship for Greeks who wanted to finish their degree in the United States that would cover his trip, food, and tuition—everything. There were only three scholarships available, but George, already brimming over with ideas and obvious native intelligence, was a shoo-in.

George was awarded the scholarship, but he still had to face his family's approbation. "All my friends and family," George explains, "thought I was always seeing things with rosy glasses." George was expected to study in France or Germany, as his uncles had. "They didn't have a very high opinion of the intellectual level [in the United States], but I did. I mean, I was really in love with this country." The first thing he did when he landed in New York in 1948 was to have his picture taken standing under a Broadway street sign. He sent it back to his friends—he had landed in the New World.

George found nothing but open arms at MIT, an academic community that had seen very few Europeans during the war. Professors and students "leaned backward," George says, to the point where he began to wonder if he was being given an unfair advantage. And as he went to class, worked in the labs, and socialized, he found reminders everywhere that he was in a very different society from the one he had known in Europe.

These weren't just the casual observations of a student in an unfamiliar land. George was collecting data as he watched Americans at work, and he places his findings on a metaphorical graph. In Europe, he believes, you can graph almost anything that makes up a society—morality, income, political ideology—and get a classic bell curve, with most of the population in the middle and very few people at either extreme. "Well," he continues with his minilecture, "in America the distribution is not like that. There are two extremes. Sure, there's a center, but there's also two other 'bounces.' The curve has three bumps, one in the center and two emphasizing the extremes. You can see that everywhere."

Among George's fellow students at MIT, he met the extremely puritanical, and the extremely decadent. There were extreme conservatives and extreme liberals. And he found plenty of cases in America where extremes coexisted within the same person. "Students who would put their feet on the chair in front of the professor," he remembers, behavior that was unheard of in Europe's staid institutes, "while on the other hand, they were really listening to the professor and were behaving very well, with their feet on their chair. Two extremes."

The force exerted by polar extremes, George believes, ensures that Americans will have a hard time sitting still. "America is a teenager," he says, echoing a sentiment common among historians and social scientists. "Other [European] countries are mature. I mean they are middle-aged. And teenagers always have extremes of behavior. This confirmed essentially what my picture of America was. So I was very pleased."

George wanted to stay in the United States. There was no more fertile ground for the company he envisioned building—a dynamic corporation that would harness technology to social need, a flexible organization of restless energy. The nucleus of his vision was his conviction that "technology really can make a major contribution in the lives of humans on earth . . . can find and give answers to our needs." But it was George's love of problem solving that propelled his dream forward. "That really makes my life. When I have a problem that I have a chance to solve—I don't care what it is, what the problem is. That is my drive." George already had his eye on any number of scientific puzzles, but first he had to solve the problem of how to stay in the United States.

George inquired about citizenship but found that there was a strict quota for Greeks and a long line to get in. Twenty-two years, he was told. "That didn't sound very good to me," George says, "so I was trying to figure out how to get around it." At the time, he remembers, there was no provision for highly skilled and educated immigrants, no way to move up the line. The idea of marrying for a green card was abhorrent to George, and besides, he wanted full citizenship.

He was still looking for a way around the closed gates when the Korean War broke out. With the draft reinstated, the government collected names from the dormitories and fraternities at MIT. George's name wound up on a list, and his number was called. "I knew I could protest because I wasn't even a resident. In fact, it even said there, if you believe there is any reason you shouldn't be drafted, let us know. Well, I decided to act dumb. And so I was called into the army."

While training at New Jersey's Fort Dix, George's visa expired and he got word that the INS was asking questions around MIT. His acquaintances there played dumb, and George reasoned that the last place the immigration agents were going to look for him was an army base. He was safe but nervous, so he asked his captain and an army lawyer for advice. They recommended that he send a letter to the INS, explaining his situation. Both assured him that INS agents couldn't come on base to arrest him.

That letter ended up causing problems. The army, having invested in and trained George, wanted to keep him and send him to Korea; the INS wanted to deport him. The two fought over who would get to do what with George in a very unusual hearing, and the army lost.

One morning at the crack of dawn, George learned that the army had been forced to give him an honorable discharge. He had to leave Fort Dix by sundown, and the immigration agents would be waiting at the gates. He spent the day calling his relatives and securing a lawyer, who got him out of INS custody before he even had to spend a moment in jail and gave the INS a dressing-down in court. Eventually they reached a compromise. He could stay on his student visa at MIT to earn a Ph.D. if he went back to Greece for a few days. Another problem immediately arose. "Don't come here," his father insisted, "because there's a civil war going on. They'll grab you and put you in the army."

The only thing to do was delay, which he accomplished by securing a position as third engineer on an oil tanker. "So I ran around South America for six months. And had a great time, really." Meanwhile, his father was pulling strings back home that would lead the Greek parliament to vote on an unusual deferment on his military service so he could come home. "And MIT sent some beautiful letters on my behalf," George says, laughing, "saying that I was the greatest thing since Columbus or whatever." The INS lived up to their end of the deal, and George was given a new student visa. "I'm back at MIT, it's 1953, having been away for almost a year and a half, and I'm in the same boat as I was before!"

Three weeks later, though, President Eisenhower took office and made good on a promise to offer citizenship to anyone who had served in the military more than six months. George had had the right idea after all when he allowed himself to be drafted. George became an American citizen just two weeks after Eisenhower's inauguration.

The problem of his citizenship solved, George set to work immediately building his company. He went back to the dreams he had recorded in his notebook as a teen. Where many if not most of us might find sophomoric and sweetly naive jottings, George came up with about a dozen feasible inventions, and he asked an uncle in New York to introduce him to a few people on Wall Street. "So I went around," he says, "and asked, 'Well, of all these inventions, which ones are you most likely to fund?' " The investors were unanimous in their choice: an idea George had to directly transform heat into electricity by a process he called "boiling" electrons. At MIT, he told his advisor that he had just chosen his doctoral thesis topic.

MIT funded the research, but when George wanted to found his company on this invention they turned around and handed him the patent. The dean explained that the budding entrepreneur didn't have to pay now, all he had to do was endow a professorship if he was successful. George says, "So we shook hands and they gave me the rights. And I started my company." In the late 1980s, George made good on his promise by endowing the Hatsopolous Chair in Thermodynamics. He even got to meet the first round of candidates, coming face-to-face with how much, and how profoundly, he was able to give back to the institution that believed in and trusted him.

George's thermionic converter, which could produce electricity with no moving parts, was a true breakthrough. And now that he owned the patent, all he needed was some cash. He got a first round of funding from a friend's father (the father thought that the venture was sure to fail, giving the son a hard lesson about the value of a dollar). Four years later, George went into another round of funding, and had his choice of investors. He went with Laurance Rockefeller, who put up a million dollars—in the early 1960s this was actually enough to start a high-tech company—and his Thermo Electron Corporation, based in the high-tech corridor outside of Boston, was not just off the ground, but flying. "When I tell that story to prospective entrepreneurs," a grateful-sounding George says, "they salivate."

Unfortunately, the thermionic converter proved too expensive for commercial use, although the invention was later picked up by the Russians for their space program (George adds that if we ever visit Mars, thermionic conversion will be the way to go.) Here's where George's innovative business sense saved him. He had envisioned a corporation that would be ever flexible and innovative, and that's what Thermo Electron would have to be. George had assembled a "great group of scientists" around the promise of the thermionic converter. Now he called them all together and told them it was time to start new businesses.

George was putting into practice the basic idea he'd had in high school: "I wanted to be a company that always searches for new businesses in response to social needs. That's the theme." With stock options, he drew the best talent he could find, but it became apparent that the central corporation's success was tied too directly to the individual fates of the subsidiaries it had spun off. "Some of them were more successful than others, and some of them did in fact fail," George says. "I had no way of discriminating the reward to people who were successful versus those who were not. Everybody was getting the benefit of the average." A new structure was called for, and it was a good thing that George also had a strong interest in the finer points of corporate administration and finance.

The new business model George devised was as novel as the ideas he'd worked up in the lab. He let each "daughter" company have its own stock, a minority of which would be sold to the public. Thermo Electron's stock price would benefit, and the spin-off companies would gain access to cheaper capital. "But most important," George insists, "is that I would give the incentive to people to have their own company. As a result, I'm the only company on Route 128 that I know of that never had any group leave and start their own business." Why would they, when they can fully satisfy their entrepreneurial yens under Thermo Electron's umbrella?

After George had put his plan into action, his ideas were published in the *Wall Street Journal,* which dubbed it the "spin out strategy." Ronald Reagan invited George to lunch at the White House to hear his ideas— at a time when scarce access to cheap capital was a national crisis—and he is still asked to give talks at Harvard, Stanford, and Cal Tech. For George, though, it keeps coming back to solving problems.

When he first got started, most of the needs he was able to isolate and address were in the space program. But when America started downsizing its space ambitions, the increased governmental focus on the environment claimed George's attention. He focused his resources on developing low-emission engines. By 1973, his company had already identified a small niche that could benefit from independence from oil—companies that use metallurgical furnaces. When the oil embargo took the nation by surprise, Thermo Electron was ready to go with efficient natural gas furnaces. After that point, George says, business grew by 25 percent a year for ten years. When terrorist attacks on airplanes became a big concern in the 1980s, his team built explosive detectors, which were bought by airports throughout Europe and eventually in the United States. But George is most proud of his subsidiary Thermocardio Systems, developer of the first artificial heart, an invention that has been used by thousands worldwide as a "bridge" to the day when a transplant becomes available. The market cap on this subsidiary, he adds after talking about the lives he says the invention has saved, is around a half billion dollars. "The more suddenly these needs appear," George says, "the better I like it."

Daedalus, the journal of the American Academy of Arts and Sciences, perhaps summed it up best with the description of Thermo Electron as "a perpetual idea machine." The fuel that keeps it running is its founder's love of the new, first sparked so many years ago by the feats of Thomas Edison. It seems strange to say, but there's still quite a bit of the teenager in this seventy-three-year-old. His spirit filters down to the twenty-five thousand employees who work for Thermo Electron and its subsidiaries—a corporate culture where everyone wants to impress everyone else with their skill at solving problems.

George has retired from Thermo Electron, but he still has plans. In his next venture, which is still too young for him to fully discuss, he'll try to correct some of the missteps he encountered with Thermo Electron—a fresh start for a serious perfectionist. "I hope I'll do it faster than the last time," he says, where "before we got the thing moving, it took about twenty, twenty-five years." He believes that his new idea, which he hopes to get "moving" within ten years, will create a company that outlasts Edison's General Electric.

If you are wondering where this man gets his energy, think of the last time you devoted all your mental effort to a single problem. That rush of discovery, that moment when an attempt is actualized, is what drives George Hatsopolous. George talks about the years that went into developing the invention that gave his business its start: he first entered the idea for the thermionic converter into his notebook in 1942 and he started working on it in earnest in 1953. He set up a whole lab, a team, and a business around it before the day of reckoning and then, "finally," in January 1958, it worked. "It's very difficult to describe feelings," George says, but for him, "the only comparable moment was when the Germans left Athens and I walked downtown from the suburbs, all the way, and there were thousands of people there celebrating the liberation. And that was roughly the same excitement."

Liberation. Freedom. A burden lifted, new opportunities granted. George Hatsopolous's perception of discovery's thrill is a part of the American dream.

Eileen Collins

One of the best things about my job is the people I get to meet. I've never been the hero-worshiping type, but you'd have to be a jaded soul indeed not to get a thrill from meeting so many folks who live on the front lines of history. And, perhaps because my reporting career got its start at the same time as America's push into space, I've always taken a special interest in meeting the men and women involved in this monumental human endeavor. So when I found myself introduced to space shuttle astronaut Eileen Collins at Game Three of the 1999 World Series in New York, I had one of those moments where the hard work seems more than worth it: the World Series and the chance to talk to an astronaut too. Only, as they say, in America.

I already knew some of Eileen Collins's story—that she'd been the first woman to pilot the shuttle and had gone on to become the first woman to command a shuttle mission. The more I learned, the more I realized that her story would be perfect for a book that celebrates the American dream. Eileen has come far in pursuit of her dream and gone even farther.

Eileen didn't set foot inside any kind of flying machine before she was nineteen. There wasn't a lot of money at home to spare for vacations, but she and her mother splurged this one time on a trip to Colorado. Her mother was scared to death, so Eileen took the window seat. "I was just loving it," she remembers. "I'm looking out the window and saying, 'Oh. So that's what it looks like from up here.'"

Eileen lived in public housing in Elmira, New York, from age seven to thirteen, where her parents, whom she refers to as her "heroes," made ends meet without much left over. It's not a time she likes to dwell on.

She talks to a lot of school groups, she says, and she likes to give "a really upbeat message versus, you know, 'I grew up in a difficult neighborhood, I grew up in federal housing where kids came over and beat on us.' There weren't gangs, but there were the beginnings of gangs, so I lived a little bit of that. And it's gotten a lot worse."

Family outings were simple affairs, but they got everyone out of the projects. And, although her parents didn't know it at the time, they made Eileen's imagination take flight. "One thing my father liked to do," she recalls, "was take us to the airport and watch the planes take off. We'd go up to Elmira Corning Airport and have a root beer or an ice cream or something. It was pretty simple. But it was inspirational."

Eileen's parents also made sure she got a chance to go to summer camp when she was a girl. The camp was at nearby Harris Hill, a spot known for its excellent gliding conditions. Eileen remembers the skies being full. "You couldn't help but see the gliders flying. I would just look up and go, 'Hey, people fly!' " After several years of these sights, it didn't make sense to her to be always stuck on the ground.

Summer camp was also where Eileen learned structure and responsibility. She adapted well to working with others and to the leadership roles in which she was placed. She found pride in following the camp routine—reveille in the morning, lining up, inspection, grace before meals, taps at night. It was "pretty rigid," she recalls, "and I liked that. I knew, as I got into high school, that I wanted to be in the military." At the time, this was a goal distinct from her dream of flying. Eileen graduated from high school in 1974, but the air force didn't train women as pilots until 1976. "Back in high school," she says, "there was no *way* I was going to be a military pilot. I thought, well, maybe I'll be a technician, or who knows—they'll find something for me to do."

Eileen believes that she feels comfortable with regimentation because of the way her brain is wired. She found that her ordered way of thinking also served her well when she entered college: she was good at math. She gravitated toward the practical, taking engineering and other related courses and absolutely loving them. "There's one right answer," she says, "and you know you're building something, you're making something." Like innovator George Hatsopolous, she enjoyed working out puzzles and solving problems. After a moment's thought, she adds another reason she enjoyed this field of study: "Math is hard!"

Eileen often says that she was at the right place at the right time, and that's how she became an astronaut. It's a modest summary of a ground-breaking career that does not do justice to all that she did to get to that right place. When she first realized that she wanted to fly, she says, "There was no way that my family could afford flying lessons for me. When my mother struggled to get clothes and things like that, you don't ask for flying lessons!"

Eileen worked a series of minimum-wage jobs at a pizza joint, a hospital, and a catalog showroom. "I learned a lot," she says, "and I saved my money. I saved it and put it in the bank." Once she had saved enough for the entry fee, between her junior and senior years of college, she went down to the same airport where she'd watched the planes take off with her father and asked for flying lessons.

Eileen admits she didn't march in and slap down her money with confidence. "I think I was a little self-conscious when I started," she says, "because when I walked up there, I thought, 'Oh, I'm a girl, and this is a guy thing.'" Eileen to this day looks like the proverbial girl next door, with an easy smile and short, bobbed hair. You might describe her as perky or cute, but physically imposing she is not—and that provides a quick lesson in how looks can be deceiving. Her instructors must have sensed her determination, though, as Eileen says she never doubted that they took her seriously.

Once in the pilot's seat, Eileen found that everything clicked into place: "You know how you find the thing that you like to do in life? I found it. Why I like to fly I don't know. It's challenging, and it's a precision kind of thing, and I found that I was good at it." And, she says, "I wanted to just keep doing it. So I overcame that little bit of shyness about the fact that I was a girl flying an airplane and I just did it because I liked it."

As she finished community college and transferred to Syracuse University, the military opened its cockpits to women pilots. Women still weren't serving in combat roles, but Eileen found plenty of other options. At Syracuse, she joined the ROTC, which gave her a two-year scholarship and put her in contact with a colonel who encouraged her to become an air force pilot. At the end of two years, she jumped at an offer to start pilot training.

Of the forty students in her class at Vance Air Force Base in Oklahoma, four were women. For Vance, even this small group was a first.

"There was still some of that 'I wonder if women can really do this' atti-tude," Eileen remembers. "And so we were watched *really* closely." Of the four women, three made it through the program to graduation—about the same rate as for men. Eileen definitely sensed the pressure of being a pioneer. "I felt like I was setting an example for women to fol-low me in the months and years later," she says. "I wanted to set a good example so it would be easier for them."

Eileen wasn't the top graduate; she admits that she wasn't even in the top 10 percent. But her superiors knew she was good, and on what was "probably one of the happiest days in my life," Eileen says, her request to stay on as an instructor was approved. For her, the post represented a hat trick of her passions: "I've always loved teaching, I like math, and there's a lot of math involved in military flying. And I love to fly, so I was able to take three things I love and put them all in one job."

The hardware was good too: the T-38 is a high-performance twin-engine jet aircraft used for training purposes, and the best plane in the air force that Eileen could get into at the time. She and other women in the military were still excluded by federal law from combat zones, so there was no reason, from the air force's point of view, to spend money on get-ting her up to speed on a fighter. But as an instructor, she could log hours, gain experience, and wait for a change while doing a job she loved.

That word, *job,* takes on a powerful meaning in the military. Focus on the job has to be laser tight; there is no room for distractions. Eileen was well trained and well suited for this deliberate mind-set, and it helped her get through what could have been some frustrating times. When her assignment as a flight instructor was up, she put in applications for assignment to all of the air force's top fighters: "I asked for an F-106, an F-16, an F-15, an A-10, I went through the whole list," she recalls, "and nothing changed." Further down the list was the Starlifter C-141, the armed forces' beast of burden. It wasn't a nimble fighter, but it was a job.

Eileen adds she was actually very happy with that assignment. After a year as copilot, she was made aircraft commander at the age of twenty-seven. Copilots, flight engineers, loadmasters, all reported to her on long trips to the Far East and Europe. Once again, her determination and focus trumped any worries of feeling out of place because of her gender. "Sometimes the women try to be a guy, but I never tried to be a guy. I just tried to be myself and always focus on the mission. Mission, mission, mission. And you have to keep your people in line, but I think I did it without focusing on myself and going, 'Boy, I wonder what they think about me?' "

Sometimes she found out what they thought, and found out she had proven herself. Once in a while, she says, one of the "old crusty flight engineers who have been around for forty-five years" would admit that they wondered at first if she could cut it. But she had, they knew it, and they told her so.

Focus on the mission during the rapid deployment in Grenada in 1983 brought Eileen into a combat zone when women were still not supposed to be there: "Nobody had time—I was copilot—and nobody had time to look at the roster and say 'Oh, there are women on this crew, let's take the women off.' " Her flight dropped off about two hundred troops from the Eighty-second Airborne and brought back thirty-six medical students and their families. Eileen took away a vivid memory of these passengers kissing American ground after they touched down.

Eileen was already thinking about NASA's astronaut training program at the time she started flying the C-141, but she wanted to enter fully prepared. She got a master's degree in operations research from Stanford, and then taught math for three years at the Air Force Academy while working on her second master's in space systems management from Webster University. Connecting the dots to the space program, she next applied to the Air Force Test Pilot School at Edwards AFB in California. After her first two applications were turned down for administrative reasons, her third one was accepted.

By the time Eileen started test pilot training school, she was a major and the senior ranking officer in her class. "So I was class leader," she says, "which was *very* challenging, because there were twenty-five of us in the class. Most were fighter pilots. And here I am, this transport pilot who was a math teacher . . . I didn't quite come from the same background as they did. But we all ended up getting along and had a pretty smooth year." Smooth, perhaps, but still a year that Eileen remembers as probably the most challenging of her life.

Test pilots don't just fly. They work closely with engineers in order to understand how an aircraft works and how to test particular design innovations. They have to keep the science in mind as they guide their planes through difficult maneuvers. As part of her training, Eileen flew thirty different types of aircraft in the span of a year. "The workload was just incredible," she says, but "manageable." She was married but did not yet have children. With the two kids she has now, she says, she's not sure she could have done it.

Despite her extensive training, Eileen never got a chance to test herself on an experimental plane. Something bigger came along. Just before she graduated in 1990, NASA called and said, "You're hired."

She'd applied to become either a pilot or a mission specialist, and says that either one would have been fine with her, but her flight experience made the choice obvious to her superiors. The training, however, was about much more than flying the shuttle. Eileen had to bone up on geology, meteorology, astronomy, and medicine—just a few of the "enrichment" courses she had to take to give her an appreciation for and basic understanding of what the scientists on shuttle flights are doing. She and her classmates were visited by people like Neil Armstrong, Buzz Aldrin, and Chris Kraft, all of whom shared their rarest of experiences. And then there was media training, something that would come in handy after each of Eileen's space flights.

After completing this program, Eileen stepped into a ground role with NASA, working on the space shuttle *Orbiter* engineering support and astronaut support teams. More training followed, in addition to work at Mission Control as a spacecraft communicator. After she was selected to pilot the shuttle *Discovery* on a complicated mission, she went through another year of training with her crew. Then she knew she was ready. The training was very good, she says, and "when you eventually go to the launchpad, you're not afraid. You're very confident."

Eileen assumed all along that when she got to the launchpad, she would be bristling with excitement. "But you know, it wasn't like that," she admits. "Maybe it was just me, being the first woman pilot. I was focused on 'Don't make mistakes, set a good example,' you know, for other women and other people watching." Anticlimactic perhaps, but her focus helped things turn out flawlessly. "I was happy that I *did* do my job right and didn't have to, you know, come back and explain," she says, laughing, "any mistakes I made."

Through her whole career, Eileen had focused on the job at hand and relied on her training. Sometimes, the poetry of what she was doing was obscured by more prosaic demands on her time and attention. That first eight-day shuttle mission was a case in point. "It was the fourth day of the flight that it finally hit me that I was in space," she remembers. "I was so busy the first and second day, and it was the fourth day that we did a rendezvous with the Russian space station, *Mir*. We were the first Americans to see *Mir*, and we got within thirty feet. . . . After we did that rendezvous, we finally had time to kind of unwind, and I thought, 'I'm in space! Hey!' "

On her second mission she got more time to look out the window; it was one of her jobs. This time they docked with *Mir*, and she spent hours photographing the space station for damage, but adds that she took a few sideways glances at home as well. "I'll tell you, looking back at Earth is . . . I mean, Earth is just beautiful. It's blue, it's white, it's tan. The jungles are a real dark green. But the islands, the atolls, there's so much water, there's water everywhere. It's just amazing that you get a different perspective on the planet. You know, it's not the same world that you drive to work on every day."

She's glad she had these moments to think about where she was, as her next mission did not allow for much reflection. Eileen boarded *Columbia* in July 1999 as the first woman to command a shuttle mission. "I don't know if my attitude about the mission changed that much," she says, "but being in the position where you're in charge gives you a different mind-set." She doesn't say what that mind-set is, but after hearing her describe two problems on the ascent, I got an idea.

Five seconds after liftoff, a power system failed for one critical second, killing the primary engine controller. A backup system kicked in, and a very serious problem was averted. "If the backup controller hadn't picked up the job, the engine would have failed," Eileen explains, "and we would have had to fly it over the Atlantic Ocean, turn around and come back and land in Florida." That "turnaround" would have been 180 degrees at several thousand miles per hour. Not a lot of room for error.

The second problem wasn't discovered until *Columbia* was in orbit. A small hydrogen leak caused the engines to shut down one second early. "We ran out of gas, basically," Eileen remarks. This put them seven miles below their target orbit. Eileen betrays no sense of the catastrophe averted as she gives a very informed and heavily technical description of these problems. She trusted the equipment with built-in redundancies; she sighs with admiration when she mentions the professionalism of the team on the ground, and then takes it back again to her training. "In fact," she says, "the last simulator that we did, we trained for that very same electrical problem and we trained many times for the nozzle leak, the hydrogen leak we had. Much worse cases."

The highlight of the mission came with the deployment of the Chandra X-ray Observatory, which went off without a hitch. Chandra is a powerful camera for taking pictures of X-ray emissions from the far reaches of space, and has already brought us closer to understanding the true nature of the universe. For Eileen, though, the real moment of truth was in the landing. Pilots on shuttle missions don't handle the controls during the landing. It's the commander who takes over and guides the spacecraft down by hand from fifty thousand feet. Another first.

Eileen says that she was "very aware" that she would be the first woman to land the shuttle. "I knew all those women pilots out there were watching me and thinking, 'Eileen, you better make a good landing.' So there was a lot of pressure on me, not really from within me, but from other women pilots. But they all meant well." She'd studied her previous commanders closely and had "practiced, practiced, practiced" in the simulator. The landing went well, but Eileen can't help pointing out that it wasn't spot-on perfect. The shuttle, she explains, is supposed to touch down at 195 knots. "I landed at 196. So I wasn't on the knot, but I was close enough to say it was a good landing."

The next three weeks brought debriefings, postflight medical exams, and reports. Then the media hit. Eileen appeared with one of her crew members on Jay Leno's show, and went on to do almost fifty interviews in a week. "*Regis and Kathy Lee, Oprah,* oh, I can't even remember all this stuff. It just kept going. And it was kind of a difficult time because I had a daughter back home." At the time of this interview, Eileen was turning down all interviews and speaking engagements that involved travel. She was expecting her second child, and trying to get her life back to "normal" again.

Of all the speaking engagements, public appearances, and television interviews Eileen has done, she finds nothing more satisfying than the chances she gets to talk to children. "Their eyes just light up," she says. For astronaut Eileen Collins, seeing these children extend their imaginations into the cosmos is just one of "a lot of intangibles that we get out of the space program." I couldn't agree more. From its earliest days, America's quest to explore space has brought out some of the best in us as a people, and has helped remind us all that even the most far-flung dreams can come to fruition. It's something we would do well to remember in this age of trimmed NASA budgets and correspondingly scaled-down expectations.

Eileen is frequently asked how she got interested in the space program. She says her answer has changed several times over the last ten years. "I've had a lot of time to think about it," she says. The answer now takes her back to her childhood, before the gliders and the airliners took hold of her imagination, to the times when she would act like a young pioneer, wandering around in the woods near her home. That spirit never went away. "I'm an explorer . . . I want to go places that are new and different, learn new things. I think that's what being human is all about. I mean, this is what *life* is all about, exploring and learning." I come back to the thought of Eileen getting her life back to "normal." If you believe that the American dream lends itself to lifelong learning, to a zest for investing in new possibilities, then I suppose Eileen Collins isn't being modest when she calls her life normal. She's simply another normal, American pioneer.

Shawn Carlson

Time was, an American could be a pioneer or innovator just by making up his or her mind. There was land to homestead and, for scientists, a seemingly limitless plain of opportunities for discovery. And it was open to just about anyone with a good idea.

In many ways, that's still true. But academia's ivory towers can also be intimidating, and sometimes their occupants defend them like a citadel. To the layperson with an avid scientific interest, it can seem as if not belonging to the club means they will never be able to take an active part in the process of discovery.

Shawn Carlson, founder and executive director of the Society for Amateur Scientists, grew up believing that his grandfather had the brains and the passion to make a serious contribution to human knowledge.

Shawn is unequivocal on this point. "I've been privileged in my career to know Nobel Prize winners and members of the National Academy of Sciences and university professors, and a sampling of some of the greatest scientists alive today," he says. "And I can tell you, out of all the people I've met, no one had a greater raw scientific talent, in my judgment, than my grandfather."

But this raw scientific talent also had an interest in art, and when he hired nude models (who, as it turned out, also worked as prostitutes) to come into an art class he was taking, his college "chunked him out," as my grandmother would have said. That sort of thing was just not done in Lincoln, Nebraska, in the 1920s. As a result, he never finished. As he went through life, he continued to pursue his interests—solar energy, geosciences, mathematics, just to name a few—and submit papers to peer-reviewed journals. "And because he didn't have the letters 'Ph.D.' next to his name," Shawn says, "his papers were rejected out of course."

The rebellious, iconoclastic "amateur" scientist never hid the way he was spurned from his grandson: "He used to wear his rejections as a badge of honor. When I came to visit him, he would show me his rejections slips, and very proudly display them." Shawn couldn't, however, share in his grandfather's sense of pride. "It used to drive me crazy," he says, "even when I was a young man, that someone with his degree of talent was locked out from making contributions." Shawn shared the same passion for science as, and got a lot of early lessons from, his grandfather but decided that he would follow a different route. He would become a "member of the club," as Shawn puts it.

Shawn earned a B.S. in applied mathematics and a B.S. in physics from UC Berkeley and his master's and Ph.D. in nuclear physics at UCLA. "I did everything I was supposed to do," he says, but like his grandfather, Shawn never really fit the standard model of what a successful academic should be. "My interests," he sums up, "were too broadly based." Shawn's experience in graduate school brought this home. On the one hand, he got his Ph.D. in "a highly specialized area of nuclear physics—subthreshold production of strange particles in relativistic heavy ion collisions, which is a very narrow, narrow, narrow field." (This reporter will have to take his word for it.) On the other hand, he felt restricted. "My professors and my advisors would often take me aside and tell me I'm never going to amount to anything because I'm not focused enough. I'm too busy growing algae on my windowsill," he says, referring to one of his "amateur" experiments in biology.

With credentials in hand, Shawn took a research job at UC Berkeley, but when his wife, Michelle Tetreault, was accepted to graduate school at UC San Diego, Shawn says, "I had a choice between taking another research job that I knew I wouldn't find fulfilling, or returning to my roots." Going back to his roots involved going out on a limb: financially, he and his wife could be sunk. Professionally, he could become a target for pointed scorn from his peers. But he would be free from the shackles of academia, free to pursue projects outside his training, and, if it worked, free to encourage nonprofessionals to pursue dreams of their own. In the end, he took the chance and founded the Society for Amateur Scientists—in large part as a tribute to his grandfather, but also as an acknowledgment that he is himself "very much the amateur scientist at heart."

Shawn and the SAS return to the Latin root of the word *amateur* to define an "amateur scientist" as someone who does science simply for the love of it. A quick glance at the SAS's membership rolls reveals that homemakers, accountants, a fireman, writers, teachers, and a member of the Canadian Coast Guard are all interested in somehow making a contribution. Then there are a wide variety of professional scientists and engineers who follow interests outside their training and day jobs.

SAS serves as a bridge between the worlds of the amateur and professional scientist. Shawn believes that if amateurs are taught about standards and procedures, the professionals are more likely to take them seriously. And Shawn also knows that amateurs often need to adapt some of the professionals' discipline. Amateur scientists, he allows, "are overflowing with passion and it doesn't always flow out in a constructive direction." He says he gets calls all the time from trained geologists upset about a site being damaged or a relationship with a landowner marred by enthusiastic amateurs. Paleontologists, too, all too often see unique fossils destroyed by untrained hands.

But Shawn has no doubts about the benefits of amateur science. Amateur astronomers are a ready example (they are often the first to find new supernovas, comets, and asteroids, and no one cares if the eyes that first spot a new celestial body belong to an amateur or a pro), but Shawn also remembers a man named Harvey Dubner, who created a very sophisticated computer for less than $2,000 and used it to discover the largest prime number, and also held the record for the largest double prime. Amateur paleontologists discovered animal tracks in New Mexico that predated the dinosaurs. And an elevator operator in Italy made what Shawn calls a fundamental contribution by providing a solution to the "strong focusing problem." "Were it not for strong focusing, there would be no particle physics as we know it." Again, this reporter and non-scientist will have to take his word for it.

Why do they do it? What drives these people to work outside their normal occupations on something for which they may not even be recognized? "Most of them," Shawn explains, "are after the thrill of discovery. They want to do something useful with their time, and many of them want to do something that's creative. And they have fun! It's a good time!" The SAS seeks to harness and hone and develop this sort of passion.

After the move to San Diego, Shawn and Michelle sunk their life savings of about $10,000 into the fledgling society. They lived off Michelle's earnings as a student teacher, which, Shawn says, "wasn't doing it." The young couple racked up huge credit card debts. The only thing that kept it all together, Shawn says, was their perfect compatibility. Despite a number of tense years, they persevered. And they knew that the lean times would not go on forever, "because when she graduated," Shawn says, "even if I was a total deadbeat and couldn't bring in any money whatsoever from SAS, she could bring in a healthy salary as a Ph.D. in physics. If she really wanted to." Having Michelle as the sole earner, however, was not something either of them wanted.

Things got a little easier when *Scientific American* called the society asking if Shawn knew anyone who could take over the magazine's "Amateur Scientist" column. "When they contacted me," he recalls, "I almost fell out of my chair." *Scientific American*'s "Amateur Scientist" column had been the only forum in which Shawn's grandfather had managed to get his work published. "I've known about it since I was a ten-year-old boy," Shawn says, "and I read it *religiously*." His byline helped raise the society's profile, and the accompanying stipend of $1,000 a month gave them something more to live on.

After two and a half years of writing the column and struggling to raise funds for the growing society, Michelle and Shawn had a baby girl. This obviously increased the financial pressure. For Shawn, the only light at the end of the tunnel was the knowledge that a nonprofit that lasts for five years has a real chance of enduring for the long haul. "Funding agencies tend to keep hands off for five years," Shawn explains. "If you survive five years they say, okay, they're serious, they're going to hang around." Shawn had attracted a prestigious board of directors and advisors, professional scientists who believed in the mission of the SAS. He had planned a number of ambitious projects that he hoped would convince funding agencies that SAS could get things done. And he had the support of his wife and that intense drive you can find in anyone who dares to set up a nonprofit agency: "I knew that I was fighting the good fight, I was doing good work. I knew we were making a difference in the world." At the same time, he admits, he sometimes wondered if he was crazy for trying.

By the middle of 1999, with another child on the way, things were getting really desperate. Michelle wanted to take time off from work to be with the children, and, as Shawn puts it, "I was at my wits' end. I didn't know where the support would come from." On the twenty-second day of June, he fell violently ill, with a fever of 105, a blinding headache, and no desire to deal with anyone. "I turned off the answering machine on the phone," he says, "and I laid there." While Shawn was laid up in bed, he remembers the phone ringing constantly: "Every fifteen minutes I would get another call. And all I wanted was for people to leave me alone. So I never checked the messages."

"The next day," Shawn continues, "I get up, and now my fever is a mere 102. That's what a child in day care will do for you. And I went downstairs and ate breakfast, and Michelle and I had a very serious talk about money. We went over our very dismal situation and I was really quite depressed not knowing where the money was going to come from. Then I get a call, this time on the home phone, and it was somebody from Michelle's work saying, 'Shawn, hi. We just got a call from some group called the MacArthur Foundation. They say you've won some kind of award.' "

Well, he thought. That changes everything. When he called the MacArthur Foundation, they told him he was about to get fame, prestige, and, most pressing at that point, money. "How does $290,000 sound?" asked the voice on the other end of the phone. "I gotta tell you," Shawn says, "it sounded pretty good."

The MacArthur Fellowship is a no-strings award given to an individual for being a committed and active genius. You can't apply for a

MacArthur Fellowship; you won't even know if you're even under consideration. The John D. and Catherine T. MacArthur Foundation hires one hundred authorities from a variety of fields each year to nominate potential fellows. The hundred authorities serve anonymously, and diligently hunt down geniuses like Shawn Carlson. It's designed to be a bolt from the blue, a reward for work done and an incentive to keep going.

Which is exactly how Shawn used his money. He hired a professional fund-raiser and set a goal to raise $150,000 in 2000. He hopes to raise $300,000 in 2001. "We think these are all very achievable goals. And we want to rent an office, hire workers, hire a staff, and continue to do the kinds of outreach programs that we're so good at." Just a few months after he was awarded the fellowship, Shawn is using words like "serious player" and "major institution" to describe where he thinks the organization is headed. And he can already sense that he's made a difference. "It's finally sinking in to the professional community," he says, "that you don't always have to have a Ph.D. next to your name to get involved and do good work."

The MacArthur grant also fortified Shawn in a battle he'd had to wage from the beginning of the SAS, against professional scientists who felt threatened by what he was trying to accomplish. The type of professional, Shawn says, whose "Ph.D. is woven into the very fabric of their sense of self-worth." Call-in radio shows provided a frequent battleground. When Shawn would appear in these forums, he'd get a lot of calls from scientists who "just excoriate me about how I'm taking funds from professionals and giving it to amateurs, and how there are limited funds available, and just really very negative stuff about how we are destroying the very fabric upon which successful research is based." It wasn't the attitude of a majority of the scientists with whom Shawn had contact, but it was definitely a strong one. "And when the MacArthur Fellowship hit," he says, "everybody shut up."

Who, after all, wants to argue with the winner of what's commonly called a "genius" grant? "Yesterday I was certifiable," Shawn says with humor, "today I'm certified! I'm a certified genius! And exactly how can you argue with that?" The MacArthur people, Shawn believes, "have legitimized what we do, and I'm very grateful to them for that." He points out repeatedly that in any case he never wanted to tear down the ivory towers, just open lines of communication to them.

He also understands why scientists would be suspicious. As someone who was trained in physics, he knows that truly disturbed individuals can try to pass as amateur scientists. Physicists, he explains, are often taken to be "the most brilliant people on the planet. So if you can make deep and profound contributions to that field, boy, you must be some super genius. And so the nuts, people who have more ego than common sense or training, who fancy themselves the new Galileo, they're all attracted to that subject." That's why, he says, physicists often have file drawers full of "nut correspondence." That also explains why they are a bit wary of the idea of science being done by amateurs. "But," Shawn adds, "these people are *not* amateur scientists. And they don't represent the amateur community."

The big, bold letters at the bottom of www.sas.org define the organization as strictly not for "nuts": "SAS is a conservative scientific organization. . . . SAS does not conduct research into paranormal phenomena. Also, we do not provide support for amateur theories of cosmology, creation, the unified field, or similar topics." Shawn himself isn't necessarily offended by those who try to use science as a means of propping up their own eccentric worldview—he reserves his indignation for those who use trickery to take advantage of others' superstitions or religious beliefs. In 1985 he published an article in *Nature* taking an extensive look at the accuracy of astrologers' abilities. He's shown how to make a religious icon look like it's crying, and worked with another skeptic to expose fraudulent faith healers. "I have no problem with people believing in miracles," he says, "but I have a lot of problems with people claiming to be a miracle worker and then doing magic and trickery to use someone's legitimate belief in miracles against them. . . . In my mind, those are the most despicable charlatans in the world and hell is too good a place for them to wind up."

Strong words, but Shawn regards exposing con artists as a public service. The SAS, though, is primarily involved with proving that anyone can make a contribution, rather than disproving "miracles." The SAS recently rallied behind a project to launch a two-kilogram payload to two hundred kilometers, hoping for a $250,000 prize from the Foundation for International Non-governmental Development of Space. After Shawn wrote about the prize in his *Scientific American* column, he started thinking, "Well, how difficult is that really to do?" He did some calculations and realized that a single-stage solid rocket could actually make it to two hundred kilometers. "So," he says, "I figured, well, heck, we've got a tremendous amount of talent in our organization, why don't we go after the prize?"

It was frustrating to find out that the technology wasn't the most challenging part of the project. "The most difficult aspect was dealing with the bureaucracies." Shawn says he sent the FAA over 250 pages of detailed calculations and diagrams. He redesigned the rocket to meet new requirements. And he says he got nothing but promises. When they finally got a launch license, they were hit with over $40,000 dollars in licensing and insurance fees from the FAA and the U.S. Air Force, and that was on top of the $35,000 they'd spent on two rockets. The fees were, Shawn says, an almost complete surprise. "It's not the technology that held us up, it was our beloved federal government." And that's a problem professional scientists, amateur scientists, and complete nonscientists can understand equally well.

Shawn's enthusiasm bubbles over when he talks about another project that he believes "has the potential to absolutely revolutionize citizen science." SAS is developing a data protocol—a universal data format and a communication protocol that will allow data collecting instruments from around the globe to be hooked directly into the World Wide Web. Once the system is in place, anyone will be able to go down to the local electronics store and buy a temperature sensor, an atmospheric oxygen sensor, a radiation detector, or a solar illumination detector and plug it into a worldwide data network. "Suppose," Shawn says, "I'm very interested in the maximum and minimum temperature in South Carolina for some reason. I can tell my computer to collect the database from the working sensors, to go out and make this running tally and give me whatever information I want. If we can pull this off," he continues, "and it's very clearly doable, then we could put into people's hands the ability to create their own international network to study any problem that might interest them. It's limited only by the imagination of the people who are doing it."

Home-based environmental research, Shawn calls this dream. If enough people are hooked into the network, the result will be a "universe of data," very accurate and free for the asking. "And once you have the ability to do interesting things," he emphasizes, "clever people will go beyond what anybody who was building the system ever imagined it could've been used for." Shawn envisions getting school kids and classrooms involved, and "curmudgeons of all ages." He believes that "it's going to really, really open up the field."

This is exactly the sort of penchant for innovation I was thinking of when I started to follow this aspect of the American dream. The way we can, as a society, build on each other's discoveries, and always be surprised. Alexander Graham Bell never could have expected that his invention would allow us to plug in to a worldwide data network like the one Shawn described. But he probably knew that someone would take his contribution further. And he might have guessed that that someone would be the type of person who was willing to go out on a limb. Shawn Carlson, who climbed far out on his own branch of the scientific family tree, now proposes to take the Internet closer to its playing-field-leveling ideal.

Shawn doesn't think he would have been able to pull off his dream anywhere but America. Someone who took on the vaunted academy of another country in the way he did would, he suspects, be squashed. "The ability to totally walk away, turn your back on academia, come up with something that's completely original and be respected *because* you are a maverick," he says perceptively, "that's very much a part of the American tradition." Turning back to his grandfather, Shawn believes still that if he'd been supported by someone on the inside—tutored or reviewed or challenged—he would have become a leading light in some field. Perhaps, through the Society for Amateur Scientists, this can happen for someone else who works a job but holds dreams of discovery. Maybe it can still happen without the letters *P, H,* and *D.*

GIVING BACK
IN THE SERVICE OF DREAMS

Our privileges can be no greater than our obligations. The protection of our rights can endure no longer than the performance of our responsibilities.

—John Fitzgerald Kennedy

*W*HEN you report the news for a living, you try to find fresh ways of expressing certain ideas and things one must describe again and again. The Vietnam War. The search for peace in the Middle East. The Supreme Court. Through sheer force of repetition, you end up developing multiple ways of referring to these touchstones of daily unfolding history—the Vietnam War becomes "America's Southeast Asian Quagmire"; the Supreme Court might reappear in a later paragraph as the "Court of Last Resort." On one level, this is mere rhetoric, a way to keep language lively for your viewer or your reader. On another, though, the effort to evoke without naming can clarify your own thoughts toward an event, or a process, or an institution.

America, of course, is one of those words and ideas that can come up in just about any kind of news story—good preparation, if nothing else, for writing a book on the American dream. Since long before I embarked on this project, though, I've looked for ways to succinctly capture our nation's essentials. One of my favorites is "a constitutional republic, founded on principles of freedom and democracy."

A little on the clunky side? Maybe so. It's something I've both added to and whittled at over the years. But I think it gets to the heart of the matter. I like the way it recognizes certain small differences in the things at our nation's core, more than, say, phrases like "land of the free" or "our democracy."

Of these, one of the most beguiling differences is that between freedom and democracy. They are not, obviously, in any kind of opposition to each other. Nevertheless, there is a tension that runs between the two, one that can be put in terms of "rights" and "responsibility." We are at liberty to do just about whatever we want, even nothing at all. Yet our very form of government demands that some of us step forward to serve, or at least to register our opinions at the ballot box. The shape of our country, and the course it will take, are very much up to us . . . and nothing but our sense of responsibility demands that we do anything about it.

How special, then, are those who exercise their freedom in a way that benefits others. By doing so, they improve not only the lot of the individuals they touch directly but also our country as a whole. Or as one of the people you'll meet here, Sister Sylvia Schmidt, put it, service is about "getting beyond ourselves . . . to do unto others as you would have them do unto me because that will come back to us—the kind of world we create is what we're going to have to live in."

Sister Sylvia, like so many who do the good work in our society, takes action rooted in religious belief. In a nation founded on the basis of God-given rights, houses of worship and their congregations have long been at the backbone of such efforts; until the turn-of-the-century settlement house movement, in fact, they were just about the only dispensers of charity and social welfare of all sorts. They fed the hungry, clothed the destitute, healed the sick.

As is often the case in America, though, it's not so easy to separate the spiritual from the secular. The Revolutionary generation believed, with some reason, that they had brought about a triumph over not only British tyranny but over tyranny in general. The idealism that welled up from what they saw as the perfection of human government translated into a desire to tackle all sorts of social ills. The new nation positively exploded with good intentions, as more charities sprung up in the first decade or so after independence than had been founded during all the colonial years. Many of these charitable societies were faith based, but their rapid growth had an undeniable spur in civic pride.

Of course, charity is not the only form of service that echoes still with the repercussions of the shot heard 'round the world. The most obvious way to contribute to a democracy, by serving in the government of, by, and for the people, was tinged in that age with a yeoman nobility that, despite some of the worst efforts of our age, we haven't yet managed to completely shake off.

Those pursuing dreams of service are all around us. They can be found in every community, because true community is impossible without such people. To return to Sister Sylvia's words, they shape our world for the better by reminding all of us of our better natures. Sister Sylvia herself is as good a personal exemplar of this ethos as you could hope to find. The work she has done on behalf of the homeless in Tulsa, Oklahoma, is not only inspirational; it is also something she has undertaken with energy that even the most secular soul might term miraculous. Her words are the equal of her deeds; she speaks with a true wisdom from which we can all learn.

Iowa state legislator Wayne Ford turned the anger that fueled a criminal youth into a productive force. He seized on to a feeling that he was destined to make a difference and established a community service center in Des Moines, Iowa, that, appropriately, is called Urban Dreams. He puts his keen intellect and utter fearlessness to good use in highlighting the problems of minorities and youth and making sure African-American issues remain on the agenda of Democratic presidential candidates.

Evelyn Sirrell of Portsmouth, New Hampshire, has a markedly different story to tell, but like Wayne, she has brought a strong personal voice to the political realm. When she saw how entrenched special interests and an "old boy" network were affecting her town, she decided that it was time for an ordinary citizen to serve on the city council. Eventually, she had become mayor of Portsmouth. Is it excessive to include two people who are, dare I say it, politicians? I don't think so. In America, I'll say it again, this is the very essence of responsibility. I'm not here to tell you that all politicians are humble public servants and nothing more—I'd be laughed out of the press club if I said that. But I think that a genuine desire to serve drives more politicians than the more cynically inclined in press and public alike would care to believe. Here, I believe it's noteworthy that Evelyn Sirrell and Wayne Ford came to politics through their beliefs and experiences, rather than the other way around.

Some are born to lives of service, and this would certainly seem to be the case with Enrique Camarena Jr. Enrique's father, a DEA agent, was brutally killed while working undercover in Mexico. This has not, however, prevented Enrique from pursuing his own career in law enforcement. Though he has minded his father's wish that he never become a policeman, Enrique works to protect the citizens of San Diego in the city's district attorney's office.

And if we fear for the future of our country, we might take comfort in the story of young Josh Marcus, a fourteen-year-old who started a non-profit when he was only ten. Today, his Sack It to You charity gives hundreds of kids a chance to get more out of school by outfitting them with quality supplies. What's more, he has spread his enthusiasm for giving to his classmates, young people still forming dreams that will now be informed by compassion in action.

It has been said that the performance of selfless acts is perhaps the only virtuous behavior that is sufficiently appreciated. This may be, but in an age when few tire of declaring their rights, it is my view that those folks who focus on responsibility cannot be praised highly enough. In fulfilling their own American dreams, they make the dreams of so many others possible as well . . . and in a nation that prides itself on its ideals, they show us how we might live up to them.

Sister Sylvia Schmidt

There are people who give, and there are people who give everything. Sister Sylvia Schmidt falls into the latter category. I first learned of this sixty-something Roman Catholic nun from a short account of her accomplishments that a friend clipped for me from the Tulsa *World*. The Tulsa Metropolitan Ministry, the National Conference for Community and Justice, the Jewish Federation, and the Islamic Society of Tulsa had just presented her with an award for her years of service and commitment to all of Tulsa's faiths, and the article told of a lifetime spent in public service. The article quoted a local rabbi who called Sister Sylvia a "prophet." Tulsa's mayor described her as the city's best-known woman, and a Muslim leader called her Tulsa's "conscience" just before presenting her with a T-shirt emblazoned with the letters "WWSSD?"—What

Would Sister Sylvia Do? It occurred to me that the object of such glowing ecumenical praise was likely to have some unique insights on the American dream.

Sister Sylvia laughed when asked about the T-shirt. She had certainly appreciated the honor and the humor behind the shirt, she said, but reports her response to the message as, "No, no, no . . . You have to ask yourself that question. I asked the question of myself. You will have different answers. You have different perspectives." For some, community service may mean a few hours a week at a local center, for others it may be collecting donations for global famine relief. For others it may be nothing more than raising responsible children. But for a few, for people like Sister Sylvia who hear the call, service is everything and all the time.

Family and community, bound by church, were strong in Sister Sylvia's early life in Divine, Texas, a small town about thirty miles southwest of San Antonio (and her lively sense of humor has made good use of her "Divine origins"). She was one of seven children growing up on a farm that had been in her family since her great- great-grandfather's day; as the youngest, though, Sylvia's farmwork was light. She'd help with the cattle, grab a hoe during planting season, haul firewood, and pitch in when the pecans were ready. But her focus was on school.

Sylvia learned her lessons in a one-room schoolhouse. She had started her education in a larger, more modern school, but her parents moved her, she recalls, because little Biry Public School was about to be closed. She remembers how her father and "a few of the Anglo farmers" in the area realized that, if the school shut its doors, the migrant farmworkers' children would no longer have a place to learn. "So they took us out of the larger school," she says, "and put their children into this smaller school." The increase in the student body—made up of children of families with influence—kept the doors open at one-room Biry Public School, and Sylvia had an educational experience that was already disappearing from the American landscape by the 1940s.

Sylvia looks back on Divine as "a place where people really cared, watched out for one another. They were friends. The children played together, you were just surrounded by people who knew one another all the time, and had the same kinds of values." Sylvia's parents were, she says, "very staunch and good Catholics." She stresses, though, that her father was not "a legalist" but emphasizes the commandment to love your neighbor as yourself. Sylvia grew up focusing on what she could do for others, and that became her way to serve God.

Sylvia's mind was set by the tender age of six: she was going to make a full commitment to the church. "I just said that's what I was going to be, and I just never wavered." Though she attended public school, she had contact with the sisters who came through town to teach a summer-school course. Sylvia remembers well their lessons about serving the needs of others, "especially children," she adds. From the age when she made up her mind to enter the convent, she carried an image of herself as teaching little children under the trees of a far-off land. She laughs when she remembers this missionary vision with overtones of *The Sound of Music*. "It certainly didn't happen in my life," she says, "but I think that kind of value was always something that drew me—that commitment."

Sylvia never wavered from her commitment, but she was aware that she was making a serious decision, and knew what she was giving up. "I didn't see religious life as greater than my mother's or sister's married life," she says. "I just had to make a choice. They couldn't do some of the things I could do because they chose to marry. But I couldn't have some of the joys of life—marriage and a husband and children—that they had. At some point, you say, 'I can't have both, and this is the one I choose.'"

She didn't find herself holding classes under a baobab tree, but after Sylvia took her habit in 1955, it wasn't long before Sister Sylvia was teaching elementary school in Shreveport, Louisiana. For several years, she prepared to teach math and science at the high school level, and received a National Science Foundation grant to attend the University of Southwestern Louisiana during her summer breaks. In 1961, Sister Sylvia started teaching high school math and physics in rural Catholic schools throughout Texas. When assigned to a school in Castroville, Texas, she found herself teaching some of her own relatives from the surrounding area. As she taught, she began master's work in theology, which in turn led to an assignment as head of the religion department at Bishop Kelly High School in Tulsa.

Tulsa in the early 1970s was undergoing the same tumult as the rest of the country, but what disturbed Sister Sylvia most was the effect it was having on teenagers. As she worked with Catholic students in public schools, she could see how drugs and runaway children were pulling at

the fabric of the community. Her first dealings with the Tulsa Metropolitan Ministry were with a small group formed to address this problem.
After she submitted a three-year report on the success of the program
and how it could be implemented in the diocese, they saw that this
teacher had the ability and drive to organize important social programs.

The pastor of a newly founded parish asked Sister Sylvia to become a
pastoral assistant, "a new position for women at that time," in which she
would minister outside the church, working with the parishioners of
southeast Tulsa. "It was there," she says, "that we really tried to think
about how to create a community so that it has that kind of extended
family concept . . . a community that cared for one another as you do
your brothers and sisters and parents." At the time, southeast Tulsa was a
catch basin for displaced working-class families migrating from New
York, New Jersey, or Philadelphia. It was a community that lacked the
bonds of a common history.

Sylvia reached back to her roots in Divine to, as she puts it, "build a
kind of community where people cared deeply about one another,
watched out for one another." She was, of course, also guided by her
faith. It calls us, Sister Sylvia believes, "not to just say, 'I'm responsible to
my own family,' but 'Everyone really is my family.' " When she started,
Sylvia worked with a group of about ninety families. When she left to
join the Tulsa Metropolitan Ministry in 1982, there were nine hundred
families in the program. "Some very deep, deep community relationships developed. They've gone through some very serious struggles, and
they've been there for one another. They've been through some great
times together, and they've celebrated."

The Tulsa Metropolitan Ministry was once known as the Council of
Churches, a group of Tulsa Protestant congregations, but after Vatican II
in 1965, a Catholic parish joined the organization. Other Catholic congregations soon followed. As the council deepened its involvement in
the era's civil rights movement, its members also began to work closely
with Jewish congregations and leaders, and by 1971 many in the organization felt the two faiths should join forces. The group reincorporated
as an interfaith organization, changed its name to the Tulsa Metropolitan
Ministry, and joined with the town's Jewish and Unitarian communities.
In 1983, the Muslim community became a part of it as well.

Sylvia was eager to work with other faiths. Her approach had been solidified by her work in southeast Tulsa, but she also found herself drawing again on what she had learned in her family. "While we came together to strengthen ourselves," she says, "the mission is not for ourselves. It's how we are defined in the community." For Sister Sylvia, the mission is not "going out and proselytizing. It's about how we live out our faith in what I call 'the prophetic role.' How do we look at what kind of laws we make, and what kind of people do we elect to make those laws? How involved are we in the kind of society we create, and how do we spend our money and for whom and with whom?"

The role of religious communities, Sylvia believes, is to issue what she calls "relational questions" to business and government. "If you do this in governance," she asks, "who's included? Who's excluded? If you do this economically, who gets rich and who gets poor? When the three of us work together strongly, then we develop a just and caring society. When any of us are corrupt, then we destroy ourselves."

Sylvia would eventually become executive director of TMM. Since the organization is committed to not having an overreaching agenda, Sylvia has been involved in interfaith efforts of all types, on local and global scales. From creating dialogues between the polarized camps of the abortion issue to gang intervention to publicizing the plight of Native Americans, TMM has under her direction remained a flexible and responsive organization. But of all the projects she's been a part of, she wanted to talk about the one she started when she first joined TMM. After devoting the better part of a decade to building community, she wanted to turn to those on its edges—the homeless.

The Tulsa Metropolitan Ministry sent Sylvia to a seminar in Atlanta led by a Presbyterian minister and a Baptist minister. The year was 1983, and Tulsa was feeling the effects of the oil bust just as urban renewal programs had created a housing shortage. Awareness of these economic factors had helped Sylvia to gain an intellectual understanding of homelessness, but the seminar made her appreciate it in her gut.

"The thing that struck me," she recalls, "was when they said, 'If you look around this room, all of you are wearing glasses. Just think about where you keep those glasses in your home. And if you're on the street, and you have no place, then you probably within a day's time would have those glasses broken either through street violence, sleeping on them, or someone just taking them. If you were then asked to read a paper, or fill out a form, then after about the third time, you'd be very frustrated.' That was so simple. It just struck me." Most of us get a chance to break in our shoes, Sylvia points out. The homeless are usually wearing secondhand shoes that are either too small or too large. Most of us can easily keep a healthy set of teeth. And most of us, it occurred to Sylvia, can rest when we're sick.

She spent a night in a shelter on the first night of the seminar. "I can remember these two old gentlemen. They were shaking, and they had tears rolling down their eyes. You knew they had the flu, and I thought, 'What's it like to be in that much pain and have no place to lay down?' Those faces never left me. They made a deep, deep impression."

At the time, several of Atlanta's congregations were opening their doors to the homeless on cold nights. But when Sylvia got back to Tulsa, she found almost no support for the idea—the ministers typically said their boards would reject it. The congregations were, however, willing to send out volunteers. The Salvation Army extended their night shelters, and Sylvia helped organize transportation to get the needy downtown and indoors. Still, she sensed that not enough was being done.

"One day," Sylvia continues, "I looked out during the daytime, and there was this woman who had rags on her feet and she was walking across the street in the snow. And I said that we have to do better. We can do better." She was also aware that several downtown businesses had been complaining about people using their bathrooms or sitting in their doorways. The library was seeing more and more people using their facilities to get out of the cold—and while they didn't want to turn them away, they were also aware that the library wasn't set up for this purpose. It had become clear that homeless folks also needed a place to spend daytime hours, especially during the winter.

The Tulsa Metropolitan Ministry began work on a day center for the homeless, a place where they could not only get out of the cold, but also be reached by other social service organizations. In 1985, they set up the first day center across the street from the Salvation Army. "I always felt that what we provided was a living and dressing room, and the Salvation Army provided the bedroom and dining room." The building could hold seventy-five people, but the first day they opened, a line of two hundred and seventy was waiting outside.

The day shelter also brought TMM staff and volunteers into much more frequent contact with the needs of the homeless, and new ideas sprung up. Working with state legislators, they brought money into a program geared for the homeless who suffered from mental illness at a time when the state was trying to shift responsibility back to the communities. At the same time, Sylvia and others were looking for ways to expand on their success.

They needed a larger site, and the older buildings downtown required enormous renovations. Besides, Sylvia says, they weren't designed as shelters. Not one of the forty-one buildings she looked at could meet Tulsa's growing needs. It turned out, she said, to be cheaper to build a new center. A call went out to the congregations for architects to work with staff and design a building that matched the day center's needs exactly. With money from the city, but mostly from private donations, they were able to build a two-million-dollar day center for the homeless, with a dozen spaces for related agencies to set up offices and reach those in need immediately. It also houses a five-day-a-week clinic, staffed by volunteer doctors and nurses.

The center's completion marked a victory for Sylvia's espoused principle of the prophetic role. The group had successfully lobbied their state legislature and convinced Tulsa businesses to contribute not only funds but also volunteers and support. They had not looked at the homeless as outcasts and criminals but rather saw them as citizens. Though Sister Sylvia's prophetic model made use of the instruments of power, it also demanded that she remain close to the powerless. Although the day center wasn't designed for overnight stays, the most powerless—women, children, the mentally ill—often found mats laid out for them when other Tulsa shelters couldn't take them, for whatever reason. She recalls her first night in the day center.

"I didn't want to sleep in the area where they were because I didn't want to embarrass them," she remembers. "So I slept in the lounge. But I went out periodically just to get a feel of what was going on. I remember at four o' clock, several people were stirring around and going to the coffeepot. So I said to the staff, 'What are they doing?' And they said, 'These are the ones'—and there were quite a number of them—'who try to get day employment, and if they're not there early, all the jobs are taken.' And so they get there at five o'clock, just to be at the front of the line."

Sister Sylvia saw women who walked across town in the dark to clean motels and hospitals, men who found day labor at construction sites. "They were just trying to hold everything together until they could make enough money for at least two months' rent. And that's really tough to do." Sylvia sighs. "And I thought, 'Oh, if people could see this.' "

As the center grew, it took on a life of its own, and Sister Sylvia and the Tulsa Metropolitan Ministry knew that they would have to let it go. "Our mission," she says, "was not to run programs. It was to enable, and to see that needs were met and to quickly fill gaps." When she was hired by TMM, the organization had a budget of $165,000 and three full-time staff. As the day center grew, TMM's budget grew to about $4 million and they hired fifty-three additional staff members. After the Ministry gave the day center back to the community, Sylvia's organization went back to a staff of three and a budget just above what they had when she started. "I think when it went out from under us, it helped people to understand that TMM really is serious about our mission not to have missions. It's to bring the interfaith and the ecumenical community together for understanding, and in that understanding, cooperation," Sylvia concludes.

TMM moved on, and so did Sylvia. She says she could see that it would need a long-term plan to remain effective, and new leadership to take it forward. In May 2000, after she received the Interfaith Award from the Jewish Federation of Tulsa, the National Conference for Community and Justice, and the Tulsa Metropolitan Ministry, she left her post and moved to San Antonio, where she's surrounded by family members. They get together twice a year, in gatherings of sixty to seventy, where Sylvia assumes "a very special matriarchal role."

Of course, you couldn't really call her retired. She's working with the National Association of Ecumenical Interfaith Organizations and has served on a Presbyterian task force addressing disintegration of community in major cities. As gang-related shootings reached a crisis point in her city, she said she would get a rocking chair and sit at a dangerous intersection and encourage gang members and drug dealers to find another way. When people told her she was going to be shot, she replied, "Well, a few of us will be shot, but then you'll do something about it."

I have to wonder how one person manages to do so much. Life presents us all with countless crises to be addressed, and America's particular list of problems can seem overwhelming at times. In Sylvia's view, though, these are opportunities for improving ourselves through service. Her advice? "Number one is not to try to take it all on." Instead, she counsels, "Say 'What is the one thing I can do?' and enjoy doing it. I think that's the most important thing, not to do it just out of a sense of guilt or obligation. It's got to be a real enrichment in our lives." With words like these, backed by a lifetime of good work, Sister Sylvia reminds us that sowing should have as prominent a role in the American dream as reaping. And as we sow, I think she would agree, so shall we all reap.

Wayne Ward Ford

Wayne Ward Ford believes we all have a destiny. Not a predetermined fate, but a place that a higher power wants us to go. When Wayne Ford talks about living the American dream, he is talking about finding his destiny.

Wayne was in eighth grade when a teacher asked his class to write their obituaries. What would they do with their lives? How would they like to be remembered? It was a critical time for Wayne and his class-mates: they were African Americans approaching adolescence in a city with a soaring crime rate and a decaying infrastructure. Washington, D.C., had been a beacon of hope for black families during the 1950s, which is why Wayne's mother came up from North Carolina to give birth to her child at the Freeman Negro Hospital. She could not have known then that the nation's capital would experience a swift decline in quality of life during the 1960s, or that her boy would turn to the streets.

Wayne's obituary carried a curious bit of specificity: he would make his mark in the Midwest. He would be active in politics, and in charge of a community center. After his death, he asserted, they would name something in his honor. Today, Wayne believes that this wasn't just a dream but a premonition.

Wayne Ford lives in Des Moines, Iowa. He is the only black member of the Iowa state legislature. He is executive director of a nonprofit com-munity center for at-risk youth. He seems to stand a good chance of having something named after him well before he dies. But why call this destiny? Wasn't this a case of simply setting a goal and striving for it?

Well, not exactly. There were some big twists and turns along the way. By the mid-1960s, Wayne was in high school in southeast Washington. He was his own worst enemy, and an enemy to the public as well. "I was running with the wrong crowd," he says with both intensity and regret, "doing drugs, selling drugs, robbing buses, breaking into apartments. I snorted cocaine in the laboratory in Ballou High School. I was wild. I was feared." It had taken only a few short years for a young boy with big dreams to turn into an urban nightmare.

Wayne refuses to blame anyone but himself for his fall. True, his mother had left him with his aunts, assuming he would have more opportunities in D.C. than in North Carolina. But he continued to have a strong connection to both his parents, and his relatives provided him with a stable home. The schools weren't the best, but they still offered a reasonable alternative. So why did he turn to such a life? "I did it for the notoriety," he says. "I would do it because my friends would say let's go do it. I did it because I was a big strong guy. . . . They needed me. I felt important. I felt powerful."

The sweetest words he could hear in those days were: "Don't mess with Wayne Ford, he'll kill you." He remembers the thrill he got hearing about his crimes on the local radio—"Bus robbed by three juveniles." He savored his nickname, Mad Dog, which he earned as the hardest-hitting defensive tackle on the high school football team. "I was on top of the world," he says. Somehow, in what he calls "a tremendous fantasy world," he was getting all the love and recognition he wanted. He had taken his dream, a dream of power and fame, and perverted it.

The American obsession with sports has resulted in some disturbing practices in collegiate recruiting, but at the same time, sports scholarships offer a second chance to a lucky and talented few. Wayne Ford was one of those few. Wayne probably wouldn't have bothered going to school at all if he weren't a powerful defensive end on the football team. And he wouldn't have been a powerful player if his six-foot-two, 210-pound frame had not been filled with anger. "Football," he says, "was where I could get all my aggression out. . . . My job was to seek and destroy. I was free. I could legitimately hit a man as hard as I could, hurt him, maim him, and not go to jail."

Wayne's partners in crime, however, were going to jail, or getting shot, or falling prey to drugs. There came a point where a football scholarship became a matter of survival. As Wayne told a college football scout, " 'I'm robbing buses, I'm doing wrong, I'm doing drugs, and I think I'm out of my mind. Send me away, as far away as you can, from Washington, D.C. Get me to a place where I can be reborn and live my life.' So he sent me a football scholarship to Rochester State Junior College in Rochester, Minnesota." Before Wayne left, his classmates voted him "most likely *not* to succeed." He doesn't blame them.

Ask Wayne Ford about his experiences as a teen, and you will get a direct answer. So direct, in fact, that it's easy to forget he's a politician. But ask him about his life after he went to college, and he will respond in the voice of a preacher. He has a religious passion about education. Wayne's college years—he started in 1969—were the first time in his life that he was really inspired to fight for himself. Failure, he realized, would mean a return to life on the edge.

The battle took place on several fronts. Wayne could barely read. He was in a community that was almost completely white. And his anger and barely suppressed violence still threatened to throw him off course. His roommate, one of the college's few black students, killed a man in a bar. "They didn't like him messing around with white girls," Wayne says. "He protected his life." Even with a former state attorney general defending him in what Wayne calls a clear-cut case of self-defense, Wayne's roommate went to prison for second-degree manslaughter.

Shortly after this incident, Wayne got an anonymous slap in the face. "I went to the bathroom," he remembers, "sat on the toilet, and looked at the wall. And it said, 'We want to kill the nigger Wayne Ford.' " Leaving the school didn't enter his mind; he fell back, rather, on his street instincts. "That's when I started carrying a twenty-two in my gym bag. D.C. mentality. If you got a gun out, I got a gun out. Me and you are equal."

The writing on the wall may have caused him to put a gun in his bag, but it also inspired him to make a difference. Wayne cofounded the Black Student Union at Rochester Junior College and started getting a new kind of attention. He was once again on the radio and in the newspaper, but this time as an activist rather than as part of a crime report. Once again, Wayne had power, but with a different feeling. "I was young, I was strong. I felt so good. It all started to come together: the worst things in my life were the things that had the potential to make me great."

So it was with confidence that he transferred to Drake University in Des Moines, still on football scholarship, but now devoted to academics. History studies took him away from feeling sorry for himself. "When I started reading that stuff," he says, "I thought, 'My God. The world has gone through hell, not just Wayne Ford. Wayne, you aren't as bad off as you think.' " In his literature classes, he devoured the explorations of darkness and evil in Dante's *Inferno* and Milton's *Paradise Lost*. And he felt a line from John Donne stir something inside him that had been dormant since the eighth grade: "Never send to know for whom the bell tolls; it tolls for thee." It was then that he decided that the hope he had carried as a child was actually destiny. That he had been called.

Wayne graduated on the dean's list in 1974 with a degree in education. "Now I'm an educated black man from Washington, D.C. God, I felt powerful. It's the same anger and power I had robbing buses or playing football, but now I could put it into my brain. I could *read*. I could *lead*. I could *think*. I could write proposals. Damn, I was scared of myself."

Is this arrogance? Wayne Ford says it certainly is. Echoing Adam Ballard, the aspiring filmmaker whom we met in the chapter on fame, and then taking it further, he says, "We all have natural gifts. If we can find those gifts, and know they are ours, we can be as arrogant as we want to be about who we are." Arrogance, he continues, allowed him to believe in himself even when he worked as a dishwasher in one of his college jobs and ate "garbage" off customers' plates. Humility, however, also has a place in Wayne's world. When he coached for the Special Olympics, for example, he was flattered when someone commented that they couldn't tell if he was an athlete or a coach. In those cases, he says, arrogance would have prevented him from doing his job.

Some ventures he's entered, however, required an arrogance supreme. In 1976, two years out of school, this young man from southeast Washington, D.C., decided that he would have an influence on a presidential election. "Basically," he explains, "I said, 'Never be denied.' " That's a message for anyone who feels alienated from American politics.

Wayne was working as minority education coordinator for the Carter campaign in Iowa, but he decided to make his influence more strongly felt. Without deep pockets, access, or experience, Wayne Ford established the state's first minority Democrat presidential forum. In one of the whitest states in the nation, he forced those who would be president to discuss minority issues during the Iowa caucuses. And he did it by sheer force of will. He simply decided that he wouldn't wait for an invitation but would make his presence felt on his own terms.

The 1976 Democratic hopefuls sent surrogates to the forum, who were grilled by panelists on their candidates' positions. In 1984, Wayne Ford joined forces with Mary Campos and formed the Brown–Black Presidential Forum. This time, John Glenn, Gary Hart, Alan Cranston, and George McGovern participated, and C-SPAN covered it. Presidential candidate Walter Mondale met with the Brown–Black coalition later that year. Bruce Babbitt, Michael Dukakis, Richard Gephardt, the Reverend Jesse Jackson, and Paul Simon showed up in 1988. And in 2000, MS-NBC covered Vice President Al Gore and Senator Bill Bradley's appearance at the forum.

Wayne Ford had decided, after graduating from Drake, to make his home in Des Moines but says he wasn't turning his back on the issues he left behind in Washington. He could see, perhaps more clearly than those who lacked his firsthand experience, that uniquely urban problems would transform the Iowa capital. In 1983, a Catholic bishop was kidnapped off the streets of Des Moines by two black youths. "The whole community went crazy," Wayne remembers, "went crazy looking for young black men." He had already seen that drugs were pouring into Des Moines, a city at the crossroads of two major interstate highways. And he had seen children of poor communities wearing the colors of Los Angeles gangs and taking on a familiar, distant, and hardened stare.

Wayne asked himself what he was doing in the Midwest. He still believes it was his destiny. Who else, at that time and place, he says, could reach out to the "young Wayne Fords" of Des Moines? In 1985, with a $10,000 grant from the city council, he founded Urban Dreams, blocks from where the bishop had been kidnapped.

Urban Dreams takes cases no one else will: gang members, ex-offenders, at-risk youth—people for whom the organization is often a last hope. The words "Don't mess with Wayne Ford" still sound sweet to him, but now he knows they mean he is making a positive difference. He is tough with the kids who come his way, unyielding in the challenge he issues them to change for their own good.

Urban Dreams is now a United Way agency with a half-million-dollar budget. The men and women on its staff have firsthand experience with the problems they try to solve—a woman who survived for years on public assistance, a former police detective, an ex-offender with a degree in criminal justice. With an eye toward prevention rather than just crisis management, Urban Dreams has expanded its programs to include after-school care for at-risk youth, community monitoring, youth sports leagues, and family unification, development, and self-sufficiency training.

Wayne was recently stopped on the street by someone who looked familiar. "Ten years ago," the man told him, "you helped me get a job. Now I'm a consultant making more money than you." That's recognition of a very different sort from the kind Wayne received as Mad Dog of southeast D.C., and for Wayne it has an almost spiritual effect. "I've always been so needy for attention and love that everything that touches me becomes a part of me," he explains. "I feel so comfortable, even when I'm in pain, to know that I'm not really Wayne Ford. I am a part of everything that has touched me."

It makes perfect sense that a former delinquent would make a great youth worker. But a politician? Conventional wisdom says politicians hide past transgressions. Even if some will guardedly admit to, say, drug use in college, how many would admit to carrying a gun in college? How many ever did such a thing? When Wayne ran for state representative in 1996, he did something unusual: "I ran as Wayne Ford," he says. "I ran on my past experiences, on my human qualities, on the rural to urban transition, on my former sports. I won the election by sixty-seven percent." Not only that, but he won in a district that includes "some of the most poor people in Iowa, and some of the richest." His next time up, he ran unopposed in the primary, and unopposed in the general election.

Once elected, Wayne did not change his style much. Indeed, he says, "Sometimes people on the Hill will come and say, 'Wayne, please soften up, we don't want to be here all day. . . . Sometimes they get tired: 'There's Wayne Ford again with his Ides of March and Julius Caesar speech.' " And in the role of elected official, he again seems to relish the fact that he doesn't quite fit in, that he rankles nerves.

He once told Iowa that Mother Goose is dead, and that the state would "no longer be a place where people can walk down the yellow brick road," meaning that the future of Iowa wasn't along a certain and shining path. For many of Iowa's minorities, that is true. Iowa's infant mortality rate for blacks is 23 per 1,000 births. For whites it is 6.1 per 1,000 births. And while one out of 110 whites in Iowa is in prison, on parole, or on probation, the proportion for blacks is one out of 12. No other state has a higher proportion, only Wayne's hometown of the District of Columbia.

So it's hard to ask State Representative Ford to lighten up. He could have been one of those prisoners. His wife, vice chair of the Iowa Parole Board, reviews those cases almost every day. But while Wayne may be in government, he refuses to see the so-called white establishment as the sole cause and solution to America's urban problems. "I can't blame it all on whites," Wayne says. "Blacks must go back and risk their lives and take the inner city back building by building. We can conquer slavery and segregation, but we can't conquer our own fear? There's no excuse. I'm not going to put it on whites and I'm not going to put it on the government. We overcame slavery and lynching. Don't tell me we can't do that now."

When you believe in destiny, you tend to also believe in legacy. Wayne Ford would like his to be a "line of young people believing in political society." To craft such a legacy, he feels he has to fight what he sees as the worst qualities of his generation. "As the baby boomers, who are the most arrogant, selfish generation in the history of the world, become old . . . I just hope that the young generation is more sensitive to our needs than we are to them." Service, he would like to remind all of us, gives us our best shot at being served when we ourselves are in need.

Perhaps Wayne believes in destiny because there is such a large disconnect between his life now and his years as a teenage tough. Sometimes he says he doesn't feel like Wayne Ford. This happened, he says, when he spoke before the Democratic National Convention in 2000. "Another person took over," he recalls. It was the person who, when he saw Barbara Jordan give her keynote speech during the 1976 convention, said, "I want to be up there," even though his past suggested he could never make it. Getting to that podium was one of the biggest achievements in his life, but he adds that it "wasn't the cherry on the ice cream. The best is yet to come."

What's the difference between yesterday's Wayne Ford and the Wayne

Ford of today? Both have confidence in their power. One fearlessly felled offensive tackles, the other revels in killing offensive legislative measures. Both have taken what they want from life. But only one Wayne Ford believes in responsibility—the responsibility of a government to its citizens, of citizens to one another, of one generation to the next, of the more fortunate to those with less. Today's Wayne Ford knows how much can be accomplished when we take responsibility for ourselves and for one another.

Evelyn Sirrell

As Sister Sylvia Schmidt points out, we stand the best chance to do good when we know our strengths. Problem is, we ourselves might not be aware of what our special gifts are. Evelyn Sirrell, the mayor of Portsmouth, New Hampshire, did not find her calling until late in life, but that hasn't stopped her from making the most of it since. If Wayne Ford can be said to have overcome himself and his surroundings in reaching for a political career, one must say of Evelyn Sirrell that she overcame a life that was by turns hard and often sad.

Her exposure to politics came early, with the talk Evelyn heard while growing up. It gave her an early lesson around the dinner table in how politicians are judged. "I was born in '31," Evelyn says, "grew up right through the Depression. I remember eating potato soup for about eight months. And I used to listen to my parents as I was growing up, and they kept saying there was no one like Roosevelt." Meanwhile, they lambasted Hoover for talking about a chicken in every basket and two cars in every garage. "This," Evelyn explains, "while we were starving to death!" While circumstances for this writer were not nearly as dire—there was always enough, though seldom a lot, to eat—Evelyn and I are of the same generation, and I can vouch for the sentiment she recalls. It ran strong in our country at a time when so many had so little and so few, too much.

Evelyn initially followed in her parents' Democratic footsteps but saw her staunch party identification erode over time. She worked hard on the New Hampshire campaigns of both John and Robert Kennedy but later registered as a Republican to vote for Reagan, twice. When Jeanne

Shaheen ran—successfully—for her first term as governor of New Hampshire, Evelyn went back to the Democrats. Now she says she's an independent, one who had yet to make up her mind about the 2000 election that at the time was just a few months away. "I don't know," she said, echoing a view that was dismayingly widespread in our last presidential contest and seemingly ratified by the too-close-to-call election, "because I don't like either one of them, if you want my truthful opinion."

When World War II broke out, Evelyn's family moved from her birthplace of Concord, New Hampshire, to Elliot, Maine, a small town near the Portsmouth Naval Yard, where Evelyn's father found work helping to build the wartime fleet. With the Allied victory, however, her father was let go. He was old enough for retirement, but with no pension to look forward to and six children to support, he took a job making deliveries for a local bakery. Of course, Evelyn adds, there was no money for college after her graduation from high school.

When Evelyn was twenty-one, she married a man who worked on nuclear subs at the naval yard while she held the same job at Montgomery Ward she'd started in high school. They bought a small house and dreamed of making enough to start a family. Eight years after they were married, those dreams were dashed when he died of a massive heart attack while on the job. "Quite a hard thing," Evelyn remembers. Her parents moved in with her, and stayed there for the rest of their lives.

It seemed to Evelyn that she would live out her days at the same job, for the same meager salary. "I was looking at my old paycheck," she remarks. "I got about seventy-five dollars a week. But I worked. I worked very hard." For ten years after her first husband died, she pressed on without really going anywhere until she met the man who would become her second husband. He was a contractor who fixed television sets at the department store and installed antennae on customers' roofs. In 1971, they married, and nurtured a small dream. "We decided why not open our own television business? And we just did it. It was slim pickings at first, but we did quite nicely."

They lived directly above the storefront in downtown Portsmouth, a classic mom-and-pop venture in a New England town with a rich history and simple way of life. While the population of the county in which Portsmouth lies has nearly doubled over the last thirty years, the population of Portsmouth itself has remained remarkably stable, at about twenty-four to twenty-five thousand. It lies on the banks of the Pis-cataqua River, offering a port used by fishing boats, yachts, tall ships, and naval vessels. Thanks to its port, its beaches, and its picturesque historic district, Portsmouth gets its share of tourists, and the small town's pop-ulation quadruples during the summer. It's been called one of Amer-ica's most enlightened cities by *Utne Reader,* and one of the top ten cities for young professionals by *Cosmopolitan,* but for Evelyn, it has sim-ply been home.

Evelyn and her husband had three children, a decent business, and a shot at a stable retirement. But when their eldest son was diagnosed with cancer at age fourteen, they were forced to let the business go. After sell-ing the building, they were able to afford a modest home and start life over. "But it was a very sad life," Evelyn says, "because our son never got over the cancer." After an eighteen-year struggle, he finally succumbed at the age of thirty-two, just two months before Evelyn made time for an interview.

After giving up the TV repair business, Evelyn picked up a job writing parking tickets for the police department—what they used to call a meter maid. Six months into the job, the chief of police approached her. "At the time I started," she explains, "they did not have women police here in this city. And the order had come down that male police officers could not search or baby-sit women prisoners. So the chief of police came to me and said, 'Would you be willing to go to school and become a part-time police officer?' And I said, 'Oh dear. I'm kind of old for that.' "

The rigors of policing Portsmouth were manageable, even for a fifty-three-year-old woman who stood at just five feet. The worst she can recall was the time an angry driver took a swipe at her after getting a parking ticket. But after almost nine years, the schedule proved to be too much. "I'd no sooner get home, start to prepare supper, when I'd have to be back at the police station. But," she says, "I had to work. My hus-band had this small social security, and in order to keep up with every-thing and pay the medical bills for my son, who had no medical insurance because they had all turned him down, I had to work." Evelyn did, however, exchange her police uniform for that of a security guard when she heard of an opening at the Portsmouth Savings Bank. The hours were easier and, unlike her meter maid duties, the new job involved very little walking.

"That is about the story of my life," Evelyn finishes. Of course, it isn't the whole story. She has, so far, managed to leave out politics. When she begins to warm to that subject, Evelyn's feisty side surfaces. It's a part of her personality that first arose when, in the 1970s, she became a habitual attendee of city council meetings.

In small towns, such affairs can offer either a fantastic study in small-scale democracy or a quick cure for insomnia. Evelyn was initially drawn to Portsmouth city council meetings as an owner of a small business, when she and her husband still owned the TV repair shop. Eventually, though, she says, "I became slowly addicted to it because I could see the wrongs that were being done." Evelyn says she saw too many bad decisions being made in an insider's arena by what she calls a "good ol' boy" network—just the sort of thing that would turn many citizens away in frustration. For Evelyn, who was also fascinated by the proceedings, the perceived injustice sparked a desire to serve. She ran for a council seat but came up short. "It was devastating to me," she admits. "It really bothered me." Her desire would then lay dormant until the next decade, when she found herself in the middle of a movement.

In the 1980s, Portsmouth completed a revaluation and established a historic district. "It affected the South End of Portsmouth very greatly. People down there couldn't live in the South End anymore," she says, adding that her home was one of the buildings that saw taxes skyrocket. "Some of the buildings quadrupled in taxes, and it was a very, very sad time. I mean, elderly people who had been there for years, you know? It just broke my heart." Evelyn became one of the founders of the Association of Portsmouth Taxpayers to fight for an equitable tax rate. She served as president for two years, until she made another attempt at the city council.

With the backing of the taxpayers' association, she won a seat on the city council in 1986. "I went in at full force, because at that time, Eileen Foley was mayor and her son was a city councilor. Now, we only have nine councilors—with the mayor included—and I felt that two from one family was just too many on a nine-member council. That was what I went on, and a lot of people felt the same way. Not that I'm saying that their decisions were the same. I wouldn't say that. But I just felt that they needed more of a selection than two from the same family." The mayor she's referring to was no lightweight in Portsmouth, or, indeed, in the state of New Hampshire. Mayor Foley left office in 1998 after eight terms and sixteen years in all, receiving a farewell from the governor at her last council meeting.

Evelyn won the seat, but she didn't fully appreciate what she was up against until she began to discern a pattern in the city council's votes. "It was rough-and-tumble," she says, "because there were only two of us endorsed by the taxpayers' association . . . two lone votes out there. And I'll tell you, it was a seven-to-two vote constantly throughout my first year sitting on that council." Evelyn, whose strong voice has held steady as she has recited the greatest of personal tragedies, surprises with her next statement: "I'd go home at night in tears. I really would, because I felt it was an endless battle, and we were not getting anyplace."

Her son's battle with cancer turned critical while Evelyn was still in her first two-year term, and she opted not to run again while he was in the hospital going through a bone marrow transplant. But in 1994, she picked up where she'd left off by reclaiming a seat on the council. "I just felt that Portsmouth needed to be cleaned up. I really did. I'm a gutsy person," she asserts. "I can take a lot. I might sit in the closet and cry, but I come out with my strength, and I just continue on. I did it with my son throughout all of these years. I'm a fighter." Evelyn ran again in 1996. At this next foray her fight met with greater success. Under Portsmouth's city charter, the city council candidate with the most votes becomes mayor; the one with the second-most votes assumes the office of assistant mayor. Evelyn polled well behind Mayor Foley, but far enough ahead of the rest of the pack to take the post of assistant mayor.

Evelyn wanted to "clean up" Portsmouth, and Mayor Foley put her in a position where she could do just that. As chairperson of the Citywide Neighborhood Committee, Evelyn helped gather concerned residents into twenty-nine neighborhood commissions. "And not without a lot of work, I'm telling you," she adds. "I had to go into these neighborhoods and turn them completely around. We had crack houses, we had slum areas, we had overdevelopment to the point where these neighborhoods had lost the quality of life." Evelyn worked with each neighborhood's residents, taking them along on note-taking expeditions up and down the city's streets with the city manager and the police and fire chiefs. Once the group assessed a neighborhood's particular needs, the city came together to put in new parks, sidewalks, roads, and sewers. In addition, Portsmouth implemented a general beautification plan for the city.

(I'm reminded of Lady Bird Johnson's response to this ugly word for a wonderful thing; as the former first lady put it in speaking of her Highway Beautification Program, "Until we come up with a better word, it will have to do.") Of the project's progress, Evelyn says, "We're out there every day. I'm not saying we haven't got any more neighborhoods that need to be done, but we're working at it."

Eileen Foley's decision not to run for mayor in 1998 brought on an open season. A record twenty-two candidates vied for nine city council seats, and one of them, Evelyn says, spent fifteen thousand dollars on his campaign. She says, though, that the increased competition didn't tempt her to change her campaign or fund-raising style. In her first successful run for council, she says, "I had almost no money. I didn't take any money from developers, realtors, or big business. And throughout all of this, I have followed in those footsteps. I did not want to get involved with any big business and especially with developers, you know, because there's too many cases of having that come back to haunt you."

Accepting only five- and ten-dollar contributions from individuals, she raised five hundred dollars for her first successful campaign, and a thousand dollars in 1998, when she was a mayoral hopeful. "That was the most I'd ever gotten," she says. "So I think they wanted me to be mayor." Her war chest, such as it was, had doubled in size, but she still did not have enough for anything but a street-level approach: "I made all my own signs and did all my own walking. I did it by mimeographing off my feelings and going door to door."

When the ballots were counted, it turned out that Evelyn had been elected mayor by the slimmest of margins. She was ahead of another incumbent council member by exactly one vote. When problems were discovered with the vote tally and a recount was begun, no one, not even Evelyn, believed she would remain mayor-elect for long. Taking the situation in stride, she quipped to a reporter that, with Mayor Foley out of town, she would at least get to hold the office a week. But when the recount was complete, Evelyn's lead actually increased. She won with 2,716 votes to her nearest opponent's 2,709.

As with our most recent presidential election, it was hardly the kind of win that could be called a mandate, but that's okay by Evelyn: she says she's found that an open approach and a spirit of compromise has made Portsmouth a better place to live.

Evelyn was anxious to talk about "one of her proudest achievements" as mayor. As a rash of school shootings stunned the nation in 1999, Evelyn and the citizens of Portsmouth wondered if it could ever happen there. Evelyn appointed a task force to find out what Portsmouth teens were doing and thinking, and what could be done to keep them safe. What began as an effort to "take back our children," as she puts it, became an ongoing dialogue, a chance for children to actually participate. When they described, at a cookout held specifically as a forum for their concerns, how they felt about violence in Portsmouth and elsewhere, how desperate they were to be a part of the community, they brought tears to Madam Mayor's eyes.

Evelyn is having a great time watching her town come together, but she feels her work as mayor isn't just about new parks and safer streets, the kinds of things everyone can get behind. When interviewed, Evelyn was in one of the toughest fights of her political career, over whether certain New Hampshire towns should have additional property taxes assessed to support schools in other parts of the cash-strapped state. One side says it's the only fair way to raise the standards of all schools, the other side says the towns that will bear the financial burden aren't necessarily "wealthy" across the board, that some citizens will suffer under the tax passed by the state legislature.

It's an issue that has her locking horns with Governor Jeanne Shaheen, for whom Evelyn voted. When interviewed, Evelyn was leading a group of towns in a tax revolt. As this book went to press, the battle had moved into the courts, and monies from the several towns were briefly placed in escrow before a judge ordered them to send it all to Concord. Evelyn has met with the governor, she says, but has failed to find a middle ground. When Evelyn is quoted in the papers on the issue, the emotion that comes across is anger, but during this interview she sounded regretful that it's come to this. "It's turned into a terrible thing," she said, adding that her preference would be for a state income tax. Though it's not what she really wants, at this point she feels as if it's "the only fair way to go." But Governor Shaheen has twice run on promises to oppose an income tax, and New Hampshire is a state well known for its tax-averse ways. Evelyn may be past the rough-and-tumble of her early days on the city council, but conflicts like the current one keep her aware that there's always a tough side to politics.

Mayors don't get paid much in Portsmouth; Evelyn didn't give up her job as a security guard at the bank when she was elected to the post but cut back to thirty hours a week. Recently, though, she's had to go on disability. "I got the good news last year that I have cancer," she says sardonically. She stood by her son's side during his long fight, and she lost her husband just four years before, but there was no panic in her voice. "I'm responding wonderfully," she says, "and hopefully I have just one more treatment, which is just swell. But I have tried to continue in the mayor's position, and I think I've done it quite well throughout all this." Maybe, when the treatment is complete, she'll again don the uniform of a bank security guard.

Evelyn would love to run for another term but only, she says, if she can "do the job right." Evelyn doesn't sound saddened by the prospect of leaving the office—she had a vision of how she would like to serve, and she has brought it to fruition. At her fiftieth high school reunion, Evelyn adds, she had a moment that reminded her of the importance of dreams. "When I graduated from high school, my English teacher said to me, 'Evelyn, you're never going to amount to anything. You just don't have any dream of what you want to do.'" The teacher was in her nineties when Evelyn approached her and told her that she had, at last, found it. "I know you found your dream," the teacher replied with a smile. "It's politics." The dream was always there, Evelyn insists, "but it finally came out when I started getting involved."

Enrique E. Camarena Jr.

Most reporters get to meet more than their share of law enforcement officers in the course of a career. The reason is simple: where there's news, you'll find men and women in uniform. This reporter has met plenty. And I've come away with tremendous respect for these people for whom risk is all in a day's work. You hear a lot of talk these days, perhaps too much, about corruption and excessive use of force among America's police officers. But it is worth remembering that these cases make news because they're the exception, not the rule. The overwhelming majority of people who do this dangerous work do so out of a true calling to, in the words of the ever-present police motto, "protect and serve."

Not long before he was interviewed for this book, Enrique Camarena saw a television documentary on forensic science. An FBI specialist used soil found on the body of an American DEA agent killed in Mexico to determine not only that he had been killed and then moved, but to determine exactly where in the world he had been killed. It was part of an all-out effort by American law enforcement to catch the agent's murderers. It is a case that Enrique remembers well. The victim was his father.

Enrique now works as a deputy district attorney for San Diego County. He's gotten as close as he can to following in Enrique Camarena Sr.'s footsteps without stepping directly into his shoes. "I wanted to be a police officer and carry a badge and a gun the way my dad did," he says, recalling his childhood dreams. Enrique's father raised him with an unbending respect for the law but at this aspiration he drew the line. "He said it was too dangerous," Enrique remembers. The elder Enrique Camarena insisted that his namesake go to college; for him he wanted a career far from the streets.

When Enrique's father was young, probably too young to have remembered, his family moved from the Mexican border town of Mexicali to Calexico, on the California side. Enrique became a citizen, married his high school sweetheart, and joined the marines. He returned to Calexico after his enlistment to serve as a police officer and start a family. In 1974, when Enrique Jr. was two, his father joined the Drug Enforcement Agency during a drive to recruit native Spanish speakers. "That's the type of person they were looking for," the son says, "and he jumped at the chance."

After completing an assignment in Calexico, the family moved to Fresno for three years. Then Enrique Sr. took a dangerous undercover assignment in Guadalajara, Mexico's second largest city. Enrique Jr., seven years old at the time, remembers missing the pleasures of America. "At that time, there were no McDonald's, no M&Ms, Butterfingers, all the things that are important to kids." With a short laugh, he describes how one classmate in the American school brought a souvenir from home: "He said, 'Look what I got!' and he opened his book and there was an empty french fry container from McDonald's, this little cardboard thing, and we sat for five minutes just smelling it."

Enrique Sr.'s work often brought him home late, but he always made a point of stopping in to see his son, even if that meant waking him up. "That was kind of our quality time. In the middle of the night. He'd not tell me about the things he did, but just chat with me about life and sports and things like that while I was half asleep in bed." As the family's return date got pushed back, the DEA agent knew that his family was not particularly enjoying their stay, but he was torn between duty and family. "He just didn't want to leave the guys there," Enrique says of his father today. "He was the one who was working with some informants, and when you leave, you can't just insert another agent. Most of the time, when an agent leaves, you exhaust those leads, and another agent has to create their own."

As the time in Mexico dragged on, Enrique Jr. became reacquainted with his first language, Spanish, which he had forgotten, and took computer classes as early as the fourth grade. One day, when Enrique Jr. was eleven, his father sat the family down to deliver news he knew would disappoint them. "He explained to us that he had asked to stay for a little while longer because he needed to finish some things. Of course we all got mad, and he said it would be soon." He came back a second time, saying he'd adjusted his timeline. They would leave, but it would take a couple of months. "Soon after that," the son recalls, "is when it happened."

When Enrique Jr. awoke on February 7, 1985, he knew right away that something was wrong: "I remember looking in and seeing only my mom there. That had happened only a few times where he came home really late or was out of town. But he wasn't there." His mother was busy placing calls to other agents in his office. No one knew where he could be. "By noon," Enrique says, "there were already agents in my house. Waiting. By noon it was already a big thing. Kind of like the light switch had been turned on. They were asking around and making calls to the people they could trust or *half* trust. They were calling Washington and the ball was rolling."

Enrique soon became accustomed to having agents in the house. From that day to the day his father was found, they never left. For about a week, the family waited . . . for the phone to ring, for a car to pull up with news, anything. There were plenty of calls, and a steady stream of visitors, but neither brought the desperately desired news. It was as if he had dropped off the face of the earth. "We didn't go to school," Enrique remembers, "we couldn't go outside to play." As hope slowly faded, Enrique's mother decided her sons should join relatives in the States. "I remember when I came out of the house, which was the first time in a week, there were a bunch of Mexican army guys with automatic weapons outside; there was a military guard around the house." Mexican military and American law enforcement personnel escorted them to the airport, where their car drove directly onto the heavily guarded tarmac. A plane was waiting with a DEA agent who was a friend of the family. The boys boarded and flew to San Diego to meet their aunt. Their mother stayed behind.

Enrique Camarena Sr.'s disappearance inspired an unprecedented search effort. Traffic was backed up for hours along the Mexican-American border as agents conducted car-by-car searches. The tactic drew harsh criticism from the Mexican foreign minister, while U.S. officials publicly accused Mexican police of dragging their feet on the investigation. Enrique Jr. knew nothing of this at the time. His mother had strictly forbidden him and his brother to watch the news.

Enrique explains that his mother "didn't want us to see any speculation and she wanted to be the first to tell us." While the search was under way, the Camarenas avoided the subject altogether. Enrique's mother would call from Mexico, and they would talk about, as Enrique recalls, "how are you doing, are you having fun, that kind of thing." Agents were stationed at his aunt's house in California, watching, waiting, monitoring calls. Any time the phone rang, everybody jumped and an agent would give his aunt the go-ahead to pick up, meaning they were ready to record. Most of the calls turned out to be from concerned friends and family looking for news. Meanwhile, the children's movements were restricted and they still weren't allowed to go to school. But the DEA agents would bring Enrique and his brother treats from McDonald's, and the candy bars they'd missed in Mexico.

About two weeks after the disappearance, Enrique's mother finally joined her sons in San Diego. "When she came," he remembers, "it kind of hit me that hey, this is pretty serious. . . . She wouldn't leave him down there if there was a chance." Enrique knew that his family needed him to be strong, so he kept his fears to himself. "It was pretty much me and my mom. My two younger brothers were a little too young to understand. I understood that someone had taken him, and they weren't nice guys. I understood his job was dangerous." Now he could see what his mother was going through, how her mood changed as they brought in new reports that made it ever harder to keep hope alive.

Not long after Enrique's mother arrived in San Diego, she spoke to two agents and then asked Enrique to join her in an upstairs bedroom. "She told me they had found two bodies and they didn't know who they were. They were going to do some tests to see who it was. But they weren't sure and she wasn't sure. So we were just going to wait." At the same time, it seemed to Enrique that everyone in the house was working on the assumption that they had found his father. It turned out to be so. Agent Camarena had not simply been killed; his body revealed signs of brutal torture, endured over a period of several days. When tapes of this horrific interrogation surfaced later, Enrique was thankful for his mother's news blackout.

The family stayed with Enrique's aunt for another two months, and then moved into a condo. Enrique Sr. was flown back and his ashes scattered west of Calexico on a mountain called Mount Signal. He wanted his ashes scattered there because half of the mountain is in Mexico and half in America. Two thousand mourners attended his memorial service. "We had some kind of closure," says Enrique in somber tones. "I think it would have been much different if we hadn't been through that. If it had just been, he's gone and we don't know whether he's dead. But we were able to put things back together as best we could."

Every year, at the San Diego Police Officers' Memorial, current and retired officers honor those who have fallen in the line of duty. The memorial lists the names of seventy officers, deputies, and agents, dating back to 1865. Enrique was recently called upon to address this gathering. "It helps us to look back, to reminisce and see how far we have come," Enrique told the crowd. "Some days, the pain just comes out of nowhere. As victims, we have a calling to encourage each other." He had found it difficult to answer that call so publicly, he says now, but he was rewarded by the praise he heard for his father, fifteen years after the agent's death. "It's amazing to see how many people still remember," he says. "I remember him because he was my dad, not because of the things his death started, or the huge international scandal. But it's still amazing." In Enrique's work space at the San Diego County district attorney's office, complete strangers still stop by after seeing his name on a phone list or on his door. Such encounters serve to remind Enrique that he is upholding a tradition.

Enrique never forgot his father's wish for his oldest son. "I had to go to college," he says. "I mean, I was remembering those conversations with him. So I knew I had to do well in school, no matter what. There was no other option."

Enrique attended Dartmouth after high school, drawn to Spanish literature and political science. During his junior year, he followed in his father's footsteps by marrying his high school sweetheart, and the newlywed Californians made plans to get away from the cold New England winter as soon as possible. When Enrique settled on law school, he chose the University of Southern California, and she chose to finish up school at San Diego State University, so the young couple could take up life back in the sun.

Once he had earned his law degree, Enrique found himself again drawn to law enforcement work. But, he says, "I had to mind the order: 'Don't be a cop.' Being a prosecutor was the next closest thing, and I considered it a happy medium." He applied to the San Diego County district attorney's office, and was hired as a graduate law clerk until he passed the bar, when he was made deputy district attorney.

"It's been very fulfilling," Enrique says from his home, where he's taken time off from work for the birth of his second son. "Not necessarily punishing people, but upholding the law that makes it safe to live here." Enrique describes what he does as a natural extension of the work his father did: "continuing what law enforcement officers do out in the field. They start the case, and we finish it." The young deputy DA has gotten a good start working on drunk driving cases, battery trials, and other misdemeanors. He'd tried one felony perjury case, and like most prosecutors starting out, he was looking forward to prosecuting serious felonies—murders, armed robberies, kidnappings, and drug cases. He knows all too well that the victims of these crimes, and their families, need his help.

Enrique says that his favorite part of the job is connecting with the citizens he helps to protect. "The array of people you meet is amazing," he says. "The witnesses come from every walk of life, and you get to chat with them, get maybe ten minutes of their lives." He notes a strong sense of civic duty among those who come to testify—a feeling that they take this seriously. He also meets many of the kin of the accused, who plead with him to go easy. And he sees plenty of cases where he can't find the right answer in a book. "You'd think," he says, "that with so many thick volumes of law, you'd have everything covered, but you know, we don't."

It's something Enrique has also learned by watching the government go after his father's killers. One suspect was snatched by bounty hunters in Guadalajara and transported to El Paso, where he was arrested by DEA agents. Another suspect faced evidence in a U.S. court that had been gathered from his home in Mexico by U.S. law enforcement agents acting without a warrant. Both instances would have been flagrant violations of the Constitution by government agencies if they had been carried out on U.S. soil. In both cases, the actions were defended by prosecutors as being necessary in the face of widespread corruption in the Mexican government. Both cases went to the Supreme Court, and in both cases the court sided with the prosecution. "The United States did a lot," Enrique says. "A few people thought they went a little bit too far. Obviously, I don't agree with that, but I guess everyone's entitled to their opinion."

In San Diego's courtrooms, however, Enrique views the rights of the accused as sacred. "The rules are there for a reason," he says. "If they don't help prosecutors out, they protect the rights of somebody. I don't think we have too many laws, although I think laws make proving things sometimes difficult. But that's just the way it is, and I have to follow the law." If he and others like him didn't respect the law, he doesn't believe that U.S. citizens as a whole would have the respect for law that they do.

He has a ready contrast. Across the border in Tijuana, he points out, the drug war has created a climate of near anarchy. "Broad daylight beatings, beatings to death, people are getting murdered left and right, the car drives off and nobody wants to say anything. One of the things my dad used to say was that nobody's really going to notice how big these cartels are or how big a problem this is until somebody gets hurt. And it ended up being him."

Enrique remembers how, during his childhood in Guadalajara, the prevailing atmosphere of insecurity caused his parents to keep him at home as much as possible. So when he returned to the United States, even though he was still young, he sensed "an inherent freedom all around." A freedom, he says, "to set your own priorities." When asked about his own prioirities, Enrique doesn't hesitate. "In my case," he says, "you put God first, your family second, and your work third. That's one of the things my dad taught me. And that was one of the reasons why, I'm sure, he immigrated to the United States and one of the reasons why he wanted to come back so much."

Enrique's memory of his father became an American dream geared to giving back through public service. "If people don't dedicate themselves to working in government and working for the public good," he says with conviction, "our freedom and our laws wouldn't be worth anything. The freedoms people fought for would all be for naught. We have to *uphold* the Constitution." Because, as We the People know from times and places where law enforcement and the courts are corrupt, no constitution can stand entirely on its own.

Joshua Marcus

The call to serve is insistent. It can be heard loud and clear as we walk down our city streets, as we talk to our children, and, I hope, as we watch the evening news. But we are a busy people, caught up in our careers and in our own lives. We hear, but we too often fail to answer. Almost all of the people who have told their stories here have made service at least a part of their American dreams. I suspect there are many more folks like the ones here, and I hope this isn't mere wishful thinking. The need for them, for you, for me and us, is great.

I think back to Michael Cruz, the business student who managed to start an SAT prep course for underprivileged children even as he was working banker's hours (and I'm using the new definition here). Folks like him, who find a privileged place for service in their busy lives, show us that there are few real excuses for not giving back. If Michael and others in this book offer patient reminders that no true success is complete without service, Joshua Marcus's story serves as a trumpet blast. If a boy can contribute so much at the age of ten, can't we all, somehow, give a little?

Josh made time for an interview the day before he started high school. In the last four years, he's gotten used to this sort of thing. He's appeared on the local news dozens of times, a short piece about him ran on *Oprah,* and he appeared before an audience of thousands at an Office Depot sales conference. It all started with a grade school assignment at the Donna Klein Jewish Academy in Boca Raton, Florida: get out in the world and help someone.

The academy's principal announced the community service requirement during an assembly, offering examples of where students could serve—at a nursing home, in a soup kitchen, at their temple. "Everything he said sounded wonderful to me," Josh recalls, "but I really knew that I wanted to help children." We all know that not everyone gets the same start in life, and some of us unfortunately accept that fact. As Josh puts it, though, "I looked at my life, I saw that I go to an expensive school, I live in a country club, everything I wanted I always got, and I knew that I had a very lucky start in life. And I realized that not everyone has the life that I do. Not everyone can be as fortunate as me."

He told his mother how he felt and asked her to take him where the needy children were. He thought he would have to go to someplace like Miami, but she explained that there were inequalities in Boca Raton as well. He couldn't believe at the time that some of his neighbors lived separate lives. Today he laughs at his naïveté, but he also knows that some people grow up without ever having this epiphany. Worse, some never care enough to even wonder.

Mother and son went down to the Florence Fuller Child Development Center in Boca Raton, and Marcus met the children for himself. They were poor, he found, but not that different in their dreams and aspirations. He knew he wanted to help but had no idea how until he talked to the director of the center. At first, Josh wanted to work with the kids, but he was still a kid himself—he found he had to be sixteen to volunteer. Then they got right down to a fundamental difference between Josh and these children. They didn't have—often could not afford—basic tools of learning. Paper. Pens and pencils. Notebooks. Backpacks.

He promised the director that when these kids started school in the fall, they would march in with materials as good as those used by Josh and his classmates. Materials Josh had, until then, taken for granted. "And so every day after school," he says, "my mom and I went to every single store that sold backpacks and school supplies and at first no one would help me." To put a professional polish on his request, Josh designed a logo, business cards, and a letterhead at home on the family's PC for his still-unincorporated nonprofit corporation and came up with the name "Sack It to You"—evoking the backpacks (or knapsacks, as we used to call them) that hold the tools of educational success.

But at first, his eagerness met with disappointment; store managers told Josh that they had already donated money to one cause or another. "I think they just wanted to get rid of me," says Josh. But some managers, and even more employees, were so impressed by the determination of this ten-year-old that they dug into their own pockets to make a donation. Josh also used his homemade letterhead to write everyone he and his parents knew, and some he didn't know. Soon he had enough cash to cover the kids at the Florence Fuller Center, and his mom, Shelly, took him to the local Office Depot to make a rather large purchase.

Josh fulfilled his promise with 130 backpacks delivered to the Florence Fuller Child Development Center, all loaded with supplies he had selected and stuffed into the packs himself. The children's reactions and the pride of the adults convinced Josh that he had a responsibility to carry on this work. But beyond the immediate satisfaction he got from giving, Josh had a broad view of how he was making a difference: "Education is the key to success," Josh says with conviction. This lecture may be coming from the mouth of a fourteen-year-old, but it's one worth heeding nonetheless. I remember hearing that his mother refers to him affectionately as "sort of this little old man," and I can only hope that he retains such mature convictions—and wish that more Americans, young and old, would do as much to act on their beliefs. Josh counts himself among those who see education as "one *big* key to the American dream." There are a lot of people in America, he says, who "gave up when they were a child because they didn't have school supplies or they didn't feel they had the tools they needed. Now I'm giving them the opportunities they might not have had."

Office Depot is headquartered in Boca Raton, so word of Josh's inspired gift to the Florence Fuller Child Development Center quickly made it to upper management where, coincidentally, there were similar ideas already afloat. As Josh tells it, "They're like, 'Waaaait a second. We were just looking to help children.' And here's a child helping other children. They said that was so great, and the timing of it all was just so perfect." When Josh met Office Depot CEO David Fuenta, the two formed an immediate partnership. Office Depot would donate supplies and backpacks, in numbers that even surpassed Josh's original order. Suddenly, Josh's school project had become a movement.

Josh has since given away almost four thousand backpacks filled with supplies. He says the material and cash donations over the last four years have added up to almost $200,000. And his inventory keeps growing. The Toppel Family Foundation has kicked in to help finance Sack It to You's rent on two storage units, one for supplies, and one for stuffed packs. Josh thought he would have to start looking for a larger space soon. His mom laughed when asked what she thought of being recruited as a driver. "I traded in my Lexus for a Durango," she says, "and now I'm getting a Yukon because the Durango isn't big enough"— something she discovered recently when a particularly large donation took six trips from the storage unit.

Now other students with community service requirements come to Josh, who always needs help filling the backpacks. Many, after their requirements are filled, "helped me even more," he says. The CEO of Sack It to You has learned that his simple idea and enthusiasm are infectious.

The packs themselves are tailored to students' needs. Those for elementary school kids include a pencil box, pencils, crayons, a ruler, a pencil sharpener, paper, safety scissors, three folders, and two glue sticks. Maybe they don't need two glue sticks, Josh laughs, but there was a mistake in one of the shipments during the summer before we spoke, and he ended up with twelve thousand of them. Preschoolers get materials printed with playful pictures, middle school and high school students get pens, index cards, and real scissors in addition to the basic materials packed for the elementary school kids. And they all get these loose materials in backpacks—high-quality backpacks—that they probably wouldn't imagine being able to spring for on their own.

Those packs are key to an intangible effect of Josh's program. Imagine living near a wealthy community, going to school with well-to-do children, and having to carry your books in a plastic bag. To a child, this can mean the difference between taking books home and leaving them in a locker, something Josh learned from a friend in public school. "They're so ashamed that they don't have backpacks and some people make fun of them," he says. "They feel left out, because Boca Raton is a very wealthy place and some of these kids who are bused in, they don't have what the other kids have." It's the kind of detail an adult might miss but a kid is sure to catch, and it underscores the value of having a kid at the head of this operation.

Josh reports that the children who get the packs are sometimes taken aback. But when they see that there are no strings attached, they learn something about service. "They want to start something like what I've got or go off and work in a soup kitchen, help in the community, or help around the house." Maybe, he says, it helps them realize "there's not all bad people in the world, and that they shouldn't follow the bad people in the world, but look for the good in the world. And most of the kids I help, they want to come and help me."

It didn't take long for the local media to start showing up at Josh's giveaways. He says he tries not to get a "swelled head" but admits that being on television is pretty cool: "It's the greatest thing in the world. It's the greatest feeling every time you do it, even if it tones down after a while." (This writer professes not to have any idea what he's talking about. That's my story and I'm sticking to it.) He's even taken time to practice his public speaking skills, which he put to good use at the international Office Depot sales convention. Four thousand employees watched him share a stage with then-CEO David Fuenta and introduce General Colin Powell, now Secretary of State Powell, who quipped that he was "being upstaged by a thirteen-year-old."

Josh says that Office Depot wants to send him around as a visiting lecturer to youth groups, with an eye to starting Sack It to You chapters across the country. "I realize," he says, "that even though I *want* to help everybody in the country by myself, I can't." As the program expands, Josh sees it staying in the hands of children. He's learned firsthand that giving carries its own rewards and hopes that other kids will discover the same. "Kids helping kids," Josh insists, will be the ongoing premise of Sack It to You.

There will come a day soon when Josh is no longer a kid. With precocious foresight, he explains that he will leave Sack It to You behind when he goes to college. He believes that his future is in litigation, after law school and undergraduate study in political science. There was a time, he laughs, when he wanted nothing more than to go to Yale and then become a fireman. Personally, I have a hard time believing that Josh won't someday be drafted or drawn into politics.

But any career is still a long way off. As it is, the demands of the present keep this teenager plenty busy. "Sometimes," he admits, "I really get overwhelmed and just want to throw it all out in the garbage. But then I realize that, in the end, the big picture is much greater than not having one game of basketball or not playing one game at the PlayStation." If you don't think that sounds like much of a revelation, try remembering back to piano lessons, or your after-school job, or anything you did in your teens that required more stick-to-itiveness than you sometimes felt you had.

Josh's talk of "the big picture" echoes Sister Sylvia Schmidt, who asks us to always keep the idea of the human family before us, even as we give our time as we can to just a few individuals. As Josh will tell you, "It's a big world out there. You might not know it, you might block it off, but there are a lot of people who are not as wealthy as you are, who don't have the same opportunities in life that you had. It's not equal. It's not a perfect society. But just because the people that don't have money maybe didn't have all those opportunities doesn't mean that they still can't have the same kind of life as the people who did." Josh puts it well, and his words seem a fitting way to close. We began this book with opportunity and freedom and, with Joshua Marcus's help, we end with justice.

Everyone in this book offered their personal take on the American dream, and their ideas were as diverse as they. All, however, were dedicated dreamers, in the best possible sense. Perhaps because of his youth, it was Josh who provided the most Utopian, the most impossibly beautiful vision. "I think the American dream is for a perfect society," he said plainly. "For everybody to be equal. For everybody to have the same opportunities in life. For the rich to give back to the poor, and for the poor to help themselves. And everyone getting along and having lots of peace." Thank you, Josh, for the answer. If I had to pick just one, that would be it.